Careers in International Affairs

School of Foreign Service
Georgetown University

Georgetown University's School of Foreign Service is the oldest and largest school of international affairs in the United States. Established in 1919 to provide "preparation for foreign service in public and private interests," the School offers a liberally based professional education in international affairs at the undergraduate and graduate levels. The School's mission is to educate professionals and train leaders with a profound understanding of the forces of change—past, present, and prospective—in the international system.

Careers in International Affairs

Sixth Edition

Edited by
MARIA PINTO CARLAND
MICHAEL TRUCANO

GEORGETOWN UNIVERSITY PRESS / WASHINGTON, D.C.

Georgetown University Press, Washington, D.C.   20007
© 1997 by Georgetown University Press. All rights reserved.
Printed in the United States of America.
10   9   8   7   6   5   4   3   2   1997
THIS VOLUME IS PRINTED ON ACID-FREE OFFSET BOOKPAPER.

Library of Congress Cataloging-in-Publication Data

Careers in international affairs.   —   6th ed.   /   edited by Maria Pinto
    Carland, Michael Trucano.
            p.   cm.
        Includes bibliographical references and index.
        1. International Relations—Vocational guidance—United States.
    2. International economic relations—Vocational guidance—United
    States.   I. Carland, Maria Pinto, 1944–   .   II. Trucano, Michael.
    JX1293.U6C28   1997
    327'.013'73—dc20
    ISBN 0-87840-630-1 (pbk.)
                                                            96–18399

Contents

v

Preface

The sixth edition of **Careers in International Affairs** is written for 20th century students who will have 21st century careers. Changes in technology, telecommunication, and transportation, in social institutions and political structures as well as demographics, will continue to transform the careers of bankers and businessmen, consultants and diplomats, public officials and nonprofit organizers at an increasingly rapid pace. Today it is a cliché to say that the world is getting smaller. Soon most careers will be global and distances will be important only insofar as we go about bridging them. Careers, then, will be about finding ways to cross those distances. As we look toward the 21st century, we cannot afford to be shortsighted about the skills and knowledge we will need to succeed.

Success in the 21st century will depend on broad-based education and insight. It is crucial, therefore, that students today realize that honing the skills to land a first job is not enough; and employers must realize that hiring to fit the needs of entry-level positions is not enough. As the bright young researcher, analyst, or organizer is promoted, the demands on his or her abilities will change. He or she will be asked to devise policies and strategies, manage people and programs, and understand technology and finance. He or she must be literate and articulate, a problem solver, a creative thinker—someone with a long view, who can access long-term trends and translate them into action in the short term. The ability to do this will depend not just on training in disciplines such as statistics or accounting—although these are indispensable—but on a combination of liberal education and experience designed to produce thoughtful men and women with solid skills and solid values.

Graduates with international education and experience are the ideal professionals for the 21st century. They are at ease with diversity in people, places, and things. They are well prepared for a future where dealing with what is different will be not only necessary, but commonplace.

Careers in International Affairs is designed to provoke thought about possibilities. It offers an introduction to and an overview of a wide variety of employment opportunities around the world. It is intended to provide:

- basic understanding of international career fields and what they offer;

- new insights into the skills and requirements employers find necessary for success;

- heightened awareness of career options; and

- broad guidelines for future career decisions.

The enthusiastic response of students and career counselors to the last edition of **Careers in International Affairs**, which featured chapter introductions by alumni/ae and friends of the School of Foreign Service, encouraged us once again to invite alumni/ae to share their personal experience and insights for this new edition. These men and women write from the vantage point of the successful professional in business, government, and the nonprofit world, and we think you will find them informative and insightful.

The organizations profiled in **Careers in International Affairs** are well-known generally or known specifically for their history of hiring international affairs graduates. The chapters devoted to the U.S. Government and International Organizations are comprehensive. The chapters on banking, business, consulting, nonprofit, education, and research are selective and contain a sampling of organizations broadly representative of their fields. The chapter on media offers general insights on work—and the prospects for work—in this competitive, exciting, and fast-changing field. Readers will certainly note the absence of some specific organizations that hire for international positions. However, our purpose here is to convey a sense of employment possibilities and hiring dynamics in many careers and not to attempt to provide an exhaustive list of employers to contact. **Careers in International Affairs**, then, is not conceived as a comprehensive guide to all international careers. In fact, we recommend that it be used as an integral part of your international career exploration in conjunction with other career resource materials. There is a final chapter on using the internet, and a sampling of books we consider helpful in an appendix to the book.

The information in the 1997 edition is the result of independent research and telephone and written inquiries to a wide range of organizations and institutions. This edition updates the areas of business, banking, consulting, and nonprofit, taking into account the mergers, acquisitions, and downsizing that have changed those fields in the last five years. The new book contains information on more than 300 organizations, all of which have been updated since the last edition and approximately one-third of which appear in **Careers in International Affairs** for the first time. Each entry provides a brief sketch of what each organization does, both in the United States and abroad. When possible, details on the skills, attributes, and experience desired in applicants is noted. The most significant exception to this is in the chapter on international business, where many job definitions have changed and the line between domestic and international often does not exist, rendering the task of describing specific profiles of attractive candidates increasingly problematic. Finally, we provide contact information—the central headquarters or the office where hiring is coordinated. Readers should realize that many organizations have branch offices close to where they are located, an important fact given the increase of decentralized hiring. Once again, we have agreed not to list human resource directors' names, as such information changes frequently. Where organizations have specifically requested that we not make such information widely available, we have not listed phone or fax numbers or e-mail addresses. However, the addresses and telephone numbers provided give the job seeker an initial contact point for further information on these organizations and the opportunities they offer. Specifically, telephone numbers should be used to identify individuals currently responsible for recruitment, and all correspondence should be directed to them. Where relevant, we have included an organization's World Wide Web site, which often contains a wealth of additional information about the organization and its current hiring practices.

A Special Thanks

This edition owes its existence to Dr. Allan E. Goodman, Executive Dean of the School of Foreign Service at Georgetown University. In his research and writing, he has always focused on the future. Within the School, he created a curriculum designed to prepare students for the next century. Outside the School, he has advanced the cause of graduate international affairs education and promoted the employ-ment of our graduates in the public, private, and nonprofit sectors throughout the world. Dean Goodman taught us that the future is something we conjure up—not something that comes to us, but some-thing we create for ourselves.

A book like this arises out of the advise and insights of many friends and colleagues. We must also acknowledge, first, the students of the School of Foreign Service, whose commitment to the education and training necessary for international careers has been the inspira-tion for this book. Next, we must express our gratitude to the interna-tional recruiters who have supported our program and shared their information and insights with us over the years. And finally, a very spe-cial word of appreciation must go to the alumni/ae of the School of Foreign Service, whose experience is an example and an inspiration to those who teach and train the graduates who will seek careers in the 21st century.

Careers in International Affairs

1

The International Affairs Job Market

MARIA PINTO CARLAND *

Retired U.S. Army General Colin Powell, at the dedication of the MBNA Career Education Center at Georgetown University on February 21st, 1996, told an audience of students and faculty that each of us needs to "reach down and reach back" to bring others forward to stand at our side. That is the essence of this book, written by alumni/ ae and friends of the School of Foreign Service to assist the students who come after them. Powell went on to say, "It's a great time to be alive. It's a great time to be in a career counseling center, trying to figure out what role you're going to play in this new world that is emerging." And his parting advice was, "Find that which you do well. Continue to serve . . . give something back."

The end of every century is a time for reflection and anticipation. It is especially true for us here and now, as we try to form a vision for the future. The public, private and nonprofit sectors are spending this last decade of the 20th century assessing what they have accomplished, whether they have been successes, and what needs to be done to remain competitive. Mergers, layoffs, and reorganizations are occurring around the world. Here in America, the U.S. business community began mergers and acquisitions in the 1980s that in turn led to layoffs and reorganizations in the 1990s. The U.S. government followed suit, with reallocations of funding, early retirements, and hiring freezes. And

---

* Maria Pinto Carland is Associate Director of the Master of Science in Foreign Service program in the School of Foreign Service at Georgetown University. Prior to joining the School, she was an administrator at the Patterson School of Diplomacy and International Commerce, and the University of Toronto Graduate History Department. She has also been a curatorial assistant at the Metropolitan Museum, the Art Gallery of Ontario, and the University of Kentucky Art Museum, and a program officer at the United Nations Association and the Foreign Policy Association. Ms. Carland holds an M.A. from Georgetown University.

most recently, the private voluntary organizations (PVOs) have realized they too need to find a special niche and reorganize to create their competitive advantage within it. Around the globe, men and women, corporations and agencies—governmental and nongovernmental—are gearing up for the new century, with all its problems and possibilities.

As General Powell suggested, this is an exciting time for young people today—you are entering a world where success is tied to streamlining. Society awaits the skills and strategic thinking you will offer to make the next century an efficient, effective one. Technology changes daily, but human dynamics never change—more sophisticated communication must go hand in hand with collaboration and teamwork. You will become masters in both fields. But the 21st century will make greater demands, and society will have higher expectations of you. Your challenge will be to bring creativity, courage, and compassion to all that you do. We are confident that you will succeed and offer this book as our way of "reaching back" to each of you.

It is imperative to consider the range of alternatives, how these alternatives relate to your interests, and how best to prepare for a career through an academic curriculum and professional activities.

Education and Experience

Information about careers has become such an integral part of the American education system that even many children in elementary schools have a day set aside to learn what firemen and farmers do. We are a can-do country, and we are urged early in our lives to discover what we want to do, and whether we have what it takes—in terms of interest, skills, education, and experience. To this end, effective career guidance and employment services are essential. Most educational institutions recognize this and offer students preparation and training, insights and advice, opportunities and contacts as well as encouragement and assistance. What they don't offer is jobs. Indeed, experience at the School of Foreign Service shows that our students' achievements are supported by our career services, but their accomplishments come through their own efforts. Here at Georgetown University we believe that career achievement is the result of the interaction between a student's character and our curriculum, a student's intelligence and our instructors, and a student's skills and our services.

Thus, it is crucial that you realize responsibility for finding a job is basically yours. It is also critical that you understand that the most difficult part of any job search—and of life in general—is knowing who you are and what you want. The answers to these questions will help you explain why you want to join a particular sector, assist you in choosing a job, and enable you to convince others that you have something to contribute to the field. *You* must create and seize opportunities for yourself. *You* must be able to present yourself as an asset to potential employers and to those whose career assistance you seek.

Preparation for the Entry Level: Education

Today it is no longer sufficient, or satisfying, to study a single discipline in isolation. Just as the line between domestic and international has blurred, so too the line between disciplines is disappearing. Historians must understand economics and science, political scientists must appreciate budgets and finance. And furthermore, educated individuals must be able to use technical skills not only to expand their knowledge but to apply it. The requirements of the 21st century have already outdistanced the curriculum of the 20th century. In the future, we will assume that the physical and behavioral sciences, the humanities and cultural and ethical studies will be part of every person's body of knowledge. Also, we will expect students to acquire a knowledge of foreign societies—their histories, norms, values, aspirations, capacities, and perceptions—and the language abilities to understand and reach them. This knowledge will come from an interdisciplinary, intercultural, and multilingual education, all aspects of which are crucial for communication and collaboration. A recent report from the College Placement Council Foundation said that employers place the highest value on skills not usually associated with specific training: generic cognitive skills and social skills. Nonacademic training and experience are rated as highly as the knowledge, principles, and practices of a particular academic discipline or trade. The same study called cross-cultural competence "the critical new human resource requirement created by the global environment."

This integrative approach of interdisciplinary, intercultural, and multilingual education will soon infiltrate and inform all the traditional fields. However, a number of enduring requirements continue to stand out:

- Knowledge of history and an awareness of patterns in international relations.

- Thorough grasp of what determines foreign policy priorities and realities.

- Solid grounding in economics and an understanding of international business.

- Familiarity with basic business and accounting skills.

- Well-developed computer skills and a high comfort level with technology.

- Understanding of policy development and implementation.

- Clarity and accuracy in speaking and writing.

- Self-awareness: comprehension of leadership and teamwork skills.

- Awareness of and commitment to ethical standards and personal values.

- Logic and objectivity in thinking, particularly the ability to identify issues, detail alternative courses of action, and establish and act on criteria for making choices.

- Ability to project possible future consequences of present decisions.

- Talent for time management.

- Personal qualities of poise, humor, imagination, compassion, and intellectual curiosity, balanced judgment, and openness to new ideas.

The utility of specialization is perhaps one of the more common questions posed with regard to educational requirements and concerns. Specialization and sophistication of knowledge and analytical techniques can be crucial to the knowledge and work of the international professional. The isolation essential for scientific study or specialist investigation, however, is a severe handicap in policy prescription and in the successful implementation of a given strategy. Coping in policy situations with the multidimensional interactions that characterize international affairs requires a holistic, conceptual approach. The requirements of a new era in international affairs demand generalists capable of understanding the work of specialists and able to synthesize knowledge from various fields. Thus, the liberally educated generalist is prepared to wrestle with complex issues, sort them out, and produce logical and responsive conclusions. Practitioners of international affairs must recognize the importance of interpersonal relations affecting the outcome of any decision-making situation.

The circulation of knowledge will be the most significant aspect of the 21st century. The ability to communicate is the essence of international relations. In order to be able to communicate and collaborate across disciplines, students will need experience in both theory and practice of international affairs. It is the capacity to resolve communication difficulties among specialists that distinguishes the international policymaker. Students eager to prepare themselves for the next century must understand that while practical training will help them land the first job, it is their theoretical training that will ensure promotion, and a long and successful career.

Preparation for the Entry Level: Internships

Most entry-level job seekers in the international field face an "experience" dilemma: they need a job in order to gain experience, but cannot get a job without experience. One solution is to find a job for a few years between undergraduate and graduate school. This is an ideal time to explore the world of work, travel, make mistakes, test yourself, and then return to the classroom. If this is not possible, however, there is a middle way: internships. Many students obtain an internship while in school. The term "internship" loosely refers to a part-time or temporary position (paid, unpaid, or for academic credit) involving some relevant professional experience. An internship ideally should be a training experience that involves mutual learning and screening by both the intern and the employer. It should be an occasion for the student to take academic knowledge out of the classroom and apply it in the professional world and use real world experience to complement academic courses.

Internships offer several advantages:

• Insights into and an understanding of a particular career field.

• Exposure to, and experience in, a professional environment, enabling the intern to make contacts and get a feel for the working world.

• The potential for an inside track to an unadvertised full-time position.

An internship's major disadvantage is the risk that off-campus involvement during the academic year may undermine academic performance, given the tendency of employers to emphasize their priorities over the intern's. The ability to handle an internship depends on the ability to manage one's time.

In seeking an internship, there are several points worth considering:

- Consult a variety of sources for leads. It pays to cast a wide net, but be discriminating—don't apply for every opportunity you come across.

- It takes time to arrange an internship since they are not high on the list of an employer's priorities. Be persistent. Be patient.

- You may be able to take on more responsibility than an internship description would first indicate. Many employers will want to test you on the job before rewarding you with pay or substantive responsibilities. Remember that if you have a particular interest you can sometimes convince an employer to create an internship where none exists.

The Employment Search

Job hunting is a testing, matching process. What makes it challenging and stimulating is the way you use your self-knowledge and your knowledge about the world of work. It is especially important that you do the necessary preparation or "homework" to acquire this knowledge. Your goal should be to learn about a career field and about your capabilities and interests in that area. The most successful job seekers generally are those who have researched various job sectors; who have done a good deal of reading; who have made many contacts, phone calls, and consultations; and who have skillfully used their academic base. They have done considerable internal preparation, self-assessment, and thinking. They know their personal characteristics, their desired job environment, their long range goals, and what they can offer an employer. How do you go about this?

There are two kinds of preparation, internal and external. Internal preparation involves some soul searching about who you are, what you have accomplished, what you do well, and what makes you happy. Career guidance and testing will help you here, as will workshops on resume and cover-letter writing. The process of putting together your resume will help you define your accomplishments and experience. Be honest with yourself about who you are and what you want.

External preparation involves investigating career fields in general, and firms and agencies in particular. You already possess the necessary tools—by virtue of your education you are researcher and analyst. You should approach career planning in the same way as you approach your studies. Just as you attend classes, attend workshops offered by your school's career office. Just as you use the library and the internet for research, consult them for information on career planning. In the same way you strive to write clear and concise prose, you should learn how to prepare an impressive resume and write a targeted cover letter. Just as you may interview various individuals for term papers and other projects, interview them for career information. Just as you expend considerable effort analyzing competing worldviews, historical interpretations, or philosophical tomes, analyze your own aspirations, skills, and credentials.

You may also wish to consult one of the many books that have appeared in recent years covering the mechanics of locating a job. While there are many witty and engaging manuals (some of which are listed in the bibliography) on the techniques of job seeking, the basic components of the employment process can be reduced to the following:

- Identify your interests;

- Prepare an effective resume;

- Develop leads and contacts; and

- Prepare for interviews.

Resumes

Resumes are useful for one purpose only—to get an interview. Job-hunting manuals all have sections on the preparation of a resume, but the form and content varies significantly. There is no standard way to do a resume, but for young people, a chronological approach is ideal. It is critical to keep it brief (one page) and neat and make sure that an employer can easily discover your assets and skills. Your resume should be technically perfect—no errors, no typos, in an easy-to-read (12-point) font that can be easily scanned into a computer database. While the resume is important, you can waste much time by reworking it. A properly worded cover letter, carefully targeted (with resume enclosed) can be just as effective. Your time is best spent honing your interview skills. In the end, the resume should convey to the employer a sense of what you know, where you have been, and what you can do for him or her as distinguished from what you know or have studied. Your cover letter should be more specific. It should emphasize why you wish to join that particular organization instead of another, what it is that attracted you, and describe an instance which demonstrates why your skills and knowledge would be a good match.

Contacts

An overwhelming majority of jobs (85 percent) are never advertised. In addition, many companies have decided that on-campus recruiting is an inefficient use of resources. Instead, an incredible number of employment opportunities are passed on only by word of mouth. Thus it is important to establish a wide circle of acquaintances who know your interests and abilities, so that when they hear of a position, they will think of you. Only by consulting with a variety of people of different ages and experience who are willing to help you (e.g., faculty or university staff members, alumni/ae of your school, family friends, relations, interviewees for past research projects) can you expect to tap into the "hidden job" network.

Networking is an overused word, but with good reason. Networking is often the most important component in a job search. Do not overuse your network, however—contacts are a valuable yet delicate and perishable resource. You need to cultivate them carefully. Be appreciative, be reasonable, be courteous—particularly about their time. Most people you will meet and speak with have full time jobs that require their attention and energy. They are doing you a favor by giving you some of that attention. Never request an information interview with a contact if you intend to ask for a job. Honesty and forthrightness are essential elements in maintaining this valuable access. Contacts, used properly, can provide you with excellent information about their own and other organizations. They may suggest job-search strategies and contacts that will assist you; they may share stories about what they did right or wrong with their education and their career decisions; and they even may find or refer you to a job. Remember, an information interview provides a showcase for your ability. Use it wisely.

Interviews

Interviews are the key to receiving employment offers and preparation is the key to a successful interview. The best interview should be like a good conversation: You should be comfortable with yourself, at ease in your surroundings, pleased to be there, interested in the issue at hand, and willing to discuss it. In any interview, you need to be able to develop a consistent theme based on your resume that explains why you are interviewing for this particular position. Despite the lengthy and sometimes convoluted path that an interview may follow, there are really only three essential questions posed: Why are you interested in our organization? What can you offer this organization (i.e., what specific functions in our organization can you perform)? What type of a person are you (i.e., what are your interests and assets)?

If you cannot answer these questions, you shouldn't be there. If you cannot give specific examples to support and illustrate your answers, you won't be convincing. The interview is not the time to begin considering the answers to these questions. Prepare for them in advance. The interviewer expects you to be able to demonstrate a considerable amount of self-knowledge: What do you think about what you know, what have you learned from your successes and failures, and how have you integrated your education and experience into the person you are today. And remember: Be interested, sound interested, and you will be interesting.

The Realities of Seeking a Job

In conclusion, the following advice should be considered carefully:

- Take the time to evaluate your education, experience, and ability. While you may be short on experience, you are long on the ability to analyze issues and make judgments in an intense, competitive atmosphere. You know how to organize your time, meet deadlines, and define and defend your ideas and interests orally and in writing. In a tight job market, you must present your assets intelligently and distinguish yourself.

- Employers may ask what have you done, but they really want to know what you can do for them. Make sure you have examples ready that illustrate what you can do for them.

- Job-search manuals, university career offices, and college deans all emphasize the value of focusing interests. This doesn't mean closing doors to other opportunities, but rather, choosing which door to open first. You must be focused. That doesn't mean your focus can never change. You can still keep your options open.

- Follow up on all your contacts.

- The overwhelming majority of people who fail do so as a result of personality, not skill, problems. You can master most jobs. The way you handle interpersonal dynamics, however, will make all the difference between an acceptable and a superior performance. Don't tell recruiters you are a "people person"—describe an incident that illustrates your interpersonal skills.

- Remember that one of the most highly valued experiences these days is teamwork. Make sure you can cite experiences—in the classroom, as a volunteer, or on the job—in which you played a meaningful role on a team. Be prepared to explain the results of that teamwork, not only in terms of success or failure, but in terms of what you learned about yourself and the situation.

- At the entry level, be willing to pay your dues. It's simply a way of demonstrating not only ability but an appreciation for the on-the-job culture.

- There is no forward movement if risks are not taken. You are young. You can afford to take calculated risks—don't just apply for jobs you know you can do without effort. Apply for the jobs that will make you stretch.

With these comments in mind, we hope that the international career information that follows will lead to a fuller understanding of the opportunities available and facilitate your career campaign. You will soon find that their are unlimited opportunities for those whose international, interdisciplinary education has prepared them for the 21st century.

2

United States Government

ANDREW BOESEL*

The purpose of this chapter is to give the reader an overview of the United States government as a potential employer of men and women in the international relations field. In addition, it will explain the way the civil service system now operates and then describe the variety of agencies and departments that offer careers to those with an international relations focus.

It is an understatement that the federal government is going through an incredible period of change and upheaval. Reinvention, reengineering, reorganization, downsizing, buy-outs, hiring freezes, furloughs, reductions in force, and abolishment of departments and agencies are only some of the terms that are used constantly when talking about the federal government. By all indications this emphasis on change will accelerate.

Early in the Clinton Administration, the first report of National Performance Review called for the elimination of 252,000 permanent positions from the federal government, a reduction to be spread over five years. Later legislation raised this number to 272,900 positions. These figures may continue to rise as the Congress and the Administration continue to examine ways to cut not only the federal budget but also the scope and impact of the government. Some of the proposals to restructure the foreign affairs agencies of the federal government will have a significant impact on employment.

---

* Andrew Boesel is with the Career Development Programs of the Graduate School of the U.S. Department of Agriculture. He manages a number of different development programs and services. He was the first director of the Presidential Management Intern Program. He has spoken to many different college and university groups about public sector employment options. Mr. Boesel is a graduate of Beloit College and earned a master's degree in governmental administration from the University of Pennsylvania.

Further complicating the employment picture is the fact that personnel decisions, including hiring actions, are becoming extremely decentralized. Individual departments and agencies are making their own decisions as to who they wish to hire, while making sure that these personnel decisions adhere to established merit-system principles. The role of the central personnel agency, the Office of Personnel Management, has been dramatically changed. It is no longer the gatekeeper of the hiring process, but now serves more as a resource and information provider.

It is important to realize, however, that the federal government, in spite of all these changes and pressures, continues to hire people, albeit at a much lower rate than in previous years. Furthermore, the federal government is by far the single largest employer in the country. Excluding the Postal Service and other quasi-government corporations and entities, the federal government still employs about two million persons.

Another significant point about federal government is the geographic diversity of its workforce. Contrary to popular opinion, the federal workforce is not concentrated in the Washington area. Although the Washington area is home for many of the senior managers, the workforce as a whole is spread throughout the country and, of course, overseas. California has the most federal employees of any state.

While total federal employment is declining for the first time since the early 1960s there have been dramatic changes within the workforce. The workforce of the 1990s is highly trained. It is comprised largely of professional and technically oriented staff. Gone are the days of large clerical staffs or blue collar workers. It says much about the government today, and the workforce in general, that there are more engineers on the government payroll than secretaries.

For individuals with a focus on international affairs, the range of potential job choices is quite dramatic. As this chapter hopes to point out, there are many different ways to go about thinking about a career with the federal government.

There are many dynamic forces at work that affect hiring prospects. As budgets change and various reorganization schemes are advanced, employment opportunities with specific agencies will be affected. As pointed out, the major impact to date has been contraction. Even without growth, however, agencies still do some hiring to replace workers lost to retirement, changes to other agencies, and departure from the civil service. In most instances, this replacement hiring has not kept up with attrition, nor are new hires at the same experience level. Hiring one new junior worker for every two or three senior employees lost is a fairly common pattern.

Organizing a job search in the federal government is not unlike the process that one would use in the private or nonprofit sector. You need to know what you want to do and where that kind of work is done in the government. There is no longer a single overarching structure or examination process for government personnel. Today, developing a job-search strategy for a federal position requires creativity and patience, perseverance, and hard work.

In the government as a whole, salaries and benefits for employees do not constitute a major expense. Total salaries and benefits come to about 10 percent of the total federal budget, but within specific departments the percent of the budget devoted to paying staff can be significantly higher. In those agencies, small changes in the budget can lead to real and immediate anxiety about loss of jobs.

The federal government career system is characterized by multiple points of entry and the maintenance of different personnel systems. The vast majority of the two million federal employees are in the competitive civil service, but even that has separate systems for foreign service, the intelligence agencies, and law enforcement. The legislative and judicial branches have their own personnel systems, but it should be noted that legislative staff totals have started to decline.

The geographic diversity of the workforce is both positive and negative. The positive aspect is obvious. One does not need to be tied to a narrow geographic area. The downside is that availability of timely job vacancy information can be fragmented and occasionally is not current.

Other general comments about federal employment are in order. Nearly every federal agency has some office, division, or identifiable group of staff that has international relations as its focus. In many cases these offices are easy to find, but in others it takes a little detective work to ferret out the appropriate staff unit. Begin with the information in this chapter. Commercially published directories of federal departments and agencies can also be valuable sources of information. So too are the departmental telephone directories that can be purchased from the Government Printing Office.

Government career systems build from the bottom up and career paths begin at the entry level. For many occupations that entry point is at the GS-5 or GS-7 level. For those with a master's degree, the beginning point is at the GS-9 level. The overwhelming majority of positions in the career service are filled from within. As agencies struggle with realigning their workforces to match budget realities this emphasis on retaining existing employees will be reinforced. The result is that employment opportunities for those on the outside will be drastically reduced.

Most federal government employment systems put a premium on the written application. Even this area has been affected by dramatic change. Gone is the Standard Form 171 "Application for Federal Employment." In its place is a vast array of agency-specific requirements, as well as a new form that agencies may use if they wish. More and more agencies are asking applicants to submit some kind of resume. Regardless of the exact written application requirement there are some general guidelines to keep in mind.

It is critical to tailor your application package to the specific job. Having a generic, one-size-fits-all resume will not work. You need to highlight specifically the knowledge, skills, and abilities (KSAs) that the position calls for. If it is a budget analyst, then you need to clearly highlight your experience in that area. Work experience descriptions should stress your accomplishments and actual skills. Reliance on action verbs is essential and putting the job experiences in the first person context is critical. Remember, you are marketing yourself.

In describing your experiences do not overlook campus and community activities, as well as political activities. Don't be concerned that you have been working for the "wrong" party. Political activities can demonstrate the kinds of work you can do. The federal employment process gives full weight and credit to volunteer experience, and affiliation with either party is a plus. Once in the government you are precluded from getting involved in a whole host of political activities. The civil service is truly nonpartisan.

Some general comments on pay and benefits are in order. Legislation was enacted a few years ago to establish locality pay for high-cost-of-living cities like New York and San Francisco. There also is a pay system in place designed to keep federal pay in line with comparable jobs in the private sector. However, the impact of the ongoing budget debate has meant that annual increases have been significantly less than what survey data would have required. An individual with a bachelor's degree and some limited work experience would begin federal employment at the GS-7 level. A master's degree qualifies one to start at the GS-9 level. Current starting salary at the GS-7 level is nearly $24,000 and at the GS-9 level just about $29,000.

There are a number of provisions being debated within the current Administration and the Congress to substantially change the federal pay and job classification system. In all likelihood the changes will mean that individual departments and agencies will have more flexibility in setting starting pay levels and also in changing the way that pay will be adjusted for employees already on board.

Federal employee fringe benefits have lagged behind changes in other parts of the economy. Suffice it to say that federal employees do have access to health and life insurance and there is a retirement system, which is based social security. The Federal Employee Retirement System (FERS) has a number of key features, most importantly because it is based in social security it is more portable than the system it replaced. Employee contributions to FERS can go up to 10 percent of your salary, and the government will contribute up to 5 percent of your salary.

One final comment about federal employment concerns its distribution among the agencies. As mentioned earlier, a relatively small percentage of the workforce, between 12% and 14%, is located in the Washington metropolitan area. Nearly half of the federal civilian workforce is employed by the Department of Defense. The largest single nondefense agency is the Department of Veterans Affairs. With nearly 260,000 employees it has more than 100,000 more employees than the next largest agency, the Department of the Treasury.

The pace of change and turmoil in the federal government was commented on earlier in this chapter. That sense of change and the use of radically new systems certainly extends to the employment process itself. Gone are the nationwide, governmentwide examinations and maintenance of registers of interested and qualified candidates. In its place are specific vacancy announcements and detailed application procedures.

The civil service hiring process can be confusing and mysterious, even to those already in the system. Agency hiring officials can no longer rely on the results of examinations such as the Professional Administrative Career Exam (PACE) and standard Form 171s. In their place are a range of application methods, including electronic approaches. The critical point to keep in mind is the need to take a great deal of personal initiative in finding offices and persons who are interested in hiring you. Having access to timely information is key to the employment process.

Instead of the nationwide exams of the past, the federal government now relies on what in the personnel business is known as case examining. Under case examining, an agency posts a vacancy, individuals apply for this position, candidates are rated and ranked against the job qualifications, and selections are made. The next time there is a vacancy the whole process is repeated.

There is one important exception to this process and that involves the outstanding scholar provisions. If a student has a 3.5 grade point average on a 4.0 scale or is in the top 10 percent of his or her class, these individuals can be hired directly by the agency without having to go through a rating and ranking process.

An often overlooked mechanism for landing a position with a federal department or agency is the cooperative education program. This program, designed for students still enrolled in school, is based on the principle of combining academic coursework with planned periods of on-the-job experience at a particular agency. One of the most important features of the program is that at the end of co-op experience, the agency may hire the student immediately without any further examination or testing. This is called noncompetitive conversion and is a key feature of the Presidential Management Intern Program.

The cooperative education program applies to both graduate and undergraduate levels. There are some important differences between the requirements at the graduate and undergraduate levels, but the principles remain the same, as does the noncompetitive conversion authority. A cooperative education program does require an agreement between the college or university and the participating federal department or agency. The agreement does not have to be in writing, but does need to address the length of the work experience and its frequency. To qualify a graduate student must work 640 hours or 16 weeks. For an undergraduate the work time must be 26 weeks or 1,040 hours. This work time can be extended over the time one is earning a degree. If there is time to consider a cooperative education assignment as part of an educational plan, it is wise to pursue it.

If you don't qualify as an outstanding scholar or the cooperative education idea won't work, let us briefly take a look at how the hiring process is supposed to work.

Beginning in 1995, Form 171 was no longer required and was not going to be printed or stocked. The new option form, "Application for

Federal Employment," is just two pages long. Unlike Form 171, it asks only for information about employment and education related to the specific vacancy for which you are applying. If written information is required, applicants will choose whether to submit a resume, use the new optional form for federal employment, or present their qualifications in some other written format. There is some general information that is needed on all written application for federal employment. These relate to citizenship, which is required for federal employment, and eligibility for veterans preference.

Agencies may develop their own forms for unique occupations with highly specialized requirements or for use in agency-developed automated application systems. Agencies may also require specific types of applications from their own employees for merit promotion opportunities.

The new 3-step process for seeking federal employment is:

1. Find out what jobs are open. You may call the Career America Connection at (912) 757-3000 (not a toll-free number) and obtain current job vacancy information. Another option is to visit the closest Federal Employment Information Center. These centers can be found in most major cities and are listed in the phone book. In the Washington area, the Federal Employment Information Center is located at 1900 E Street, NW. Vacancy information also can be downloaded from an OPM bulletin board. The phone number for that is (912) 757-3100. There are a number of commercially published federal job vacancy directories that either can be found in libraries and career placement centers or purchased at major bookstores and newsstands.

2. Select a potential job and request an application and/or vacancy announcement from the hiring agency. From the previously mentioned information sources you can request more detailed information about the job and/or any specific instructions for applying for a position. In most cases you will also get the name and phone number of a contact point in that agency.

3. Follow the instructions on how to apply.

Is the federal hiring system really that simple? Probably not. Having access to current information and knowing what agencies are actually looking are the keys to unlocking the federal employment process.

The agency-specific vacancy announcements are absolutely vital to the new process. Knowing when agencies will be issuing vacancy announcements and then being able to tailor your application to match the requirements are the essential features of the process.

Unfortunately, the actual conduct of a federal government job search can sometimes seems as daunting as the employment outlook and hiring process seems daunting. Thus one needs to be persistent, patient, and determined. In organizing a job search, one should focus on the kinds of work one likes, where one wants to be located, and the type of organization in which one wants to work. For example, does working in a staff office doing research and analysis sound interesting or does being involved in day-to-day program administration sound more appealing? The choice between staff and line assignments can sometimes be difficult to change later in a career. Don't be distressed if it is not possible to obtain a job in the agency in which you are most interested. Keep in mind that your first job is not your last job. A first job in the Department of Commerce might well lead to another job offer later on from a different agency. Always remember that for a recruiter, it is much easier to hire from within government than it is to bring people in from outside government. Be flexible. Agencies may find it easier to get a person on board through some type of temporary or noncareer appointment and attempt to convert this position to a permanent, career position at some later date.

A lot of the job search depends on personal contact with interested agency officials. This will require making appointments with agency personnel, and these appointments will require advance notice. Security arrangements at the vast majority of federal office buildings preclude casual visits. Always bring some form of identification with you when going to a federal building.

It is difficult to predict how long the job-search process will take because it varies with each person's goals and opportunities. Four to six months is not an unrealistic time frame. If the position requires a background check and security clearance, that time period can almost double. This is especially true if you have lived or studied abroad for any length of time. Be prepared to cope with a great deal of uncertainty in the job-search process. This has never been more true than now as agencies face dramatic changes in budgets and program responsibilities. This is especially true for foreign affairs agencies. The political climate is chilly these days.

Paperwork in large bureaucracies has a life of its own and is subject to movement in fits and starts. The office seeking to hire you may need to get approval from other places in the organization. The office extending a formal job offer may be different from the one in which you are going to work. As budgets change constantly, what once seemed like a great prospect may disappear overnight.

In spite of a gloomy immediate forecast, one thing remains constant: Public service is part of what democratic government is all about. We need young men and women who wish to serve their government. Dedication to public service is both rewarding and honorable. The federal government always needs an infusion of new talent. If you are diligent in pursuing job leads and can be creative in selling yourself the results can be extremely worthwhile. The committed job-hunter should be aware that current reductions in the federal workforce combined with desires to restructure the scope of the government will mean, in particular, an extended period of limited hiring and, in general, a period of great change. Competition for vacancies will be extremely high. This should result in the hiring of only the best and the brightest.

CIVIL SERVICE

Agency for International Development

The United States Agency for International Development (USAID) is the independent federal agency that administers and coordinates U.S. foreign economic and humanitarian assistance programs around the world. The agency was created by an executive order of President John F. Kennedy in 1961. Employees of USAID work with individuals, governments, and other organizations to support sustainable development—economic and social growth that can maintain itself without exhausting the resources of a host country or damaging the economic, cultural, or natural environment. USAID coordinates programs and operates missions in Africa, Asia, the Near East, Central and Eastern Europe, Latin America and the Caribbean, and the Newly Independent States of the former Soviet Union.

USAID's sustainable development program focuses on many interrelated areas. By supporting economic growth, through such program investments as microenterprise development and poverty lending, USAID creates markets for American goods and services. USAID supports economic development that is environmentally sensitive and programs that use natural resources wisely. USAID supports long-lasting approaches to health and population problems, including vaccination and immunization programs, AIDS prevention, child and maternal nutrition programs, and family-planning services. USAID programs promote democracy through free and fair elections, teach the skills of democratic governance, and empower citizens so that they are full participants in their own development. In the belief that sustainable development is not possible without integrating all aspects of human development, USAID is committed to improving early childhood development, basic education, adult literacy, and the empowerment of women. Humanitarian relief and disaster planning are also integral to sustainable development. By helping nations acquire the means to plan for and respond to disasters, USAID can measurably contribute to a more peaceful and prosperous world.

Candidates for employment with USAID should have a background in one or more of the following areas: development, economics, international relations, health, business/accounting, or public policy. Hiring is uncertain for the foreseeable future, however, because of uncertainty of budget cuts.

USAID   tel. 202/647-1850
320 21st Street, N.W.
Washington, D.C. 20523–0056

Agriculture, U.S. Department of

The United States Department of Agriculture (USDA) has a wide variety of international functions. USDA's international work includes negotiating on farm products, running major export market development programs, and administering import regulations.

The **Foreign Agricultural Service** (FAS) has prime responsibility for administering export promotion programs and some agricultural import regulations. FAS operates worldwide with staff located at more than 70 posts abroad covering more than 100 countries. Through a global network of agricultural counselors and attaches, FAS helps build markets overseas, gathers and assesses information on world agricultural production and trade, and provides that information to U.S. farmers and traders. FAS manages USDA's export credit program and the food for peace program that help finance $6 to $8 billion in agricultural exports each year. FAS maintains more than 12 overseas trade offices that draw together the resources of private-sector agricultural trade promotion groups to ease access for foreign buyers and provide services to U.S. exporters. FAS coordinates and directs USDA's responsibilities in international trade agreement programs and negotiations.

As a career field, international agriculture has good employment prospects for applicants with strong backgrounds in economics, agriculture, and trade. With a current staff of about 300 professionals based in the United States and 100 overseas, FAS hires about 15 professionals a year. Most career opportunities are in the field of agricultural economics and require a graduate degree (or equivalent experience) with substantial economics coursework and work experience in agricultural economics. FAS has both a competitive career civil service and an excepted foreign service thereby offering a broad range of activities and opportunities for promotion.

The **Office of International Cooperation and Development** (OICD) is charged with planning and implementing the USDA's international development and technical cooperation efforts in food and agriculture as well as coordinating the department's international organization affairs and scientific exchange programs. Staff professionals have backgrounds in either agricultural economics, international relations, or agricultural sciences.

Within the **Economic Research Service (ERS)**, the **Agriculture and Trade Analysis Division** studies the agricultural economies and policies of foreign countries and the agricultural trade and development relationships between foreign countries and the United States. The division relates economic, technical, and political factors to agricultural trade between countries. The structure, efficiency, and performance of foreign economies are major research interests of the division. Most of the division's employees are economists with backgrounds in either agricultural or international economics. While the division prefers applicants with Ph.D.s, it will consider candidates with lesser degrees. The ability to speak and read one or more foreign languages is increasingly important for potential candidates.

A number of other USDA offices also are concerned with international affairs. The **Federal Grain Inspection Service** performs grain export inspections and the **Food Safety and Inspection Service** monitors import grades. The **Animal and Plant Health Inspection Service** checks imports for disease and examines plants, meat, and poultry at ports of entry. Technical assistance for overseas forestry programs, research on international forests, and arrangements for the training of foreign forestry experts are provided by the **International Forestry Staff** of the **Forest Service**. The **Office of Transportation** identifies transportation problems in areas of export and foreign trade and initiates remedial action. The **Agricultural Research Service** engages in cooperative research with foreign nations and the **Extension Service** works on extension programs with foreign nations. The economists and meteorologists of the **World Food and Agricultural Outlook Board** compile all agricultural and food data used to develop USDA outlook and situation material.

U.S. Department of Agriculture tel. 202/720-2791
14th Street & http://web.fir.com:80/web/fed/agr
   Independence Avenue, S.W.
Washington, D.C. 20250

Arms Control and Disarmament Agency

The U.S. Arms Control and Disarmament Agency (ACDA) operates under the direction of the Secretary of State and works closely with the Office of the President to formulate and implement American arms control and disarmament policies and to assess the effects of these policies on the U.S. economy and national security. The agency manages U.S. participation in international arms control forums, produces and disseminates public information about arms control and disarmament, and conducts U.S. participation in international compliance and verification regimes. The agency comprises four bureaus and four offices. Each bureau, under the direction of an assistant director appointed by the President and confirmed by the Senate, is further broken down into divisions, each responsible for specific areas of ACDA's mandate.

Career opportunities with ACDA are limited due to the small size of the agency. Specialists in military strategy and technology, disarmament, weapons technology, foreign policy, and Soviet and East European studies are employed.

U.S. Arms Control and tel. 202/647-8677
   Disarmament Agency
320 21st Street, N.W.
Washington, D.C. 20451

Commerce, U.S. Department of

The U.S. Department of Commerce encourages, serves, and promotes American international trade, economic growth, and technological advancement. In order to fulfill its task, the department provides a great variety of programs.

The **International Trade Administration** (ITA) carries out the U.S. government's nonagricultural foreign trade activities. It encourages and promotes U.S. exports of manufactured goods, administers U.S. statutes and agreements dealing with foreign trade, and prepares advice on U.S. international trade and commercial policy. The agency is divided into four main offices: International Economic Policy, Trade Administration, Trade Development, and the Foreign Commercial Service. The **Office of International Economic Policy** has specialists for each country and region of the world, as well as a multilateral affairs office. It devises and implements trade and investment policies and agreements of bilateral and multilateral nature. The **Office of Trade Administration** is concerned with the development of export policies for sensitive commodities and products with emphasis on the prevention of the illegal transfer of high technology to other nations. It administers programs to protect U.S. products from unfair competition and it enforces antiboycott provisions. The **Office of Trade Development** handles most departmental efforts to promote world trade and to strengthen the international trade and investment position of the United States.

The ITA is headquartered in Washington, D.C., and operates 47 district offices. The agency employs about 250 people in various positions. International trade specialists should have a strong academic background in marketing, business administration, political science, sales promotion, economics, or related fields. Applicants for international economist positions should have completed a full four-year course with substantial attention to economics and statistics, accounting, or calculus. Other professional positions at ITA include specialists in trade, industries, import and export administration, compliance officers, electronic engineers, trade assistants, and criminal investigators. All these positions require a degree in political science, economics, finance, history, electronic engineering, business or commercial law, business administration, international trade, or international relations. A bachelor's degree is accepted; however, a master's degree is preferred. In some instances, appropriate work experience (such as market research, sales promotion, advertising, industrial production operations, commercial law, administrative law enforcement, or application of investigative skills) can qualify a person for certain positions.

An important part of the International Trade Administration with independent personnel procedures is the overseas component of the U.S. and

Foreign Commercial Service (US & FCS) known as the **Foreign Commercial Service** (FCS), which is part of the foreign service of the United States. The FCS is a career foreign service and has officers stationed in over 80 foreign nations as well as in the United States. The mission of the FCS is to support and represent U.S. trade and investment interests abroad, particularly in export expansion. FCS pursues these goals in three primary ways: promoting trade and facilitating investment; developing market and commercial intelligence; and representing the rights and concerns of U.S. commercial and investment interests abroad. The FCS professional profile emphasizes three elements: experience; commercial, policy, and linguistic skills; and behavioral characteristics. Junior officer entry is through the foreign service written examination. Competition for positions in FCS is extremely intense and many officers come from within ITA or the Department of State.

The Commerce Department's **Bureau of the Census** is the world's largest statistical organization and generates a considerable quantity of international demographic and foreign trade statistics. Approximately 105 professionals in the **Foreign Trade Division** compile current statistics on U.S. foreign trade, including data on imports, exports, and shipping. The **Center for International Research** has a staff of 62 people and gathers in-depth current data on a broad range of socioeconomic and demographic indicators for individual nations as well as particular world regions. Employment with the census bureau requires a background in statistics, demography, mathematics, economics, or area studies combined with a reading knowledge of a foreign language.

The **National Oceanographic and Atmospheric Administration** (NOAA), part of the Department of Commerce, is involved in a number of international activities in connection with its responsibilities for the weather service; civilian satellites; ocean fisheries; charting and mapping; and oceanic and atmospheric research. Each of these activities has an office specializing in international affairs. The **National Marine Fisheries Service** collects extensive data on foreign fishing and acts as staff in connection with negotiation of bilateral fisheries agreements. A small **Office of International Affairs** coordinates the work of the line organization, represents NOAA in certain international negotiations, and acts as a point of contact on international matters. A few positions with NOAA overseas also are available at weather stations and observatories for scientists with meteorological, electronic, or geophysical backgrounds.

The **Bureau of Economic Analysis** (BEA) monitors the state of the U.S. economy including international transactions. BEA's **International Investment Division** measures U.S. direct investments abroad and studies the economic impact of multinational corporations. Accountants and economists constitute the majority of the division's 30 member professional staff. The bureau's **Balance of Payments Division** employs about 45 professionals who prepare current statistics and analyses of the U.S. balance of international payments and international investment position.

International matters are dealt with by a number of other offices within the department. The **Maritime Administration** compiles statistics on U.S. seaborne trade, manages U.S. maritime relations with foreign countries, and administers the development and operation of the U.S. Merchant Marine. The **National Bureau of Standards** represents the United States in several international standards-setting organizations, maintains contacts with individual agencies in policy-making on international science and technology issues and offers technical assistance to nations wishing to engage in standards research. The secretary is advised on policy for the U.S. telecommunications industry by the **National Telecommunications and Information Administration**. The **Patent and Trademark Office** processes international trademark laws and regulations and represents the United States in international efforts to cooperate on patent and trademark policy.

U.S. Department of Commerce
Personnel Division
14th Street & Constitution
   Avenue, N.W.
Washington, D.C. 20230

tel. 202/482-2000
http://www.doc.com
http://www.ita.doc.gov

Bureau of the Census
Personnel Division
Room 1412-3
4700 Silverhill Road
Suitland, MD 20746

http://www.census.gov

National Oceanographic &
   Atmospheric Administration
Personnel Division
Silver Spring, MD 20910

tel. 301/413-0900
tel. 301/713-3050 (Personnel)
http://www.noaa.gov

Commission on Security and Cooperation in Europe

Also known as the Helsinki Commission, the Commission on Security and Cooperation in Europe is a U.S. government agency created in 1976 to monitor and encourage compliance with the Final Act of the Conference on Security and Cooperation in Europe, which was signed in Helsinki in 1975 by the leaders of 33 European countries, the United States, and Canada. The addition of Albania, the Baltic States, the Newly Independent States of the former Soviet Union, and several of the former Yugoslav republics has increased the number of participants to 53.

The Commission consists of nine members each from the U.S. House of Representatives and the U.S. Senate, and one member each from the departments of State, Defense, and Commerce. The posts of chairman and co-chairman are shared by the House and Senate and rotate every two years when a new Congress convenes. A professional staff of approximately 15 persons assists the commissioners in their work.

The Commission carries out its mandate in a variety of ways. It gathers and disseminates to the U.S. Congress, nongovernmental organizations, and the public information about Helsinki-related topics. Public hearings and briefings focusing on these topics are held frequently. The Commission also reports on the implementation of the Organization for Security and Cooperation in Europe (OSCE) commitments by the countries of Central and Eastern Europe, the former Soviet Union, and the United States. Some meeting reports are published. The Commission plays a unique role in the planning and execution of U.S. policy in the OSCE, including member and staff participation on U.S. delegations to OSCE meetings and in certain OSCE institutions. In addition, members of the Commission have regular contact with parliamentarians, government officials, and private individuals from OSCE-participating states.

Commission on Security and   tel. 202/225-1901
    Cooperation in Europe   fax 202/226-4199
234 Ford House Office Building   e-mail: csce@hr.house.gov
Washington, D.C. 20515

Council of Economic Advisors

The Council of Economic Advisors (CEA) is the President's key advisory panel on economic issues. The CEA has a staff of about 20 economists who analyze economic issues, provide economic advice, evaluate the federal government's economic programs and policies, and make recommendations concerning economic growth and stability. Employment opportunities are extremely limited.

Council of Economic Advisors   tel. 202/395-5084
Old Executive Office Building
Room 314
Washington, D.C. 20500

Defense, U.S. Department of

The United States Department of Defense (DoD) and related establishments offer a variety of opportunities to pursue careers in military, strategic, and intelligence activities. Although many positions are filled by military personnel, most of the offices and agencies related to the defense establishment also require civilian employees. For the sake of simplification, the related establishments will be treated as distinct from the main department.

The DoD is responsible for giving the United States the military forces it needs for its security. The department's organization and civilian recruitment procedures are extremely complex. For a better understanding of the structure of the department, consult the latest edition of the United States Government Manual (available from the U.S. Government Printing Office) for assistance.

The DoD and the military services (Army, Navy, Air Force, and Marine Corps) have their own separate personnel offices that independently recruit civilians for domestic positions. In general, all of the offices seek candidates with broad-based academic training. International affairs majors with a strong preparation in history and applied economics and an understanding of defense issues make attractive candidates.

The **Office of the Assistant Secretary of Defense for International Security Affairs** (ISA) develops and coordinates DoD policies and research in international political, military, and economic affairs. It studies general problems of international security as well as arms control and disarmament issues; administers overseas military assistance programs and arms sales to foreign powers; and provides policy guidance for U.S. military abroad and for U.S. representatives to international organizations and conferences. The office is also responsible for negotiating and monitoring agreements with foreign governments concerning equipment, facilities, operating rights, and the status of forces. The ISA administers an extensive external research program with emphasis on identifying and analyzing alternative defense policies to cope with international problems likely to affect the security of the United States.

The **Office of the Assistant Secretary of Defense for International Security Policy** (ISP) formulates and coordinates security strategy and policy and political-military policy on issues of DoD interest that relate to foreign governments and their defense establishments in Russia, Ukraine, and the other states of the former Soviet Union.

The **Office of the Secretary of Defense** (OSD) itself has limited occasions for hiring master's graduates with previous work experience. Typically, foreign affairs specialists are hired at GS-13 or GS-14 levels. Positions filled at the entry level are done through the Presidential Management Intern Program.

There are also many other DoD offices with significant international responsibilities. The **Office of the Secretary of Defense for Acquisition and Technology** oversees DoD research and development activities and exercises export control responsibilities. The office is involved in export licensing decisions; technology transfer policy; review of foreign military sales proposals from a technical military viewpoint; security assessments of proposed exports; munitions control cases; and technology training and sharing programs with allies. The **Office of the Secretary of Defense for Force Management Policy** develops policies, plans, and programs for employing foreign national employees with the DoD and participates in the negotiations of status of forces agreements with foreign governments. The **Army Material Command** operates an **Office of International Cooperative Programs**. Policy papers and estimates for the Joint Chiefs of Staff relating to U.S. security interests overseas are prepared by the **Director for Strategic Plans and Policy** of the Joint Chiefs of Staff.

Each of the military services has two offices where domestic employment opportunities in the international field are most numerous: intelligence and operations. Each service runs its own intelligence unit that gathers information on the activities of foreign elements as they relate to the interests of each organization. Each branch also has an office concerned with operating and planning. Within each of these offices are desk officers who follow political and military developments abroad and who prepare policy papers on issues confronting the particular service.

Division for Personnel & Security
Washington Headquarters Services
Room 3B347—The Pentagon
Washington, D.C. 20301

tel. 703/614-4066 (Employment Information Center)
tel. 703/697-9205 (General Employment Information)
http://www.dtic.mil/defenselink (DoD)

Personnel & Employment Service/
    Washington
Department of the Army
Room 1A881—The Pentagon
Washington, D.C. 20301

tel. 703/693-7911
tel. 703/693-6781

Human Resources Center Naval
    Sea Systems Command
Department of the Navy
2531 Jefferson Davis Highway
Arlington, VA 22242–5161

tel. 703/607-1816

Civilian Personnel Office
Department of the Air Force
Room 5E871—The Pentagon
Washington, D.C. 20330–1460

tel. 202/767-5449

Human Resources Office   tel. 703/614-1046
United States Marine Corps
Code ARCA, Room 1215
2 Navy Annex
Washington, D.C. 20380–1775

Defense Advanced Research Projects Agency

The Defense Advanced Research Projects Agency (DARPA) is the central research and development organization for the Department of Defense and has the primary responsibility for helping to maintain U.S. technological superiority over its potential adversaries and to prevent unforeseen technological advances by those adversaries. DARPA pursues research offering significant military utility to support and manage projects assigned by the Secretary of Defense and to marshal advanced research through a demonstration of its feasibility for military application. Research is conducted in such fields as advanced vehicle systems; tactical technology; advanced manufacturing, information sciences, and technology; and defense electronic, materials, and electromagnetic sciences. A vast majority of the technical professionals at DARPA have advanced degrees in one of the scientific or engineering disciplines. Applicants are required to establish eligibility with the Office of Personnel Management to be considered.

Office for Personnel & Security   tel. 703/697-9205
Washington Headquarters Services   http://ftp.arpa.mil
DARPA
Room 3B347—The Pentagon
Washington, D.C. 20301

Defense Security Assistance Agency

The Defense Security Assistance Agency (DSAA) develops and executes security assistance programs that support U.S. foreign policy and national security. The focal point for military assistance programs and foreign military sales, DSAA monitors direct weapons sales, technology transfer issues, budgetary and financial arrangements, and legislative initiatives. DSAA is divided into three directorates. **Plans Directorate** maintains an overview of the entire security assistance program, manages security assistance, and participates with the State Department in formulating and presenting to Congress the security assistance budget proposal. The **Operations Directorate** directs and supervises military assistance programs worldwide. Operations provides the interface between foreign governments, international organizations, U.S.

industry, and key elements of U.S. national defense. The **Comptroller** is responsible for overall financial management of security assistance programs. These three directorates are supported by a legal counsel and a professional congressional relations staff.

The agency's professional staff comprises over 100 security staff assistants, program analysts, country managers, comptrollers, budget analysts, and data analysts. Academic preparation in international relations, national security studies, or area studies provides good training for positions as security staff assistants and country managers. Expertise or experience in defense issues, military sales programs, or weapons systems is an asset for any potential recruit.

Defense Security Assistance Agency   tel. 703/695-7015
Room 4E841—The Pentagon
Washington, D.C. 20301–2800

Defense Technology Security Administration

The Defense Technology Security Administration (DTSA) develops and implements Department of Defense policies on international transfers of defense-related goods, services, and technologies to ensure that: (1) critical U.S. military technological advantages are preserved; (2) transfers of defense-related technology that could prove detrimental to U.S. security interests are controlled and limited; (3) proliferation of weapons of mass destruction and their means of delivery is prevented; and (4) legitimate defense cooperation with foreign allies and friends is supported. DTSA manages and implements the programs through four line directorates: Policy, License, Technology, and Technology Security Operations. A Resource Management Directorate provides information technology, human resource, financial, security, contracts, internal management controls, and general administrative support.

DTSA employs approximately 100 professionals. Employment opportunities are limited.

Defense Technology Security   tel. 703/604-4805
   Administration
Suite 3010
400 Army-Navy Drive
Arlington, VA 22202–2884

Drug Enforcement Agency

The Drug Enforcement Agency (DEA) enforces the controlled substances laws and regulations and investigates and prepares for prosecution those individuals suspected of violating federal drug-trafficking laws. The DEA also regulates the manufacture, distribution, and dispensing of licit pharmaceuticals. On an international level, the DEA attempts to reduce the supply of illicit drugs entering the United States from abroad, conducts investigations of major drug traffickers, exchanges intelligence information with foreign governments, stimulates international awareness of the illicit drug problem, and assists foreign nations with the development of institutional capabilities to suppress drug trafficking.

In addition to DEA's domestic field offices, the agency has special agents, diversion investigators, intelligence analysts, and support personnel stationed in offices around the world. About half of the agency's 7,000 employees are special agents. Minimum qualifications for these positions are a combination of experience, college education, and previous law enforcement training.

Students of international affairs may be particularly interested in the **Intelligence Division** and the **Operations Division**. The Intelligence Division is responsible for constructing a complete picture of the international drug-trafficking situation; the Operations Division is responsible for conducting enforcement operations. Many of the employees in these offices have investigative, foreign affairs, and intelligence backgrounds.

Personnel Division   tel. 202/307-1000
Drug Enforcement Administration
700 Army-Navy Drive
Arlington, VA 22202

Education, U.S. Department of

The United States Department of Education's international activities are primarily the concern of two offices. The **Office of Postsecondary Education's Center for International Education** administers programs supported under the Fulbright-Hays and the Higher Education acts. These programs serve to develop and maintain high levels of expertise in foreign languages and area studies and increase the general understanding of other languages and world areas. Less commonly taught languages and related cultural and area studies are emphasized. The **Office of Intergovernmental and Interagency Affairs** provides overall leadership in establishing and directing effective intergovernmental and interagency affairs for the department through communication with intergovernmental, interagency, and public advocacy groups and constituencies.

Department of Education   tel. 202/708-5366
400 Maryland Avenue, S.W.   tel. 202/401-0559 (Employment
Washington, D.C. 20202   Information)
                                            http://www.ed.gov

Energy, U.S. Department of

The United States Department of Energy (DOE) coordinates and develops national energy policy and administers the federal government's energy research and development functions. DOE also prepares long- and short-range national energy estimates and plans concerning supply and utilization of energy resources of all types.

International energy policy, emergency preparedness, and export assistance are the principal responsibilities of the **Office of the Assistant Secretary for International Affairs and Energy Emergencies.** Major initiatives are undertaken through subordinate organizations that focus on international energy policy, technical cooperation, U.S. participation in appropriate organizations, emergency preparedness planning, emergency operations, analysis of energy price and supply trends, and the encouragement of free trade in energy resources. Professionals assigned to the office generally are trained as economists, analysts, and engineers. Individual backgrounds range from international relations and international economics to foreign area studies and contingency planning and business administration. A significant number of the staff have earned master's and/or doctoral degrees.

Personnel Division
Department of Energy
Forrestal Building
1000 Independence Avenue, S.W.
Washington, D.C. 20585

tel. 202/586-5000
http://www.doe.gov

Environmental Protection Agency

The Environmental Protection Agency (EPA) is responsible for executing federal laws for the protection of the environment. EPA's mandate covers water quality, air quality, waste, pesticides, toxic substances, and radiation. Within these broad areas of responsibility, EPA program efforts include research and development and the development, implementation, and enforcement of regulations. EPA is involved in many policy and technical aspects of transboundary, regional, and global environmental and health-related issues. These international activities also include information-sharing within many international organizations and directly with other countries on common issues, problems, and solutions.

EPA involvement in international efforts is coordinated by an **Office of International Activities.** This office employs about 60 professional staff. Qualifications for employment with the office preferably should include education and experience in one or a combination of the following areas:

international affairs, environmental issues, or management with a demonstrated ability to work on policy and technical issues that are responsibilities of EPA.

Environmental Protection Agency
Office of International Activities (A-106)
401 M Street, S.W.
Washington, D.C. 20460
tel. 202/260-2080 (Public Information)
tel. 202/260-3144 (Personnel)
tel. 202/260-4870 (Office of International Activities)
tel. 202/260-5550 (Office of International Activities Job Hotline)
http://www.epa.gov

Export-Import Bank of the United States

The Export-Import Bank of the United States (ExImbank) is an independent agency of the United States government that facilitates the export financing of U.S. goods and services. It supplements and encourages, but does not compete with, commercial financing. By neutralizing the effect of export credit subsidies from other governments and by absorbing risks that the private sector will not accept, ExImbank enables U.S. exporters to compete effectively in overseas markets on the basis of price, performance, delivery, and service.

ExImbank has three main programs. The **Foreign Credit Insurance Association** offers several types of credit insurance policies to cover the risks of nonpayment on export credit transactions such as sales of products and services, leasing of equipment, and consignments in foreign countries. The **Working Capital Guarantee Program** helps small companies obtain critical pre-export financing from commercial lenders. The bank's **Loan and Guarantee Programs** cover up to 85 percent of the U.S. export value, with repayment terms of one year or more. The loans provide competitive, fixed interest rate financing for U.S. export sales facing foreign competition backed with subsidized official financing.

ExImbank is a small but dynamic agency with about 360 employees working in Washington, D.C. It offers many career opportunities in the fields of accounting, computer science, economics, financial analysis, law, marketing, and public affairs. Competition for jobs is keen. Staff vacancies generally are filled through individual vacancy announcements that outline specific job duties, salary, and qualification requirements. The announcements are widely distributed to colleges and universities, federal job information centers, professional organizations, and newspapers. About 25 professional positions are filled annually. Most jobs at ExImbank require Office of Personnel

Management competitive eligibility. They are filled from a federal listing of qualified candidates, which is open to those with undergraduate degrees or significant work experience. For interested applicants with a graduate degrees or relevant experience, there are some trainee positions open to those with majors in finance, accounting, or economics. The bank also employs a small number of students during the year under various intern programs.

Export-Import Bank of the
   United States
Room 10005
811 Vermont Avenue, N.W.
Washington, D.C. 20571

tel. 202/622-9823
tel. 202/566-8834 (Personnel)

Federal Bureau of Investigation

The responsibility for investigating violations of most federal laws and civil matters of interest to the United States government rests with the Federal Bureau of Investigation (FBI). In addition to these duties, the FBI provides the executive branch with information relating to national security and inter- acts with cooperating foreign police and security services.

The principal professional position within the FBI is that of special agent. Applicants for this position must be U.S. citizens who have reached their 23rd but not their 37th birthday and qualify under one of four entrance programs: The Law Program, for those with a law degree; the Accounting Program, for those with an accounting degree; the Language Program, for those with at least a bachelor's degree and fluency in a foreign language for which the FBI has a current need; and the Diversified program, which covers any academic program. Applicants must possess either a four-year college degree and three years of full-time work experience, or an advanced degree and two years of full-time work experience. There are currently more than 10,000 special agents within the FBI. All special agent applicants must pass a battery of written tests (Phase I) and a structured interview and written exer- cise (Phase II) of the special agent selection system. Applicants must also undergo a drug test, polygraph examination, and physical examination. Besides special agents, the FBI employs language specialists who possess the ability to translate foreign languages.

Those interested in a position with the FBI should contact the applicant coordinator at the nearest FBI office, listed under United States Government in the telephone directory, or visit the FBI Web site at http://www.fbi.gov.

Federal Communications Commission

The Federal Communications Commission (FCC) is responsible for U.S. tele- communications policy. FCC's **International Bureau (IB)** was established in order to create an effective organization in which to centralize and consolidate the FCC's international telecommunications policies and activities. The Bureau's mission is to administer FCC's international telecommunications policies and obligations; enhance the competitiveness of U.S. industry domestically and abroad; promote a high-quality, reliable, globally interconnected and interoperable international infrastructure; and promote U.S. interest in international communications and competitiveness. The Bureau consists of three divisions: Telecommunications; Satellite and Radio Communication; and Planning and Negotiations.

The **Telecommunications Division** develops, recommends, and administers policy, rules, and procedures for the authorization and regulation of international telecommunications facilities and services. It also represents the FCC at international conferences and meetings involving non-radio-related telecommunications matters. The **Satellite and Radio Communication Division** develops, recommends, and administers policy, rules, procedures, and standards for licensing and regulation of satellite and earth station facilities, both domestic and international. It also represents the FCC in international conferences and meetings involving radio-related telecommunications matters such as satellites, spectrum allocation, standards, broadcasting, aviation, maritime and safety of life at sea in the International Telecommunication Union (ITU) and other international forums. The **Planning and Negotiations Division** conducts long-range market and industry analyses for international policy development, provides advice on specific policy issues and agenda items, maintains information resources, undertakes planning studies on issues important to the development of international policy, and assists in planning for special activities. It also ensures that FCC regulations, procedures and frequency allocations comply with international and bilateral agreements.

Personnel Division   tel. 202/418-0500
Federal Communications   http://www.fcc.gov
   Commission
1919 M Street, N.W.
Washington, D.C. 20554

Federal Maritime Commission

The Federal Maritime Commission regulates the ocean-borne foreign commerce of the United States, ensures that U.S. international trade is open to all nations on a reciprocal basis, and protects against unauthorized activities in U.S. ocean-borne commerce. The commission's work includes accepting or rejecting tariff filings, attempting to eliminate the discriminatory practices of foreign governments against U.S. shipping and trying to achieve comity between the United States and its trading partners.

The commission employs about 200 people in its headquarters and field offices. Most of the professionals have backgrounds in law, transportation, business administration, and economics.

Federal Maritime Commission   tel. 202/523-5725 (Public
800 North Capitol Street, N.W.   Information)
Washington, D.C. 20573   tel. 202/523-5773 (Personnel)

Federal Reserve Bank of New York

The Federal Reserve Bank of New York (FRBNY) is one of 12 regional Federal Reserve banks that, along with the Federal Reserve Board in Washington, D.C., and the Federal Open Market Committee (FOMC), comprise the Federal Reserve System, the nation's central bank. The role of the FRBNY is unique within the system. At the direction of the FOMC, the top policy-making unit of the system, the FRBNY conducts open market operations on behalf of the entire Federal Reserve System. Open market operations—the purchase and sale of U.S. government securities—is the means through which the system conducts monetary policy by influencing the cost and availability of credit. The FRBNY is responsible within the Federal Reserve System for relationships with foreign central banks as well as all intervention within the foreign exchange market that is conducted on behalf of the Federal Reserve and the U.S. Treasury. The presence in the New York region of many of the nation's largest banks as well as the majority of foreign banks that operate in the U.S. ensures the FRBNY an active and important role in bank supervision and regulation matters.

Many career opportunities exist at the FRBNY with a significant international component. The **Foreign Banking Organizations** unit of the **Bank Supervision Group** analyzes the financial condition of the foreign parent banks that have a banking presence in the U.S. and their home-country financial systems to determine the strength of support the parent bank can provide to its U.S. operations. The **Research and Markets Analysis Group** of the **Financial Markets and Institutions Function** (FMI) specializes in research, current analysis, and policy studies of developments in financial markets and issues involving nonbank financial institutions. The **Banking Studies Department** conducts policy-oriented research on developments in the banking industry, the behavior of banks, and the structure and health of U.S. and foreign banking systems. The **Payments System Studies Staff** (PSSS) provides analytic support for the development of Federal Reserve payments risk reduction initiatives, monitors domestic and international developments related to payment systems, and analyzes trends in the clearance and settlement of securities. The **International Macroeconomics Function** monitors, analyzes, and interprets economic and political trends in foreign countries; projects U.S. current account developments; and reports on international issues.

Candidates for positions with the FRBNY should have a master's degree in business administration, economics, finance, or public policy and possess highly developed qualitative and quantitative skills. Strong financial analysis, writing, and research abilities and a background in finance, accounting, and economics is desirable.

Professional Recruiter
Campus Recruitment Staff
Federal Reserve Bank of New York
59 Maiden Lane, 39th Floor
New York, NY 10038–4502

Federal Reserve Board

The primary function of the Federal Reserve Board is the setting of monetary policy to foster stable economic conditions and long-term economic growth. International career opportunities exist with the **Division of International Finance**. The division analyzes the international policies and operations of the Federal Reserve System; major economic and financial developments abroad that affect the U.S. economy and U.S. international transactions; and a wide range of issues connected with the working of the international monetary system and the balance of payments adjustment process. The staff produces both analysis and interpretation of recent developments and research projects of a longer-run nature. Staff members regularly serve on U.S. delegations to international financial conferences and maintain liaison with central banks of foreign countries.

The division has a continuing need for economists who have already achieved or are working toward their doctorates and for exceptionally qualified economists holding a master's degree. In addition, many opportunities exist for applicants with a bachelor's degree in economics, strong quantitative skills, and a knowledge of computer programming to work closely with the economists and assist in basic research projects.

Supervision and regulation of foreign banks operating in the United States and of foreign branches of state member banks are provided by the **Division of Banking Supervision and Regulation**. The division also analyzes specific issues of monetary and international financial policies that have a bearing on regulatory policy. Individuals interested in pursuing employment opportunities as a financial analyst in Banking Supervision and Regulation should possess an M.B.A. in a related field or an undergraduate degree with one to three years of relevant work experience.

The Federal Reserve Board, located in Washington, D.C., has a staff of over 1,500 employees. Most professional positions require formal education or specialized equivalent experience in such fields as economics, finance, law, and data processing.

Board of Governors of the   tel. 202/452-3000 (Information)
   Federal Reserve System   tel. 202/452-3880 (Personnel)
20th Street and   tel. 202/452-3108 (Job Hotline)
   Constitution Avenue, N.W.
Mail Stop 156 (Human Resources)
Washington, D.C. 20551

General Accounting Office

The General Accounting Office (GAO), an independent, nonpartisan agency in the legislative branch, assists Congress in its legislative and oversight responsibilities. GAO examines virtually every program or activity funded by the federal government and provides a variety of services, the most prominent of which are audits and evaluations of federal programs and activities. GAO's reports and recommendations frequently result in agency actions to improve their operations or legislation to improve program objectives and management. Its issue areas cover a wide range of topics, including international activities such as foreign aid, trade, energy, defense, environment, agriculture, transportation, and financial systems.

Of particular interest to those searching for an internationally oriented career is the GAO's **National Security and International Affairs Division** (NSIAD) that oversees the operations of the Department of Defense, NASA, and the federal government's departments and agencies directly managing foreign affairs and national security issues. Relevant subdivisions include those that focus on specific military activities (Army, Navy/Marines, Air Force); four that review defensewide issues (manpower programs; logistics; procurement; and command, control, and intelligence); and one that reviews NASA programs. Additional subdivisions focus on international trade, energy, and finance; security and international relations; and foreign economic assistance issues. Work in other GAO divisions such as the **Resources, Community and Economic Development Division** (RCED) or the **Information, Management and Technology Division** (IMTEC) frequently involves international issues. In addition, GAO's regional offices increasingly are involved in carrying out work in an international environment.

The GAO employs approximately 5,000 professionals, most of whom are called evaluators. GAO's professionals come from a variety of educational backgrounds including public administration, computer science, business, political science, international affairs, and accounting. GAO also employs specialists in the social sciences, economics, computer science, mathematics, and other specialties. Approximately 200 new professionals are hired each year to work in the GAO Washington headquarters or in regional offices. GAO maintains a personnel system separate from the executive branch. Employment at GAO requires a bachelor's degree or equivalent work experience as a minimum. Candidates with master's degrees and doctorates increasingly are preferred for positions with GAO.

Office of Recruitment
General Accounting Office
441 G Street, N.W.
Room 4043
Washington, D.C. 20548

tel. 202/512-3000
tel. 202/512-4500 (Personnel)

General Services Administration

The General Services Administration (GSA) manages the federal government's real and personal property. Its responsibilities include construction and management of federal buildings, procurement and management of supplies and services for the government (including automated data processing and telecommunications services), and promulgation of federal policy concerning acquisition and management of property and services. It employs about 20,000 people nationwide. Most of GSA's international work involves the administration of a small amount of U.S. property located overseas and some overseas engineering projects.

The majority of the professionals with GSA have academic backgrounds in business, finance, economics, engineering, and computer sciences.

General Services Administration
18th and F Streets, N.W.
Washington, D.C. 20405

tel. 202/501-1231 (Public
   Information)
tel. 202/501-0370 (Personnel)
http://www.gsa.gov

Health and Human Services, U.S. Department of

The United States Department of Health and Human Services (HHS) is responsible for the health, welfare, and income security plans, programs, and policies of the federal government. Within HHS, the **Office of International Health** has overall departmental responsibility for policy and coordination of international health activities. The office's functions can be divided into three broad areas: multilateral programs involving liaison and representation responsibilities to the World Health Organization and Pan American Health Organization; bilateral programs that include binational programs of health cooperation with more than 20 countries; and cooperation with the Agency for International Development in those areas in which HHS has special competence.

The office currently has a professional staff of 14. Several hold master's degrees in public health or health care administration. Most have had previous work experience ranging from teaching and research to service with other government agencies and private enterprises.

HHS's **Social Security Administration** (SSA) has a number of international career opportunities. The **Office of International Operations** processes the social security claims of those living overseas. The work of the division's 500 employees falls into two main categories: claims adjudication and authorization processing (providing authorization for the payment of benefits). The professionals on the staff represent virtually every academic discipline conceivable. The **Office of International Policy** employs approximately 40 professionals on three staffs. The international activities staff trains foreign nationals in the administration of social security systems. The international studies and organizations staff—which also serves as the administration's liaison with international organizations—studies various social security systems throughout the world. The division of international program policy and agreements negotiates international agreements on social security and studies the effects of these agreements on domestic programs. Most openings occur at the medium-grade level (GS 12 and above). The majority of staff members have law or economics degrees as well as social security program experience or international agreements expertise.

The SSA's **Old-Age, Survivors and Disability Insurance** (OASDI) program is primarily domestically oriented but has several international aspects. It employs several federal benefits officers stationed abroad; these positions are traditionally filled by federal career employees with SSA technical and managerial experience.

The **Fogarty International Center** of the **National Institutes of Health** promotes study and research on the international development of science as it relates to health; administers several programs for advanced study in health sciences; facilitates linkages through which NIH interacts with scientists, institutions, and organizations around the world; and coordinates exchanges of scientists around the world.

There are a number of other HHS divisions concerned with international matters. Research, consultation, and training programs in international statistical activities are conducted by the **National Center for Health Statistics**. The **Alcohol, Drug Abuse, and Mental Health Administration** conducts and finances extensive international research in the areas of alcohol, drug abuse, and mental health and the associated problems of AIDS and homelessness. In Atlanta, the **Center for Disease Control and Prevention** directs and enforces foreign quarantine regulations, provides consultation to other nations in the control of preventable diseases, and participates with international agencies in the eradication or control of preventable diseases. The **Food and Drug Administration's** (FDA) international affairs staff employs about 10 people to facilitate communication between FDA and similar organizations overseas.

U.S. Department of Health &   tel. 202/619-0257
   Human Services
200 Independence Avenue, S.W.
Washington, D.C. 20201

Office of International Health   tel. 301/443-1774
Office of Public Health & Science
5600 Fishers Lane
Rockville, MD 20857

Personnel Division   tel. 410/965-1234 (Public
Social Security Administration   Information)
6401 Security Boulevard   tel. 410/965-4506 (Personnel
Baltimore, MD 21235   Division)
                               tel. 410/965-9321 (Office of
                                 International Operations)
                              tel. 410/965-7389 (Office of
                               International Policy)
                              http://www.ssa.gov/
                               SSA_Homepage.html

Fogarty International Center   tel. 301/496-2075
National Institutes of Health   http://www.nih.gov
Building 16, Room 306
9000 Rockville Pike
Bethesda, MD 20892

Human Resource Management Office tel. 404/639-3311 (General
Center for Disease Control   Information)
   and Prevention   tel. 770/488-1725 (Job
4770 Buford Highway MS K05   Information Center)
Atlanta, GA 30341–3724   http://www.cdc.gov

Housing and Urban Development, U.S. Department of

The United States Department of Housing and Urban Development (HUD) has a small international staff in the **Office of Policy Development and**

Research responsible for coordinating HUD's participation in international activities. Its major aims are to facilitate exchanges between senior officials responsible for large-scale housing and urban development programs by maintaining regular channels of communication with foreign governments and to share U.S. research and experience in housing and urban development with other countries. Employment opportunities are limited.

U.S. Department of Housing
and Urban Development
451 7th Street, S.W.
Washington, D.C. 20410

tel. 202/708-0770 (Office of
Policy Development and
Research)
http://www.hud.gov

Immigration and Naturalization Service

The Immigration and Naturalization Service (INS) administers federal laws covering the admission, exclusion, deportation, and naturalization of aliens in the United States. Specifically, the service investigates aliens to ascertain their admissibility into the country; adjudicates aliens' requests for benefits under the law; guards against illegal entry into the United States; investigates, arrests, and removes aliens residing in the nation illegally; and examines aliens wishing to become citizens. The service maintains liaison with federal, state, local, and foreign officials (in consulates and embassies).

About 85 percent of the service's employees are located outside the Washington, D.C., area. The service primarily employs immigration and naturalization officers and examiners who are trained at the Government Law Enforcement Training Center. Because of the complexity of U.S. immigration law, most administrative positions are held by former officers or examiners.

Immigration and Naturalization
Service
425 I Street, N.W.
Washington, D.C. 20536

tel. 202/514-4330 (Public
Information)
tel. 202/514-2530
(Headquarters Personnel)

Inter-American Foundation

The Inter-American Foundation was established to promote social change and development in Latin America and the Caribbean. It provides support through grants and the financing of projects for private, community-level, self-help efforts in solving basic social and economic problems. This approach springs from the belief that only the recipients themselves can define their communities' problems and needs. The wide variety of projects funded by the foundation has included workers' self-managed enterprises, peasant associations, informal education, credit and production cooperatives, cultural awareness programs, self-help housing, legal aid clinics, and worker-run bank and agricultural extension services.

The foundation employs about 40 professionals with an average turn-over of one or two positions per year. There is a tendency to hire generalists rather than people with specific, technically oriented backgrounds. The skills needed by the foundation are defined by its wide array of activities. Employees have backgrounds in such diverse fields as economics, rural and urban development, finance, agriculture, housing, banking, law, labor relations, nutrition, education, statistics, and industrial management. Although not a prerequisite for employment, virtually all professionals on the staff have at least a master's degree.

Inter-American Foundation   tel. 703/841-3800
901 N. Stuart Street   tel. 703/841-3868 (Personnel)
Arlington, VA 22203

Interior, U.S. Department of the

The responsibility for most nationally owned public lands and natural resources rests with the United States Department of the Interior. The department's **Office of Insular Affairs** administers federal programs and regulations relating to territorial and trust territory matters and oversees the various international activities of the department. The backgrounds of the professionals in this office—including education, economics, sociology, and law—reflect the diversity of the office's programs. The element most have in common is experience in territorial matters gained in any number of ways, including Peace Corps work or previous employment with congressional committees involved in territorial issues. The office also employs two program officers who coordinate the department's international activities.

Other offices with international duties can be found throughout the department. The **Bureau of Mines** exchanges mining-related information and experience with a wide variety of international organizations and foreign governments. The bureau's **Branch of Foreign Data** employs mining engineers, geologists, economists, and statisticians who collect and publish information (production, trade, legislation, technology, and so forth) on minerals and mining in foreign countries. About 40 specialists with the **U.S. Geological Survey** furnish technical and training assistance to foreign geological, hydrological, and cartographic services. The survey also publishes technical studies on the geology, hydrology, and mineral resources of foreign countries. The **Minerals Management Service** administers the mineral resources of the outer continental shelf. It is responsible for jurisdictional issues involving the resources of the continental shelf that arise in international negotiations; studying the possible effects of a domestic ocean mining program; and managing departmental activities relating to deep seabed mineral resources. In an effort to protect endangered wildlife, the **U.S. Fish and Wildlife Service** engages in international research, foreign importation enforcement, and consultation to foreign countries. The **National Park Service** operates training programs in park management and conservation for foreign country representatives and gathers research on foreign park lands. Imparting technical assistance to foreign nations in water resource development and utilization is the job of the **Bureau of Reclamation**.

Despite the many offices within the department with some form of international responsibilities, employment opportunities for graduates in international affairs are extremely limited. In most cases, the professionals are trained in the particular discipline of the office involved rather than in international studies. An information packet on general career opportunities with the department is available from the Office of Personnel.

U.S. Department of the Interior
1849 C Street, N.W.
Washington, D.C. 20240

tel. 202/208-7220 (Public Information)
tel. 202/208-5065
http://info.er.ousgs.gov/doi/avads/index.html

International Trade Commission

The United States International Trade Commission (ITC) studies and makes recommendations on international trade and tariffs to the President, Congress, and government agencies. The major thrust of the commission's work is the analysis of all possible effects of imported products on U.S. industries. Special emphasis is placed on the effects of imports from countries with non-market economic systems. The commission also conducts studies on a broad range of topics relating to international trade and publishes summaries of trade and tariff information. In order to carry out its responsibilities, the commission must engage in extensive research and maintain a high degree of expertise in all matters relating to the commercial and international trade policy of the United States.

The staff of ITC, which numbers about 240 professionals, provides six commissioners with the expertise required to carry out the responsibilities of the organization. International economists form one of the largest group of employees on the staff. They must have a minimum of 21 credit hours in economics and three credit hours in statistics earned at the bachelor's and/or master's level. Of particular importance are courses in microeconomics, industrial and labor economics, and international economics and trade. Other prevalent staff positions include international trade analysts, investigatory economists (both frequently require course work in accounting and international economics), and attorneys (especially patent, antitrust, and customs). Additional academic specializations of special interest to the commission are marketing, international law, international trade, business administration, and regional studies.

U.S. International Trade Commission tel. 202/252-1000
500 E Street, S.W.   tel. 202/252-1651 (Personnel)
Washington, D.C. 20436   http://www.usitc.gov

Justice, U.S. Department of

Within the Department of Justice, most international issues are handled by four of the six department divisions: Antitrust, Civil, Criminal, and Environment and Natural Resources. The **Antitrust Division** is responsible for the enforcement of federal antitrust laws. The **Foreign Commerce Section** of the division is responsible for the implementation of division policy on issues of trade and international antitrust enforcement. The section is active in the interagency process of administering the trade laws and assessing the competitive aspects of U.S. trade policy. The section is the division's liaison with international organizations, including antitrust enforcement agencies of the European communities, Canada, and other countries. In conjunction with the State Department, the section exchanges information with foreign governments concerning investigations and cases that the division initiates involving foreign corporations and nationals.

The **Civil Division** represents the United States in virtually all types of civil proceedings. Litigation based on international maritime agreements is handled by the division's **Torts Branch**. **Commercial Litigation Branch** attorneys within the **Civil Division** represent the United States in virtually all cases initiated in the Court of International Trade. These cases include challenges brought by domestic and foreign producers contesting antidumping and countervailing duty investigations, as well as actions commenced by the government to enforce civil penalties for customs fraud. Attorneys in the **Civil Division's Office of Foreign Litigation** pursue claims on behalf of the United States and defend the government's interests in foreign courts. Foreign litigation attorneys frequently become involved in white-collar crime cases and recovery of offshore assets. Decisions in this area often have significant foreign policy implications. The **Civil Division's Federal Programs Branch** handles the defense of challenged government activity ranging from domestic welfare programs to international agreements. The **Federal Programs Branch's** responsibilities include matters as diverse as litigation involving federal banking statutes and regulations, and suits raising national security and foreign policy issues.

In enforcing most of the nation's criminal laws, the **Criminal Division** participates in criminal justice activities involving foreign parties where a centralized national approach is desired. The **Internal Security Section** supervises the investigation and prosecution of cases affecting national security, foreign relations, and the export of military and strategic commodities and technology. The **Criminal Division's Office of International Affairs** supports the department's legal divisions, the U.S. attorneys, and state and local prosecutors regarding questions of foreign and international law, including issues related to extradition and mutual legal assistance treaties. The office also coordinates all international evidence gathering. In concert with the State Department, the office engages in the negotiation of new extradition and mutual legal assistance treaties and executive agreements throughout the world. Office attorneys also participate on a number of committees established under the auspices of the United Nations and other international organizations that are directed at resolving a variety of international law enforcement problems such as narcotics trafficking and money laundering.

The **Environment and Natural Resources Division** is the nation's environmental lawyer. The **Policy, Legislation and Special Litigation Section** of the **Environment and Natural Resources Division** coordinates and directs the division's legislative program, including representing the department on interagency groups that develop the Administration's position on legislation, and at meetings with Congressional staff. The section's attorneys coordinate the division's international environmental activities and environmental justice activities.

The **Foreign Claims Settlement Commission** is an independent, quasi-judicial agency within the department, responsible for adjudicating claims of U.S. nationals against foreign governments that have nationalized, expropriated, or otherwise taken property of those nationals without paying compensation as required under international law.

The bulk of the professionals employed by these offices and divisions are attorneys assisted by paralegals and other support staff. Attorneys and law students interested in employment with any department organization may contact the Office of Attorney Personnel Management. A current **legal activities** book (LAB) is available on the internet at the address given here. The LAB describes the department's legal employment programs and the legal responsibilities of each organization in the department.

Attorney and Law Student Employment:

U.S. Department of Justice	tel. 202/514-3396
Office of Attorney Personnel	TDD: 202/616-2113
Management	
Room 6150, Main Building	
Pennsylvania Avenue at 10th Street, N.W.	
Washington, D.C. 20530	

General Employment:

U.S. Department of Justice   tel. 202/514-6818
Justice Management Division   http://www.usdoj.gov
Personnel Staff   gopher://gopher.usdoj.gov
Suite 1175
1331 Pennsylvania Avenue, N.W.
Washington, D.C. 20530

Labor, U.S. Department of

The United States Department of Labor's international activities are concentrated in the **Bureau of International Labor Affairs**. The bureau's major
duties include helping formulate international economic and trade policies;
carrying out overseas technical assistance projects; arranging trade union
exchanges and other programs for foreign visitors to the United States; fur-
nishing directions to U.S. labor attaches at embassies abroad; assisting with
the representation of the United States in bilateral and multilateral trade
negotiations and in various international organizations; evaluating U.S.
immigration policy; representing the United States in the International Labor
Organization and in the Manpower Committee of the Organization for Economic Cooperation and Development; and reporting on and analyzing the
activities of foreign trade unions. To handle these responsibilities, the bureau
is divided into three offices: foreign relations, international economic affairs,
and international organizations.

The majority of professional positions with the bureau require a strong
economics background (especially microeconomics) combined with some
knowledge of statistics, international trade, and/or labor relations. In addition, those with backgrounds in area studies, international organizations, and
comparative politics may be hired. Employment opportunities are limited.

The only other office dealing with international issues is the **Bureau of
Labor Statistics**. The bureau's small Division of Foreign Labor Statistics and
Trends collects data and conducts research on topics such as foreign employ-
ment and wage levels, labor forces, costs, benefits, and productivity.

Department of Labor   tel. 202/523-7316
200 Constitution Avenue, N.W.
Washington, D.C. 20210

Bureau of International Labor Affairs   tel. 202/523-6717
Office of Operating Personnel Services
Room C-5512
U.S. Department of Labor
Washington, D.C. 20210

Management and Budget, U.S. Office of

The United States Office of Management and Budget (OMB) performs a wide variety of functions. OMB prepares and administers the federal budget; analyzes proposed legislation and executive orders; reviews all major administration testimony and all legislation enacted by Congress; assesses federal program objectives, performance, and efficiency; and tracks the progress of government agencies with respect to work proposed, work actually initiated, and work completed. The Associate Director for National Security and International Affairs holds paramount responsibility for OMB's review of international programs. The director's staff is partitioned into three divisions: international affairs, national security, and special studies.

The **International Affairs Division** is concerned with trade, monetary, and investment policy and deals with such specific issues as international energy policy and commodity agreements. The division reviews all foreign aid, trade financing, grant military assistance, and foreign military credit and cash sales programs as well as the budgets of the agencies primarily responsible for international economic activities and the conduct of foreign affairs. Reviewing and advising the Defense Department budget and national security policy is the task of the **National Security Division**. The **Special Studies Division**, while principally concerned with defense issues, also coordinates administration responses to congressional inquiries in the international field.

OMB employs over 630 professionals. Candidates for entry-level positions are expected to have graduate training in economics, business administration, public policy, law, or (to a lesser extent) science and mathematics. Previous experience in budget analysis or management is considered helpful but not essential. Applicants should possess an ability to analyze problems and communicate effectively both orally and in writing. All potential recruits must meet Office of Personnel Management eligibility requirements. Paid summer internships are available for graduate students with the same qualifications.

Office of Management and Budget   tel. 202/395-7250
Executive Office Building
Room 9026
Washington, D.C. 20503

National Aeronautics and Space Administration

The National Aeronautics and Space Administration (NASA) ensures that activities in space are devoted to peaceful purposes for the benefit of all humankind. In addition, the act that created NASA in 1958 charged the agency to conduct its activities "so as to contribute materially to . . . cooperation by the United States with other nations and groups of nations." In fulfillment of this mandate, NASA has entered into more than 1,000 agreements with more than 150 countries and international organizations. These relationships have covered a broad spectrum of collaborative endeavors, ranging from the development of major space hardware to the sharing of space data among scientists around the globe.

The **International Relations Division** is responsible for all international activities of the agency. The staff consists of about 14 professionals with backgrounds in international relations, political science, or related fields. A graduate degree is preferred and communications skills are emphasized. The ability to speak a foreign language is preferred. The staff assignments include responsibility for relations with particular countries and/or space projects.

National Aeronautics and
Space Administration
400 Maryland Avenue, S.W.
Washington, D.C. 20546

tel. 202/453-1000 (Public
    Information)
tel. 202/453-8440
    (International Relations
    Division)
http://hypatia.gsfc.nasa.gov/
    NASA_homepage.html

National Science Foundation

The National Science Foundation (NSF) was established in 1950 to promote and advance scientific progress in the United States. The foundation does this primarily by sponsoring scientific and engineering research and by supporting selected activities in science and engineering education. NSF does not itself conduct research.

NSF's **Division of International Programs** complements other foundation activities in support of scientific research. The programs are designed to support the work of U.S. scientists cooperating with scientists in other countries in research and related activities. Four types of activities may receive support: cooperative research projects designed and conducted jointly by principal investigators from the United States and a foreign country; international research fellowships; research-oriented seminars or workshops; and scientific visits for planning cooperative activities or for research.

The division has a staff of about 25 professionals and fills approximately two vacancies a year. Scientists with Ph.D.-level training and with six to eight years of postdoctoral research experience as well as an international background are sought by the division to fill these senior-level positions. Whenever vacancies at the entry- or middle-levels do occur, they are normally handled through the Office of Human Resources Management. The booklet *NSF Guide to Programs* contains helpful information on the division's operations.

National Science Foundation
4201 Wilson Boulevard
Arlington, VA 22230

tel. 703/306-1070 (Public Affairs)
tel. 703/306-1180 (Human Resources Management)
tel. 703/306-1710 (International Programs)
e-mail: intpubs@nsf.gov
http://www.nsf.gov

Nuclear Regulatory Commission

International activities at the United States Nuclear Regulatory Commission (USNRC) are directed at contributing to the safe operation of licensed reactors and fuel-cycle facilities and the safe use of nuclear materials; improving worldwide cooperation in nuclear safety and radiation protection; assisting U.S. efforts to restrict U.S. nuclear exports to peaceful use only; and supporting U.S. foreign policy and national security objectives.

The **Office of International Programs** is the commission's primary organization for coordinating international activities and policies, as well as licensing U.S. exports and imports of nuclear materials and equipment. The USNRC's international bilateral cooperation efforts traditionally have focused on power-reactor safety, but increased attention also is being given to broader radiation protection matters, waste-management activities, and other areas of materials safety. International Programs also works with the International Atomic Energy Agency (IAEA) in Vienna, Austria, in promoting effective international safeguards and cooperation on nuclear safety.

The Office of International Programs helps recruit qualified U.S. citizens for IAEA positions by listing the positions in the USNRC's weekly vacancy announcements. Of the approximately 100 vacancies that occur each year at IAEA—the majority of which are technical positions—the United States fills approximately 20 percent.

The Office of International Programs is staffed by 22 professionals, most of whom have backgrounds in public administration or international relations. A technical background combined with international relations is highly desirable. A language ability in French, Spanish, Russian, German, or in the languages of the Pacific Rim is useful. Very few openings are expected in the future.

U.S. Nuclear Regulatory Commission

tel. 301/415-7536 (Personnel)
tel. 301/415-8550

Office of Personnel   (Vacancy Information)
Mail Stop T-3 D29   http://www.nrc.gov
Washington, D.C. 20555

Overseas Private Investment Corporation

The Overseas Private Investment Corporation (OPIC) provides political risk insurance, financing, and a variety of investor services to encourage U.S. private investment in more than 130 developing nations and emerging economies around the world. Although wholly owned by the U.S. government, OPIC is organized along the lines of a private corporation. OPIC has six departments: Insurance, Finance, Investment Development, Legal Affairs, Management Services, and Financial Management. OPIC insurance protects investors against the risks to property and income of political violence, expropriation, and inconvertibility of U.S. currency into U.S. dollars. OPIC's financing assists U.S. businesses through direct loans, loan guaranties, and equity investments. OPIC's investor services are designed to assist small- and medium-sized "new-to-market" U.S. firms in successfully identifying, planning, and implementing overseas investment projects. These services include business and advisory services; investment missions; a computer data system that matches a U.S. investor's interest with specific overseas opportunities; and an information clearinghouse that provides basic economic, business, and political information and data on developing countries.

OPIC employs approximately 160 employees, of whom about 60 percent are professionals. OPIC's requirements for professional personnel generally include training in law, finance, business, economics, or international affairs. Based on the job requirements, foreign language skills may be required. Computer skills are often important. OPIC has only occasional vacancies, but welcomes applications for employment from qualified U.S. citizens.

Office of Human Resources   tel. 202/336-8400
  Management   tel. 202/336-8882
Overseas Private Investment   (Job Information)
  Corporation
1100 New York Avenue, N.W.
Washington, D.C. 20527

Peace Corps

The Peace Corps seeks to promote world peace and friendship, help the peoples of other countries meet their needs for trained manpower, and promote mutual understanding and cooperation between U.S. citizens and other peoples. To meet these goals, the Peace Corps trains volunteers in the appropriate local languages, technical skills necessary for the particular task they will be performing, and cross-cultural skills needed to work with peoples of a different culture. Following successful completion of the two- to three-month training, volunteers are sent to various sites within a country where they spend a period of two years aiding in the country's economic and social development.

There are over 5,000 Peace Corps volunteers in 85 developing countries. Assignments vary according to volunteers' qualifications and host-country needs. Volunteers work primarily in the fields of agriculture, forestry, fisheries, education, health, engineering, business, the skilled trades, and community development-related activities. In greatest demand are those with degrees and/or backgrounds in forestry, fisheries, mathematics, science, and agriculture. It is important to remember that education is not the only avenue to acquiring the background necessary for these positions; such backgrounds can be obtained through a variety of experiences.

Although host countries have asked for volunteers with practical training, the Peace Corps still recruits volunteers with no specific skilled experience. Many of these volunteers work on forestry and fisheries projects, teach handicrafts, establish cooperatives, or teach community nutrition and maternal child care. Foreign language proficiency (especially in Spanish or French), past experience living or working abroad, or extensive volunteer/community service work would greatly increase a generalist's chances of acceptance.

Applicants to the Peace Corps must be U.S. citizens, have no dependents under the age of 18, and be at least 18 years of age. It is extremely rare that anyone under 20 has the skills or experience to qualify. While specific skills or work experience and foreign language proficiency are highly desired in potential volunteers, the Peace Corps also looks highly upon those who demonstrate a desire to serve others, a sense of dedication, emotional maturity, and a great deal of flexibility and adaptability. The Peace Corps covers round-trip transportation from the United States to the country of assignment and provides medical care. It also provides each volunteer with a living allowance to cover basic necessities such as housing and food including a modest amount of spending money. Upon completion of service, each volunteer receives a $200 readjustment allowance for every month he or she has served. The Peace Corps recruits approximately 3,000 volunteers per year.

In addition, the Peace Corps has approximately 1,000 employees stationed in Washington, D.C., in 15 regional recruiting offices around the United States, and in Peace Corps offices abroad. These employees are involved in such fields as volunteer recruitment, program development, support, and personnel. The Peace Corps has exhibited a tendency to hire former volunteers for many of these positions. The Peace Corps usually hires about 250 employees annually and maintains over a dozen area recruiting offices in the continental United States and Puerto Rico.

Peace Corps Volunteer Recruitment Information:

Peace Corps	tel. 202/606-3000
Office of Recruitment Resources	tel. 202/606-3940 (Public
9th Floor	Information)
1990 K Street, N.W.	http://www.peacecorps.gov
Washington, D.C. 20526	

Peace Corps Staff Recruitment Information:

Peace Corps	tel. 202/606-3950
Office of Personnel	tel. 202/775-2214 (Dial-a-Job)
1990 K Street, N.W.	tel. 800/424-8580, ext. 2214 or
Washington, D.C. 20526	2225 (Dial-a-Job, toll-free)
	tel. 202/606-3400 (Personnel)

Postal Service, United States

The United States Postal Service (USPS) furnishes mail processing and delivery services to U.S. and foreign individual and business mailers. The USPS operates an International Postal Affairs (IPA) function that is responsible for coordinating relations and activities with foreign postal administrations, international postal organizations (such as the Universal Postal Union), and U.S. government agencies concerning international postal issues. IPA supervises the exchange of mail with other countries based on multilateral and bilateral treaties.

IPA has 15 professional positions for the following functions: developing overall USPS international mail policies; conducting bilateral and multilateral postal business negotiations; representing the USPS at international postal organization meetings; and coordinating technical cooperation and postal development activities with other postal administrations and international development institutions like the United Nations Development Programme and the World Bank.

Graduate degrees in international relations constitute the most relevant background for a career in IPA. Fluency in foreign languages, particularly French and Spanish, is extremely useful.

International Postal Affairs	tel. 202/268-2444
Room 4400-E	fax 202/268-4871
475 L'Enfant Plaza	
Washington, D.C. 20260–6500	

Science and Technology Policy, U.S. Office of

The United States Office of Science and Technology Policy (OSTP) serves as a source of input for the President on scientific, engineering, and technical issues. The office advises the President of scientific and technological consid-erations involved in areas of national concern including the economy, national security, and foreign policy. In executing its mandate, OSTP fre-quently deals with such issues as export controls, arms control, technology transfer, foreign aid, energy, space cooperation, transborder data flows, and oceans policies.

From a total staff of around 40, about one-fourth deal directly with inter-national affairs. Candidates must have strong technical backgrounds com-bined with relevant experience. Employment opportunities are limited.

Office of Science and Technology   tel. 202/456-7116
   Policy
Room 360, Old Executive
   Office Building
Washington, D.C. 20506

Securities and Exchange Commission

The Securities and Exchange Commission (SEC) is responsible for the admin-istration and enforcement of federal securities laws. The commission regu-lates the nation's securities markets, stockbrokers, and investment companies that issue stock or other securities. The international duties of the SEC entail handling the disclosure of improper corporate payments abroad, governing the issuance and trading of foreign securities in the United States, and over-seeing the international operations of mutual funds and activities of foreign brokers in the United States.

The internationalization of securities markets has resulted in increased efforts by the SEC to work and cooperate with securities regulators around the world. The commission's **Division of Corporate Finance** supervises filings by foreign issuers of securities, oversees foreign tenders and takeovers of regis-tered companies, and monitors possible improper corporate payments over-seas. Such improper payments are investigated and violators are prosecuted by the **Division of Enforcement** which also investigates and maintains enforce-ment actions in a variety of areas that require obtaining information from for-eign countries. The **Division of Market Regulation** supervises brokers and securities exchanges, including accountants, financial analysts, securities com-pliance examiners, attorneys, financial economists, and investigators.

The SEC's **Office of International Affairs** has primary responsibility for negotiating memoranda of understanding between the SEC and foreign secu-rities regulators as well as for coordinating activities relating to enforcement programs pursuant to those agreements. It also operates in a consultative role regarding the significant ongoing international programs and initiatives of the SEC's operating divisions and offices.

Securities and Exchange Commission   tel. 202/272-2650 (Public
450 5th Street, N.W.   Information)
Room 1C45   tel. 202/272-2550 (Personnel)
Washington, D.C. 20549

Smithsonian Institution

The Smithsonian Institution is the world's largest museum and research complex, a trust instrumentality of the federal government and repository of the
U.S. national collections. It was established in 1845 with funds left to the people of the United States by English natural scientist James Smithson. Today
the Smithsonian consists of 16 museums and galleries, the National Zoo, and
various program divisions, research institutes, and support offices. Smithsonian researchers have ranged the globe, assembling unique collections, form-
ing a worldwide network of friends and correspondents and organizing
research or participating in cooperative museum projects in almost every
country of the world. It has facilities in eight states, Panama, Honduras, and
Kenya.

Given the nature of the Smithsonian's activities, there are a number of its
divisions that are significantly international in scope. Research, exhibition,
and program staff conduct their work in many countries, and foreign colleagues regularly come to Smithsonian facilities to work with its staff and
members. The **Office of International Relations** (OIR) serves as the point of
contact for the Smithsonian with foreign institutions or individuals, international organizations, and government agencies. It administers two modest
funding programs and provides information to Smithsonian staff about possible hazards and implications of undertaking activities in particularly sensitive areas of the world. OIR has a staff of less than a dozen people, with
infrequent turnover, although other parts of the Smithsonian do appoint support, research, and program staff involved with international operations.
Required training or experience varies: the majority of curatorial, research,
and exhibitions positions require specialized training or experience, while
candidates for liaison officer positions generally have practical experience in
international exchanges and advanced training in a relevant academic discipline. About 70 percent of staff positions are federal civil service and hiring
for them involves adherence to U.S. Office of Personnel Management guidelines.

Office of Human Resources   tel. 202/287-3100
Smithsonian Institution   http://www.si.edu
955 L'Enfant Plaza
Suite 2100
Washington, D.C. 20560

Trade and Development Agency, U.S.

The United States Trade and Development Agency (TDA), an independent U.S. government agency, has two objectives: to assist in the economic development of friendly developing and middle-income countries, and to promote the export of U.S. goods and services to those countries.

TDA accomplishes these objectives by providing grants for feasibility studies, consultancies, training programs, and other project-planning services for public sector development projects. TDA assists U.S. firms by identifying major development projects that offer large export potential and by funding U.S. private sector involvement in project planning. TDA activities serve as a catalyst to encourage U.S. private sector involvement in fewer infrastructure projects. This approach helps position U.S. firms for follow-on contracts when these projects are implemented. TDA grants are not tied to follow-on procurement, yet TDA-funded feasibility studies have led to more than $6.5 billion in direct exports for the United States.

TDA activities cover a wide range of sectors of high priority to host governments and international development efforts. U.S. technological expertise can help accelerate the development process in all these sectors.

A small staff of 38 individuals runs the program. Virtually all entry-level positions are at the higher grade levels and are usually filled by candidates with an advanced degree and previous experience.

U.S. Trade and Development Agency tel. 703/875-4357
SA-16 Room 309   e-mail: info@tda.gov
Washington, D.C. 20523–1602

Trade Representative, Office of the U.S.

Working out of offices in Washington, D.C., and Geneva, the employees of the Office of the United States Trade Representative (USTR) are responsible for setting and administering overall U.S. trade policy. This objective includes multilateral trade negotiations implementation, import remedies, East-West trade, international investment, energy trade, international commodity, and export expansion policies. Furthermore, USTR plays the lead U.S. role in bilateral and multilateral trade, commodity, and direct investment negotiations involving the General Agreement on Tariffs and Trade (GATT), the Organization for Economic Cooperation and Development (OECD), and the U.N. Conference on Trade and Development (UNCTAD).

Employment opportunities are limited and highly competitive. Notable skill in economics with expertise in negotiations and trade is required of all applicants. A doctorate in economics or trade is preferred. A nonremunerated, year-long University Intern Program exists for graduates and undergraduates with concentrations in economics, international relations, law, political science, business, and finance. Typically, 40 to 50 students are selected from a pool of 275 to 325 applicants.

Director, Office of Management   tel. 202/395-7360
Office of the U.S. Trade   tel. 202/395-3350
   Representative
600 17th Street, N.W.
Washington, D.C. 20506

Transportation, U.S. Department of

The United States Department of Transportation (DOT) is responsible for planning and administering the nation's overall transportation policy. The **Office of Policy and International Affairs** provides departmental leadership for international transportation policy issues and assesses economic, financial, technological, and institutional implications. The office coordinates international transportation cooperative research; organizes technical assistance programs for developing nations; formulates and presents the U.S. position on transportation matters before international conferences; develops, coordinates, and evaluates international air and marine transportation policy in concert with various elements from government, industry and labor; and negotiates and implements multilateral and bilateral aviation agreements.

The educational experiences of the 80 staff professionals varies widely. Most common backgrounds are law, international relations, and public administration. Many of the professionals have joined the staff with previous work experience in areas such as bilateral negotiations, aviation and maritime policy, cooperative technical exchange programs, and technical assistance programs.

The **Federal Aviation Administration** (FAA) has an **Office of International Aviation** that promotes aviation safety and civil aviation abroad by managing the FAA's foreign technical assistance programs, providing training for foreign nationals in areas of the agency's expertise, developing and coordinating FAA's international policies, and exchanging information with foreign governments. In addition, the office provides technical representation to international organizations and conferences and participates in cooperative efforts with other U.S. government agencies and the U.S. aviation industry in order to promote aviation safety abroad. The office's 41 professionals stationed in the United States fall into two broad categories: international specialists and those with technical backgrounds. The international specialists have degrees or backgrounds in economics, international relations, or international marketing. For the people with technical aviation backgrounds, the emphasis is on experience. The majority are former pilots, air traffic controllers, and flight safety inspectors. Some have engineering degrees, but many others have nontechnical degrees in areas such as the liberal arts.

There are three other major offices within the department involved in international issues. The **Federal Highway Administration** (FHWA) employs highway design, construction, maintenance, and bridge engineers and specialists to provide assistance and advice to foreign governments in various phases of highway engineering and administration. It also is active in a number of international organizations interested in road-related affairs. FHWA's **National Highway Institute** trains foreign highway officials interested in American highway practices. The **Saint Lawrence Seaway Development Corporation** operates that portion of the seaway within the territorial limits of the United States and coordinates its activities with those of its Canadian counterpart. International maritime and related U.N. matters are dealt with by the **U.S. Coast Guard**, which falls under DOT's jurisdiction during peacetime. The Coast Guard maintains an Office of Public and International Affairs. Additional Coast Guard offices are concerned with the enforcement of international laws and treaties, the international impact of environmental questions, and the operation of deep-water ports.

U.S. Department of Transportation   tel. 202/366-4000
400 7th Street, S.W.   tel. 202/366-9395 (Employment)
Washington, D.C. 20590   http://www.dot.gov

Office of International Policy   tel. 202/366-4898
   and Programs
Room 10232
Department of Transportation
400 7th Street, S.W.
Washington, D.C. 20590

Federal Aviation Administration   tel. 202/366-4000 (Public
800 Independence Avenue, S.W.   Information)
Washington, D.C. 20590   tel. 202/267-3229 (Personnel)
   tel. 202/382-6151 (Office of
    International Aviation Affairs)

Treasury, U.S. Department of the

The United States Department of the Treasury develops and recommends economic, financial, tax, and fiscal policies; serves as the federal government's financial agent; performs many law enforcement activities; and manufactures coins and currency. The **Office of the Assistant Secretary for**

International Affairs (OASIA) offers the most attractive international career opportunities. OASIA is concerned with the development and implementation of international monetary, financial, and economic policy and programs. The office is divided into groups responsible for monetary affairs, developing nations, trade and investment policy, and Arabian peninsular affairs. The functions of OASIA include conducting financial diplomacy, attempting to improve the structure and operations of the international monetary system, monitoring international gold and foreign exchange markets, coordinating U.S. participation in bilateral and multilateral development lending programs and institutions, monitoring and formulating policy concerning international indebtedness, formulating policy concerning financing of trade, coordinating policies toward foreign investments in the United States and U.S. investments abroad, analyzing balance of payments information, and monitoring energy developments.

OASIA has about 140 professionals on its staff, including those stationed overseas. The vast majority of these employees have advanced degrees. Approximately 10 professional economists are hired each year. A strong background in economics, finance, statistics, or trade is the single most important requirement for any position with OASIA. While these are the predominant academic specializations, M.B.A.s and foreign affairs specialists are represented on the staff.

The Department of the Treasury serves as the focal point for international tax policy questions. Under the Assistant Secretary for Tax Policy is the small **Office of International Tax Affairs**, composed of economists and lawyers who study and formulate international tax legislation and regulation, negotiate tax treaties and perform economic analyses of international tax matters.

The **Office of the Comptroller of the Currency** (OCC) has two offices with responsibilities in the international area. The **Office of the Deputy Comptroller for Multinational Banking** is responsible for the direct supervision of the nation's largest national banks, foreign banks, federal licenses and international examination activities. The other office, headed by the **Deputy Comptroller for International Relations and Financial Evaluations**, focuses on the assessment of the international financial situations to determine the impact of global economic problems on OCC's regulatory functions in international banking institutions. Professional positions within OCC number over 2,000. About 100 positions are filled annually. Candidates must have either three years' experience in positions requiring a thorough knowledge and application of commercial accounting or auditing principles and practices or a college or university degree with a minimum of 24 semester hours in accounting, banking, business administration, commercial or business law, economics, finance, or a directly related field.

U.S. Department of the Treasury
15th Street & Pennsylvania
    Avenue, N.W.
Washington, D.C. 20220

tel. 202/566-2000 (Public
    Information)
tel. 202/566-5061 (Personnel)
http://www.ustreas.gov

Office of the Assistant Secretary
    for International Affairs
U.S. Department of the Treasury
Room 3430, Main Treasury
Washington, D.C. 20220

tel. 202/566-5363
tel. 202/566-5953 (Personnel)

Office of the Comptroller of
    the Currency
490 L'Enfant Plaza, S.W
Washington, D.C. 20219

tel. 202/447-1810 (General
    Information)
tel. 202/447-1621 (Personnel)

PRESIDENTIAL MANAGEMENT
INTERN PROGRAM

JOSEPH A. MCMASTER, JR. *

The Presidential Management Intern Program is designed to attract to the federal service high-caliber graduates with advanced degrees. The program offers a special means of entry into the federal government for students completing an advanced degree who have demonstrated an interest in the management or analysis of public policies and programs.

The path to becoming a Presidential Management Intern consists of two steps. The first step is nomination by a graduate program. The graduate program is responsible for developing a competitive nomination process that ensures consideration of all interested students and choosing those who will be nominated.

Step two is a review of each person's nomination package that includes two essays as well as letters of recommendation. This review is done by an outside committee of experts who are looking for strong and demonstrated management and leadership abilities.

This two-step selection process leads to the identification of the group of finalists who will be eligible for placement. Up to 400 PMI positions may be filled each year. Since the program was established in 1978, all cabinet departments and more than 44 agencies have hired PMIs.

Interns are given diverse and challenging assignments within their chosen agency. On-the-job training, rotational opportunities, mentoring, and attendance at regularly scheduled conferences are features of many agency programs.

PMIs receive an initial two-year appointment at the GS-9 level. They are eligible for promotion to GS-11 after successfully completing one year as a PMI. After successfully completing the second year, the PMI is eligible for conversion to a permanent government position and eligible for promotion to GS-12.

---

* Joseph A. McMaster, Jr., a friend of Georgetown University's School of Foreign Service, is the Presidential Management Intern Program Coordinator with the Office of Personnel Management's Philadelphia Service Center. He has 29 years of federal service, all with OPM and its predecessor agency, the Civil Service Commission. He has worked in a variety of program areas including staffing, and college relations.

The percentage of each class of PMIs who have completed graduate studies in the field of international relations has been steadily rising. At the same time, the number of positions filled at the agencies that are the most obvious choices for PMIs with that background (e.g., State Department, Agency for International Development, International Trade Administration) has been relatively stable.

In preparing for the steps of the PMI screening process, it is important to keep in mind that the PMI program is designed to provide its participants with unique exposure to a wide range of public management issues. It is important to know the direction you want your career to take, but be aware that PMI officials do not want applicants whose focus is too narrow.

One of the keys to a successful application is a clear indication of how one plans to put an international relations background to work in the broader arena of public service. Nearly every agency has international activities that may not be readily apparent. In addition, all these agencies are looking for PMIs in whom to develop transferable, general management skills. Keep an open mind. No matter what agency or type of position you choose, you will be able to put your knowledge to work in the service of your country.

Announcements about the PMI program are available each year to graduate schools and students nationwide. Additional information and application materials may be obtained from the heads of graduate programs and career guidance and placement offices, or by contacting the U.S. Office of Personnel Management's Career America Connection at 912/757-3000.

FOREIGN SERVICE

KATHRYN CABRAL*

Living abroad and representing the government of the United States is as much of an adventure today as it ever has been. But more than a spirit of adventure and a desire to serve your country, the Foreign Service requires dedication and persistence from its corps of professionals—women and men who are willing to work hard to represent the interests of the United States and to look after the needs of U.S. citizens in other countries. The basic role of American diplomats is to provide information and recommendations to policymakers, implement U.S. foreign policy overseas, advance U.S. interests, and provide services to U.S. citizens and businesses.

The Foreign Service is not just a job: it is a way of life. While there is occasional glamour—state receptions, for instance—most Foreign Service officers spend long hours working on issues that many might not be aware of, from implementing prisoner exchange agreements and maintaining an embassy, to reducing barriers to trade and reporting on local political news. Of course, the Foreign Service offers unique opportunities—whether it is helping U.S. citizens in distress abroad or laying the groundwork for successful economic or political agreements. And while not all Foreign Service officers have a chance to work on headline-grabbing peace initiatives, they all have the opportunity to contribute every day to the safeguarding of U.S. lives and interests overseas. Some of the newer areas covered by Foreign Service officers include human rights, refugees, narcotics and environment, and science and technology issues.

There is no one Foreign Service career. No two officers are likely to follow the same career path or have the same experiences. State Department Foreign Service officers generally specialize in one of four areas: administrative, consular, economic, or political. All four areas

* Kathryn Cabral, a 1986 graduate of Georgetown University's Master of Science in Foreign Service program, joined the U.S. Foreign Service in 1987. In addition to assignments in Guatemala and Madrid, she has participated in negotiations on international trade agreements such as the Uruguay Round and NAFTA, and served on the Board of Examiners of the Foreign Service. Ms. Cabral was a Presidential Management Intern at the Department of Commerce prior to becoming a Foreign Service officer. The views and opinions expressed here are solely the author's and do not necessarily represent those of the U.S. Department of State.

are vital to the success of a U.S. Embassy. The Department increasingly expects that officers specializing in one area will gain substantial experience in at least one other area, making true generalists of all officers. The State Department also employs hundreds of Foreign Service specialists, including diplomatic security agents, information management specialists, secretaries, health professionals, and engineers.

The United States Information Agency, the Departments of Agriculture and Commerce, and the Agency for International Development all have their own Foreign Service officers. A number of other federal government agencies, including the Treasury and the Federal Aviation Administration, also assign employees to embassies overseas.

At present, almost every new Foreign Service officer is assigned a first tour of duty overseas in a consular section. Many new officers will spend a second tour doing the same kind of work. To be realistic, it is unlikely that junior officers will find themselves advising senior department officials on matters of high foreign policy, regardless of their education or work experiences prior to joining the Foreign Service.

Some of the advantages of a career in the Foreign Service can also be considered the disadvantages. Living abroad offers the excitement of travel and meeting new people; it can also mean long separations from extended family and friends and having to figure out all over again such everyday tasks as grocery shopping and dry cleaning. Having a new assignment every two or three years offers great variety in your career; it also means you are the "new kid on the block" over and over again, having to prove yourself to new colleagues and bring yourself up to speed on new issues, all the while trying to make sure that you and your family are settling in to a new home life! It is a demanding balancing act, and while many people in the private sector face similar challenges, the Foreign Service adds the dimension of frequent overseas assignments.

A Foreign Service career requires a great commitment to public service and sometimes personal sacrifice from both the officer and family members. For example, many Foreign Service assignments entail living in overseas locations where American amenities are scarce if they are available at all. Housing, employment opportunities for spouses, and educational and medical facilities at some locations may not be what Americans have come to expect. Hardships at some embassy locations, and danger—in the form of terrorism—at others, will continue to be everyday concerns for Foreign Service officers.

It takes time, energy, and strong skills to make it through the selection process to become a Foreign Service officer. The process starts with a written exam, usually offered once each year, which is open to U.S. citizens between 20 and 59 years of age. Candidates who pass the written exam are invited to participate in a day-long oral assessment that tests a variety of skills deemed essential to a career in the Foreign Service. Successful oral examination candidates, currently about 8 to 10 percent of those who take the orals, go on to a graded personal interview. Most candidates are then invited to complete the process with security and medical clearances and a final review. Candidates successful at that stage have their names entered on a ranked register, from which individuals are offered appointments as new "classes" of Foreign Service officers are formed.

Budget constraints have kept the number of new hires low in the last few years, in the range of 90 to 120 per year, and the situation is not expected to change greatly in the near future. The State Department is currently considering alternative methods of identifying appropriate candidates for Foreign Service careers, but there have been no decisions about what those methods might be or when they would be implemented.

There is no one way to prepare yourself for a career in the Foreign Service, and no specific educational background is required. Most successful candidates have a broad knowledge of both domestic and international affairs, U.S. and world history and government, as well as foreign policy and culture. While most successful candidates have a B.A. degree, it is not a requirement. Recently, about 65 percent of successful candidates have had advanced degrees, in areas such as international relations, economics, business administration, law, or journalism, and most have had work experience in various fields before their appointment to the Foreign Service. Many have had overseas experience.

There is no doubt that the Foreign Service will continue to offer challenging career opportunities in the years ahead. Dedicated Foreign Service officers will continue to staff our embassies around the globe, observing dramatic changes in global politics and economics and engaging in diplomatic activities as diverse as conflict resolution, nuclear nonproliferation, human rights and democracy, environmental issues, world trade, and the protection of the interests of U.S. citizens and businesses abroad. But indications are that those Foreign Service officers will be doing all this, and more, with fewer resources, and at times, little public support.

A career in the Foreign Service offers rewarding and unique work, and demands a great commitment. If you seek challenge, growth and responsibility in an international setting, the Foreign Service may be the career for you.

Information Agency, United States

The United States Information Agency (USIA) is responsible for the conduct of international education, culture, exchange, and communication programs designed to promote understanding between Americans and other peoples of the world. USIA accomplishes its goals through a variety of activities ranging from academic and cultural exchanges to international broadcasting to press, film, seminar, library, and cultural center programs abroad.

USIA's staff number about 9,200, of whom 4,400 are domestic employees working principally at the agency's Washington headquarters and at the Voice of America. More than 3,800 are foreign nationals hired abroad to work at agency offices around the world. Another 1,000 are foreign service officers (FSOs).

Most FSOs serve as generalists and are expected to move into the social and cultural environment of the locale where they are stationed and cultivate personal contact with key individuals in government, education, media, arts, and professions. In the course of their work, FSOs must define and explain U.S. policies and society, correct misconceptions, and analyze and report on public perceptions of the United States. USIA's overseas posts range in size from a single officer to two dozen.

The FSOs stationed overseas fall into one of three categories: public affairs officer, information officer, or cultural affairs officer. The public affairs officer has responsibility for the management and supervision of all public affairs activities of the embassy. The officer participates in the formulation of embassy objectives and advises the ambassador on trends in local public opinion and the implications for U.S. foreign policy. Information officers are responsible for those activities that directly concern the "fast" media: press, publications, radio, and television. The role of embassy spokesperson also is filled by an information officer. Cultural affairs officers administer the post's educational and cultural exchange programs, arrange lectures and seminars with U.S. speakers, manage U.S. libraries, organize exhibits, assist local publishers with the publication of reprints and translations of U.S. books, and work closely with bilateral educational-exchange commissions.

FSOs are recruited through the foreign service examination conducted jointly with the Department of State. Candidates should demonstrate a broad knowledge of American civilization including literature, the arts, history, and current events. In addition, a background in cross-cultural communication, journalism, area studies, languages, international relations, or business administration is highly desirable. On average about 35 new officers are hired annually.

USIA has established a Foreign Service Mid-Level Minority Recruitment Program for which there are a limited number of openings for well-qualified individuals to enter as mid-level Foreign Service officers (salary range: $36,147 to $65,510). The successful applicant is appointed as a Foreign Service officer (career candidate) for a four-year period, extendable to five, after which the candidate will be considered for conversion to career status. Applicants for this program must be U.S. citizens, at least 21 years of age, and member's of a minority group (American Indian, Inuit, Aleut, Asian, Pacific Islander, Black, or Hispanic). A rigorous medical exam and complete background check also must be completed successfully. Applicants must hold at least a bachelor's degree and five years of professional education or work experience of which three years must be related to the foreign service. Backgrounds in international relations, foreign area studies, American studies, history, journalism, political science/government, public administration, or business administration are particularly relevant. Candidates who meet the basic requirements must participate in a half-day assessment process similar to that administered to those passing the foreign service written exam.

USIA also offers a variety of career opportunities outside the Foreign Service, most of which are located in Washington, D.C. (For more information about civil service positions in general, see the section on Civil Service careers.) From here, USIA operates the government's programs of educational and cultural exchange and athletic and artistic exchanges. Most non-Foreign Service professionals have specialized backgrounds in technical and information areas such as journalism, radio and television production, cinematography, graphic arts, and library science. USIA offers opportunities in administrative and management fields such as budget, personnel, procurement, and contracting. Applications for non-Foreign Service positions may be made by submitting a completed SF-171 form for a specifically advertised vacancy to the USIA personnel office.

One source of non-Foreign Service USIA employment of particular interest is the **Voice of America (VOA)**. VOA is the official U.S. overseas radio network charged with pursuing the goals of USIA. Employees generally fall into one of three categories: technicians (operating radio hardware), broadcasters and producers, and auxiliary personnel. Most successful applicants have a journalism or broadcasting background coupled with a strong interest in international affairs. VOA operates an intern program designed for recent graduates with communications degrees. The program provides on-the-job broadcast training and job opportunities upon completion.

U.S. Information Agency	tel. 202/619-4539 (24-hour Job
Office of Personnel	Line)
301 4th Street, S.W.	tel. 202/619-4659 (General
Washington, D.C. 20547	Employment Information)

For additional information on the Mid-Level Minority Recruitment Program:

U.S. Information Agency   tel. 202/619-4702
Foreign Service Division
Room 506
301 4th Street, S.W.
Washington, D.C. 20547

Voice of America   tel. 202/619-0909 (24-hour Job
330 Independence Avenue, S.W.   Line)
Washington, D.C. 20547   tel. 202/619-1092 (Personnel
                                   Office)
                                 http://www.usia.gov

State, U.S. Department of

The United States Department of State advances U.S. objectives and interests through formulating, representing, and implementing the President's foreign policies. It carries out its mission through overseas posts, its Washington, D.C., headquarters, and other U.S. offices. The **Foreign Service**, America's diplomatic corps, fosters international relationships through the exchange of official representatives and supports the President and Secretary of State in planning and pursuing the United States' foreign policy goals. It represents U.S. interests; administers overseas missions; assists U.S. citizens abroad; conducts public diplomacy; and reports, communicates, and negotiates political, economic, consular, administrative, cultural, and commercial affairs.

Foreign Service Officers (FSOs), generalists who promote U.S. interests at diplomatic posts overseas and in Washington, D.C., advocate and explain U.S. objectives; report on political, economic, and scientific developments; assist U.S. citizens overseas; interpret and administer the United States' immigration and nationality laws; and promote U.S. business. **Administrative** officers manage the complex operations of an overseas post. **Consular** officers handle passports and visas and assist U.S. citizens in distress. **Economic** officers negotiate international civil aviation, trade policy, fishing rights, and multilateral lending policies; pursue agreements for scientific, environmental, and technological cooperation; and defend the interests and rights of U.S. businesses. **Political** officers assess the support for U.S. policies; advocate policy consistent with U.S. interests; and seek to maximize cooperation among governments and nations in areas of mutual concern. The first step to becoming an FSO is a written exam administered nationwide and at all U.S. embassies and consulates. The exam tests job-related knowledge, including U.S. and world history, systems of government, economics, and English expression, and includes a biographic information questionnaire. Those who pass are invited to a day-long oral assessment, which includes exercises in which a candidate presents a demarche to the examiners; resolves three hypothetical problems based on administrative, consular, and public affairs scenarios; writes an essay; and participates in a group negotiation. The exercises are closely correlated to tasks frequently performed by FSOs. Candidates who pass are interviewed to assess their motivation and expectations and must pass a background investigation and medical clearance. **Foreign Service Specialists** provide technical support and administrative services worldwide in a variety of occupations. Like generalist FSOs, Foreign Service Specialists go through a competitive selection process and must be willing and able to serve worldwide, based on the needs of the service. Specialist candidates do not take the Foreign Service exam but must meet specific education or work experience requirements and pass an oral assessment, background investigation, and medical clearance. Opportunities are announced on the Foreign Service job hotline.

Civil Service employees work with Foreign Service colleagues to ensure the efficient operation of the department and provide continuity for the United States' diplomatic efforts with expertise in a range of capacities. Civil Service employees primarily work at the State Department in Washington, D.C., or at a passport agency, despatch agency, or diplomatic security office in one of several major U.S. cities. Many Civil Service opportunities are similar to those found in the private sector, including budget officers, secretaries, and attorneys, but specialized positions exist as intelligence analysts, passport examiners, interpreters, and foreign affairs specialists. Qualifications vary according to specialization. Openings are announced on the Civil Service job hotline.

The State Department offers high school, college, and graduate student internships; cooperative education; work-study programs; and fellowships. Most are in the Washington, D.C., area. These programs offer an opportunity to gain firsthand knowledge of foreign affairs operations through performing duties such as conducting research, preparing briefing papers, working in computer science, drafting correspondence or assisting in legal cases.

For brochures and applications for the **Foreign Service officer, Foreign Service Specialist,** and **Student Employment Programs,** write:

Recruitment Division
U.S. Department of State
P.O. Box 9317—GT
Arlington, VA 22219

tel. 703/875-7490 (Foreign
Service/Student Employment
Job Line)

Office of Civil Service Personnel
  Management
U.S. Department of State
P.O. Box 18657
Washington, D.C. 20036-8657

tel. 202/647-7284
(Civil Service Job Line)

International Organization Affairs, Bureau of,
U.S. Department of State

The Department of State's Bureau of International Organization Affairs and other federal agencies assist U.S. citizens interested in employment with international organizations by maintaining a roster of interested and qualified candidates for referral to organizations for senior positions. The final selection of the candidate, of course, is always the prerogative of the international organization and often is based on a desire to maintain a geographic balance among member countries. As a very large number of applications from all over the world are normally received for a given opening, competition is always keen.

It should be kept in mind that while the government's service may be very useful, the selection of candidates is rarely confined to those proposed by national agencies and no sponsorship is required. Citizens may always apply directly to the organization in which they are interested and in some cases that may be the only procedure. Normally, however it would be to the candidate's advantage to pursue as many avenues as possible to ensure that the application is received. Many organizations stress that individual initiative may often have a significant impact on the recruitment and hiring process.

The respective U.S. government agencies responsible for liaison with international organizations constitute an important source of information and serve as contact points for interested candidates.

The State Department bureau maintains a computerized roster of senior applicants listed according to academic disciplines, work experience, languages, service abroad and other relevant factors. In addition to positions with the U.N. Secretariat, the bureau also collects vacancy announcements for the agricultural agencies in Rome (Food and Agricultural Organization [FAO], International Fund for Agricultural Development [IFAD], World Food Program [WFP]); the agencies in Vienna (International Atomic Energy Agency [IAEA], United Nations Industrial Development Organization [UNIDO]); the health, labor, refugee, telecommunications and other agencies in Geneva (International Labor Organization [ILO], International Telecommunication Union [ITU], United Nations High Commissioner for Refugees [UNHCR], World Intellectual Property Organization [WIPO], World Health Organization [WHO]); and the economics-oriented commissions throughout Europe and elsewhere (Economic Commission for Africa [ECA], Economic Commission for Europe [ECE], Economic Commission for Latin America and the Caribbean [ECLAC], Economic and Social Commission for Western Asia [ESCWA], General Agreement on Tariffs and Trade [GATT], Organization for Economic Cooperation and Development [OECD]).

Positions range from entry to senior levels. At a minimum, candidates for U.N. junior positions must have advanced degrees, at least one foreign language and five years of relevant work experience; occasionally, three years of experience are adequate for entry-level vacancies. Senior positions require at least 16 years experience including some international work. There is also a mandatory retirement age of 62 for most secretariat personnel, and most agencies will not appoint persons who have reached or nearly reached that age.

For those interested in applying for positions in the United Nations and many of its associated agencies (not including language specialists who must apply directly), a resume and a letter describing specific interests should be sent to:

Bureau of International Organization   tel. 202/647-6414
   Affairs
UN Employment Information &
   Assistance Unit
IO/S/EA—Room 4808 Main State
Department of State
Washington, DC 20520–6319

INTELLIGENCE

CAROLYN EKEDAHL *

The intelligence community has long been a major employer of graduates in international relations, languages, and the sciences. As the world becomes more interdependent and challenges to U.S. policymakers become more complex, the intelligence community must become more sophisticated. This will require the maintenance of a diverse workforce with backgrounds in virtually every academic discipline and professional field.

The mission of the U.S. intelligence community is to provide policymakers, particularly the President, with the information they need to inform their decisions about foreign policy. Intelligence is simply information—in this case, information relating to U.S. national security interests.

The issues important to policymakers are changing. During the Cold War, the intelligence community focused on the political and military threat posed by the Soviet Union. Now its focus is on a wider range of issues that includes ethnic conflict, proliferation of weapons of mass destruction, economic trends, drug trafficking, and international terrorism. Previous consumers of intelligence were overwhelmingly part of the national security apparatus (the National Security Council, State and Defense departments); in the post–Cold War era, law enforcement agencies such as the Federal Bureau of Investigation and the Drug Enforcement Agency are becoming major consumers of foreign intelligence.

Whatever the issues of concern, the primary functions of the intelligence community will remain constant: providing warning of situations that may pose a threat to U.S. interests, such as an impending Iraqi attack on Kuwait or a terrorist attack on the World Trade Center;

* Carolyn Ekedahl, a friend of Georgetown University's School of Foreign Service and former Associate at Georgetown's Institute for the Study of Diplomacy, works for the Central Intelligence Agency. Ms. Ekedahl spent most of her career in the CIA's Directorate of Intelligence focusing on Soviet foreign policy and currently serves as Chief of Public Communications in CIA's Public Affairs Staff. Ms. Ekedahl has been a senior fellow at the Atlantic Council of the United States and served as an adjunct professor at Georgetown University's School of Foreign Service. She is the is co-author of *Moscow and the Third World under Gorbachev* and *The Wars of Eduard Shevradnadze*. Ms. Ekedahl holds a B.A. from Wellesley College.

monitoring issues of concern such as arms control agreements, weapons proliferation, and drug trafficking; and tracking long-term trends that may affect U.S. interests, such as political events in Russia or China or the development of nuclear programs in North Korea and Iraq.

The basic business of intelligence is information management—collecting and analyzing data, then disseminating finished intelligence products to policymakers in a timely and relevant fashion. Significant information has always been readily available from the reporting of diplomatic and military officers, trade and economic data, the normal exchange of information between nations, and the huge amounts of information published and broadcast openly.

Nations use other means to gather information that is not freely available:

- Signals intelligence (SIGINT) is information derived from intercepted communications, radar, and telemetry.

- Imagery intelligence (IMINT) includes overhead and ground imagery.

- Measurement and signature intelligence (MASINT) is technically derived intelligence data other than IMINT and SIGINT. MASINT employs a wide range of disciplines including nuclear, optical, radio frequency, acoustics, seismic, and materials sciences.

- Human resources intelligence (HUMINT) involves clandestine and overt collection techniques.

Collection in all of these areas requires sophisticated systems developed by highly capable scientists, engineers, and trade or craft specialists. The U.S. intelligence community has always been in the forefront of developing technologies designed to enhance its collection capability.

Once information has been collected, it must be processed, exploited, and transmitted using secure communications. Exploiting imagery, decoding messages, translating broadcasts, reducing telemetry to meaningful measures, preparing information for computer processing, storing and retrieving data, and placing human-source reports into context are all examples of processing intelligence.

Intelligence analysis focuses on many issues, including strategic issues, science and technology, economics, politics, and societal problems—virtually every international issue of national security interest. Most intelligence organizations assign analysts to a particular geographic or functional specialty. Analysts absorb incoming information, evaluate it, produce an assessment of the current status of their particular subject, and then forecast future trends or outcomes. Analysts also develop requirements for the collection of new information.

Finished intelligence is available to consumers in many forms:

- Current intelligence addresses day-to-day developments and is presented in a variety of publications as well as in ad hoc written memorandums and oral briefings.

- Estimative intelligence deals with what might happen in the future. The highest level estimative products are the intelligence community's coordinated National Intelligence Estimates.

- Warning intelligence gives notice of some impending development to policymakers and may be issued by a phone call, an oral briefing, or a warning memorandum.

- Research intelligence provides in-depth analysis on a wide variety of subjects. It may consist of structured compilations presented in maps, atlases, and handbooks. It may be operational support to planners and operators. It may be in-depth research on scientific and technical developments provided in detailed systems handbooks, assessments, or automated databases.

The intelligence community requires administrative support for all of its functions. This includes security, logistics, medical, financial, personnel, facilities construction and maintenance, legal, and secretarial support. These are functions found in all other organizations. What makes them unique in the intelligence community is that they must be conducted in a secure environment, and they are often carried out covertly and overseas.

While most intelligence analysts jobs are in the Washington, D.C., area, there are an increasing number of rotational assignments overseas, and travel to relevant foreign countries is common. Both intelligence operations officers, whose mission is the collection of information, and many support personnel serve tours overseas. Foreign language competence and living experience overseas are highly valued for those seeking positions in the intelligence community.

Employment within the intelligence community requires a security clearance. Clearance requirements may vary among the agencies, but the process typically is lengthy and includes several steps: background investigation, medical screening, and, at some agencies, a polygraph interview. The process may take nine months to a year, so those considering a career in intelligence should begin the process early in their academic programs. For additional information, call the recruiting office of the appropriate intelligence agency.

Central Intelligence Agency

The Central Intelligence Agency (CIA), while not the largest intelligence agency, has the broadest responsibility. It produces national intelligence, that is, all-source, all-subject finished intelligence for the President, the National Security Council, and Congress. It is a unique institution in that it is neither a policymaking nor a law enforcement agency; it has no domestic authority.

CIA is charged with collecting, analyzing, and disseminating information needed by policymakers making foreign policy and law enforcement decisions. It is also responsible for clandestine collection of foreign intelligence, counterintelligence abroad, and the research and development of technical collection systems.

The CIA is headquartered in McLean, Virginia, and offers careers to individuals with backgrounds in virtually every academic discipline. After several years of low recruitment because of general government downsizing, CIA is again hiring. Those interested in careers in analysis should have a graduate degree; foreign language ability and some experience living abroad are also highly valued. Those wishing to enter the operations field should have completed some area studies program and have some foreign language capability and some experience living abroad. For careers in the support and development offices of the CIA experience is needed in a wide variety of areas, including engineering, computer science, systems analysis, library science, modeling and simulation, public administration, and accounting.

The Foreign Broadcast Information Service (FBIS) offers careers as foreign language officers for those with strong language capability. FBIS is responsible for collecting, translating, and disseminating foreign print and broadcast material relevant to analysts and policymakers in the foreign policy community.

Summer internships and cooperative education programs are available for undergraduate as well as graduate students, offering flexible schedules, varied work opportunities, and tuition assistance. The programs enhance students' academic study while enabling the CIA to assess potential for permanent employment.

Those interested in career opportunities or student programs at CIA or FBIS should send a resume and cover letter to the appropriate address below.

Central Intelligence Agency   tel. 703/482-4119
Personnel Representative
P.O. Box 9065
McLean, VA 22102

Central Intelligence Agency   tel. 703/482-4119
Office of Student Programs
Department T, Room 220
P.O. Box 1925
Washington, D.C. 20013

Central Intelligence Agency   http://www.odci.gov
Recruitment Center
P.O. Box 12727
Arlington, VA 22209–8727

Foreign Broadcast Information   tel. 703/481-6226
  Service
Personnel Office
P.O. Box 2604
Washington, D.C. 20013

The largest part of the intelligence community (over 75 percent) is subordinate to the **Department of Defense (DoD)**. Agencies that are part of DoD include the **Defense Intelligence Agency (DIA)**, the **National Security Agency (NSA)**, and the tactical intelligence units attached to each of the military services.

Defense Intelligence Agency

The Defense Intelligence Agency (DIA) provides strategic military intelligence to the Secretary of Defense, the Joint Chiefs of Staff, and major military commands. It also has responsibility for the military intelligence component of national intelligence. DIA, through its National Military Intelligence Collection Center (NMICC), manages all DoD non-SIGINT intelligence collection. It directs all DoD human collection activities, including the defense attache system.

DIA is located at Bolling Air Force Base in the Washington, D.C., area. Most DIA jobs are in the Washington area; there are few overseas positions. The agency has a mix of civilians and military personnel who serve rotational tours.

Intelligence research specialists at DIA have educational backgrounds in foreign area studies, international economics, physical geography, transportation and logistics, and civil structural engineering. A bachelor's degree is sufficient for those with a technical or scientific background; otherwise an advanced degree is necessary. DIA also recruits for support positions, particularly in the fields of computer science and library science. DIA offers career opportunities to college graduates through its two-year career development plan.

Civilian Personnel Director   tel. 202/231-2700
Recruitment Branch
Defense Intelligence Agency
The Pentagon
Washington, D.C. 20301

National Security Agency

The **National Security Agency (NSA)**, located at Fort Meade, Maryland, collects, processes, and reports SIGINT to the intelligence, policy, and operating elements of the government. It provides its SIGINT product directly to military commands worldwide, to other government consumers, and to producers of all-source finished intelligence. The SIGINT product is very sensitive and is provided only to specifically designated people. NSA is also charged with protecting U.S. communications and providing computer security for the Department of Defense.

NSA hires college graduates with degrees in computer sciences, language, communications security, cryptography, signal analysis, intelligence research, management, and administration.

National Security Agency   tel. 301/688-6311
College Recruitment Program
ATTN: Office of Employment (M322)
Fort George G. Meade, MD 20755–6000

Military Intelligence

Each of the military services has an intelligence organization that focuses directly on the needs of that service. In particular, each has a strong scientific and technical intelligence component for the analysis of foreign weapons systems. These organizations are staffed by permanent civil servants and military personnel on rotation. Headquarters of these agencies are in the Washington, D.C., area, but the scientific and technical centers are located in various locations in the eastern United States. There are a few overseas positions.

Department of the Air Force   tel. 703/695-5206
Civilian Personnel Office
11 MSS/DTC SS
1460 Air Force
The Pentagon
Washington, D.C. 14600

Department of the Army   tel. 703/697-2140
Personnel and Employment Service—
  Washington
The Pentagon, Rm. 1B924
Washington, D.C. 20301

Department of the Navy   tel. 703/607-2497
Human Resources Center
Naval Sea System Command
1921 Jefferson Davis Highway
Arlington, VA 22242–5161

Department of the Marine Corps   tel. 703/614-1046
Civilian Personnel
Code ARCA, Rm. 1215
Washington, D.C. 20380–0001

Bureau of Intelligence and Research, U.S. Department of State

Among several civilian agencies that have intelligence units are the Bureau of Intelligence and Research (INR), which produces political and economic intelligence to meet the State Department's needs and to support the Secretary of State. It also coordinates State's relations with other foreign intelligence operations, disseminates reports received from U.S. diplomatic and consular posts abroad, and participates in the preparation of National Intelligence Estimates.

INR is located at the Department of State in Washington, D.C. It is staffed by permanent civil servants and foreign service officers on rotation. It has no overseas positions.

U.S. Department of State   tel. 202/647-6845
INR/EX/PER
Washington, D.C. 20520

The **Federal Bureau of Investigation** (FBI), which is part of the Justice Department, has responsibility for counterintelligence within the United States. The **Treasury** and **Energy departments** both have small intelligence units that serve their agency's respective intelligence focus. The former tracks monetary issues such as foreign financial markets, currencies, stock exchanges, and banking practices. The latter collects and analyzes information on energy issues, including nuclear proliferation and global energy resources. For additional information, contact the relevant agencies at the addresses listed in the Civil Service section of this chapter.

LEGISLATIVE BRANCH

MICHELLE MAYNARD *

While much of the day-to-day work on Capitol Hill focuses on domestic policy, the Hill also offers opportunities to those with an interest and background on foreign affairs. Most members have at least one staff person who spends part of his or her time on issues such as defense, intelligence, trade, and/or foreign policy. Committees such as the Senate Foreign Relations Committee, the House International Relations Committee, and the Senate and House Select Committees on Intelligence have entire staffs devoted to foreign policy and defense issues. Other committees—Agriculture, Appropriations, Finance, and Budget, to name a few—also have staff who devote time to international issues.

The pace is often frenetic, the hours unpredictable, job security nonexistent, and issues can change from day to day. Hill staffers are compensated for these uncertainties, however: they draft legislation, have access to top policymakers, have opportunities for foreign travel, and influence the national agenda, often unencumbered by the layers of bureaucracy found in the executive branch.

Hill Job-Seeking Strategies

Hiring practices vary from office to office, and there is no magic formula for landing a Capitol Hill job. Some staff—usually those right out of college or graduate school—start off as unpaid interns or as paid support staff or legislative correspondents and work their way up through the ranks. For example, one graduate student with an eye toward advancement started out in 1986 in a personal office as an intern/driver for a senator who was poised to take over a key committee chairmanship. Upon graduation, he took a low-level job in the senator's office and, when the senator became chairman, the staffer

Michelle Maynard, a 1986 graduate of Georgetown University's Master of Science in Foreign Service program, formerly a professional staff member with the U.S. Senate Committee on Foreign Relations, is now minority staff director on the U.S. House of Representative's Special Subcommittee investigating Iranian Arms transfers to Croatia and Bosnia. Prior to joining the committee staff in 1989, she worked at the State Department's Bureau of Public Affairs. Ms. Maynard is a 1984 graduate of the College of the Holy Cross.

transferred to the committee, where he is now a professional staff member. Another graduate student, using her home state connection and foreign policy background, landed an entry-level job as a legislative correspondent with a committee after two years at the State Department. After several months, she was given increased responsibilities because of staff turnover and, within a couple of years, also became a professional staff member.

Others at more middle or senior levels with no previous Hill experience may make a lateral move by bringing to their new job a great deal of substantive experience in a particular field such as arms control, trade policy, or foreign aid. Still others manage to land professional Hill jobs right out of school or with little previous work experience. As with any job search, finding a job on the Hill often boils down to talking to the right person or being in the right place at the right time.

Internships do not always lead to permanent work, nor do all entry-level paid staff work their way up the Hill ladder. For those still in school, however, an internship is probably the best way to try out Capitol Hill, gain some experience, and build up your resume. Those with an advanced degree or substantive experience may want to weigh the costs of investing several months in unpaid or entry-level work knowing that the time invested may prove to be no more than a good experience. For a young man or woman hoping to work in Washington, D.C., Hill experience is an asset in many areas of the public, private, and nonprofit sectors.

While Senate and House offices mostly do their own hiring, both branches operate placement offices to which individual offices may turn for resumes. More often than not, the placement office helps fill offices for support staff, but anyone interested in a Hill job should invest the few minutes it takes to drop off a resume and take a typing test at the placement offices. When job hunting, leave no stone unturned.

The offices of the home state delegation should be one of the first stops of any job seeker, as many members prefer to hire natives of their home state. Even if members don't have an opening, they do want to be responsive to their constituents, so job seekers should take advantage of this resource, if only for job tips. Constituents have an automatic foot in the door that is unavailable to others and should arrange a meeting with the administrative assistant, chief of staff, or legislative director as a first resort.

After approaching one's own senator and representative, job seekers should identify members serving on committees of jurisdiction over foreign policy, defense, and intelligence or those who, although they might not serve on one of those committees, have a high profile on or particular interest in certain foreign policy issues. Before mailing resumes and knocking on doors, it is wise to learn something about a particular member: his or her political views, ideology, and work ethic, as well as something about the office's hiring needs and practices.

Those seeking a job on Capitol Hill should have some sense of their own ideological persuasion—and on what core principles they will not compromise—before approaching members' offices. By way of example, an applicant who is deeply opposed to increased defense spending should think long and hard before accepting a job with a hawk. A prospective staffer should never approach employment thinking he or she can influence the member into changing positions on an issue.

Most committees are divided into majority and minority staffs, with the majority staff significantly larger than the minority. Some are further divided into full committee and subcommittee staffs, while others limit their staff to full committee. When targeting committees or members who serve on committees of jurisdiction, it is best to know their staffing policies; while staff on some committees may serve all the members on the committee, staff on other committees may serve only the chairman or the ranking minority member. In the latter case, members who serve on the committee may hire staff to do committee work directly out of their personal offices.

Job seekers should talk to as many current and former staffers as possible for tips on job strategies and openings—find out which of your university's alumni/ae are on the Hill and look them up. Vacancies are often not advertised, and offices that do advertise usually are flooded with resumes. Most candidates are recruited by word of mouth, so personal contacts are critical. While job seekers may wish to drop off resumes by hand, making an appointment will guarantee being taken seriously. Congressional recess periods or days when there are no votes are the most convenient times to talk to Congressional staff about job opportunities.

A Glossary of Job Titles

The following job descriptions are of professional positions and do not include administrative or support positions. Someone right out of school or with limited work experience seeking a nonadministrative position may wish to focus on getting a job in one of the following categories:

- Legislative correspondent (LC): Staff member who drafts responses to a member's mail and deals with constituent requests. LC positions are not just limited to personal offices—some committees hire LCs to answer the chairman's or ranking member's mail.

- Legislative assistant (LA): Staff person who handles legislation for a member on various substantive issues. In offices with little or no foreign policy focus, an LA may juggle five or six unrelated issues—such as taxes, women's issues, the environment, or post office—in addition to foreign affairs. House members, as a general rule, are more apt to hire people right out of school for an LA position.

- Legislative aide/research assistant: Staff person hired to do research for and provide support to legislative assistants. These slots are available in only a handful of Hill offices and fall somewhere between legislative assistant and legislative correspondent. Confusingly, they are sometimes also referred to as LAs.

- Press assistant: Staff person who provides back up and assistance to the press secretary. This position is more common in the Senate than in the House.

Someone seeking a more mid-level position might also wish to look for jobs in the following categories:

- Professional staff member: Committee staff member whose portfolio may include following regional issues, such as Asia or the Middle East, or functional issues, such as arms control or a particular piece of legislation like Foreign Operations Appropriations or State Department Authorization bills.

- Press secretary: Staff person who is the key link between the member and the media. In the Senate, the press secretary usually focuses exclusively on media relations, while in the House, press and legislative duties may be combined.

- Counsel: Lawyer who serves on committee staff and deals with matters such as nominations and treaties.

As a rule, personal staff serve the member and much of the agenda is driven by the member's personal interests, committee assignments, and election cycle. They draft legislation for the member, advise the member on what positions to take and how to vote on particular issues, write statements and speeches for the member, and assist the member during meetings with constituents, lobbyists, other members, and Administration officials.

Committee staff conduct oversight of matters within the committee's jurisdiction and serve as the primary connection between Congress and Administration on policy matters. In addition to conducting the same types of activities described above, committee staff also arrange for briefings and hearings with government officials and private sector witnesses. They draft legislation, write reports explaining the legislation, and provide staff support for committee members during committee mark-ups and floor consideration of legislation. They may also conduct and report on international fact-finding missions.

What It Takes

Working on Capitol Hill requires a great deal of flexibility. Staff are often called on to perform a juggling act, work simultaneously on several different issues and perform a variety of different tasks well, from drafting legislation to representing the member to constituents to meeting foreign dignitaries. Flexibility is also required in dealing with members and other staff who may be difficult or antagonistic but hold key positions.

A Hill staffer should also possess initiative, creativity, and motivation. Ever aware of the member's interests, strengths, and limits, a good staffer will devise initiatives for the member to take, from introducing legislation to writing an op-ed or initiating a letter-writing campaign. The goal is to promote the member. Good staff work is done behind the scenes, often with little credit or glory for the staff members themselves.

Good written and oral communication skills are essential. Most members of Congress are not interested in academic treatises. They prize staff who write clear and concise background papers and policy memos. Staff should also be prepared to adapt their writing to a member's style when drafting statements and speeches for the member to deliver or letters for the member's signature. Oral skills are often very important, as on some occasions a staffer can spend an entire day on the phone. Staff are called upon to negotiate the fine points of legislation; represent the member's interests in conversations with the Administration; make presentations to lobbyists, school groups, and constituents; and deal with the media.

Substantive knowledge in some area of foreign policy is also helpful, particularly for committee positions, but perhaps even more

important are a keen political sense, the ability to assimilate information quickly and easily, and the talent to translate ideas into practice.

Foreign policy has never been a high priority for most members,
who usually reflect their constituents demands that they focus on domestic issues. With the end of the Cold War and in the current political
atmosphere, this is more true than ever. In addition, most committee
staffs and some personal offices have been downsized. Job seekers may
wish to focus, therefore, on areas with the most potential for cross-over
between domestic and foreign policy, such as trade or international
economics.

On the other hand, the proliferation of term-limitation measures,
as well as increased member turnover in the House and Senate, will increase the importance of experienced staffers and ensure the availability of employment opportunities. Experience on Capitol Hill can be as
rewarding as it is exciting. Most Hill staffers are young and energetic,
and while their jobs may be stepping stones on their career path, they
are also playing a central role on Capitol Hill.

Senate Committees/Subcommittees
Dealing with International Affairs

Committee on Agriculture, Nutrition, and Forestry

Committee on Appropriations
    Subcommittee on Commerce, Justice and State, the Judiciary, and
        Related Agencies
    Subcommittee on Defense
    Subcommittee on Foreign Operations
    Subcommittee on Military Construction

Committee on Armed Services (all subcommittees)

Committee on Banking, Housing, and Urban Affairs
    Subcommittee on International Finance and Monetary Policy

Committee on the Budget

Committee on Commerce, Science, and Transportation
    Subcommittee on Consumer Affairs, Foreign Commerce, and
        Tourism
    Subcommittee on Science, Technology, and Space

Committee on Finance
    Subcommittee on International Trade

Committee on Foreign Relations (all subcommittees)

Committee on the Judiciary
Subcommittee on Immigration

Select Committee on Intelligence

House Committees/Subcommittees Dealing with International Affairs

Committee on Agriculture

Committee on Appropriations
Subcommittee on Commerce, Justice, State, the Judiciary, and Related Agencies
Subcommittee on National Security
Subcommittee on Foreign Operations, Export Financing, and Related Programs
Subcommittee on Military Construction

Committee on Banking and Financial Services
Subcommittee on Domestic and International Monetary Policy

Committee on the Budget
Task Force on Defense, Foreign Policy, and Space

Committee on Government Reform and Oversight
Subcommittee on National Security, International Affairs, and Criminal Justice

Committee on Judiciary
Subcommittee on Immigration and Claims

Committee on National Security (all subcommittees)

Committee on Ways and Means
Subcommittee on Trade

Permanent Select Committee on Intelligence (all subcommittees)

Placement Offices

Senate Placement Office
Room SH-142
Senate Hart Building
Washington, D.C. 20515

House Office of Human Resources
Room 263
Cannon House Office Building
Washington, D.C. 20515

Capitol Hill Web Sites:

http://policy.net/capweb/congress.html
http://thomas.loc.gov
http://www.house.gov

3

International Organizations

IZUMI NAKAMITSU *

The United Nations is currently the focus of renewed attention due to its role in the turbulent changes in the world these last few years. This attention, however, has not always been positive or favorable toward the United Nations. Why did the United Nations "fail" in its peacekeeping missions in Somalia? In Bosnia and Herzegovina? Leaving detailed academic analysis of those questions to students of international affairs, the simplified answer is that the new problem sets of the post–Cold War period go beyond the scope of what the U.N. system was established to deal with after World War II. The U.N. is now searching for new approaches to the new problems it faces, which makes the work of those who seek careers in the U.N. all the more challenging and rewarding.

The end of the Cold War has helped bring about resolutions of a number of conflicts around the world, such as those in Central America, Cambodia, Mozambique, and (hopefully) Angola. In those places, the U.N. developed and continues to maintain successful postconflict peace-building activities, returning hundreds of thousands of refugees, bringing about national reconciliation and greater stability, and assisting in the rehabilitation and reconstruction of communities. The key to those successes has been the fact that peace agreements had been achieved and that the parties involved had the political will to end

---

* Izumi Nakamitsu, a 1989 graduate of Georgetown University's Master of Science in Foreign Service program, has held a number of positions with the United Nations High Commissioner for Refugees (UNHCR). Currently the Executive Assistant to the Assistant High Commissioner at UNHCR headquarters in Geneva, Ms. Nakamitsu has also worked in the former Yugoslavia, where she was the head of the UNHCR offices in Sarajevo and Mostar and served as Senior Humanitarian Affairs Officer to the Special Representative of the Secretary-General. Prior to that, Ms. Nakamitsu served as a personnel officer in the Division of Human Resources Management in Geneva and as a legal officer in the UNHCR branch office in Ankara, Turkey.

those conflicts. These developments owed a lot to new approaches to the consolidation of peace that are emerging in the U.N. system.

These new approaches call for greater cooperation between, or even integration of, political, military, developmental, economic, humanitarian, and human rights components of the U.N. system. They recognize that the root causes of a conflict must be dealt with comprehensively in order to prevent a recurrence. Multifaceted peacekeeping operations now include the U.N. peacekeeping force, which implements and monitors peace, and the U.N. High Commissioner for Refugees (UNHCR), which repatriates refugees and then monitors and assists their reintegration into new communities. These agencies are joined by other U.N. humanitarian organizations and nongovernmental organizations (NGOs); development organizations, such as the U.N. Development Programme (UNDP), which assists in institutional capacity building; and human rights organizations, which promote respect for basic human rights. International financial institutions, such as the World Bank and other bilateral donors, also collaborate in the international effort to reach the common goal of consolidating and building peace.

If peace-building activities in postconflict situations are producing a new approach to tackling root causes of conflicts, and peacekeeping operations in the midst of conflicts present difficult challenges, yet another kind of partnership, or division of labor, is emerging between the U.N. and regional organizations in ever more complex peacemaking and peacekeeping operations. For example, in Tajikistan, the U.N. has been pursuing political settlement of the conflict with the Central Asian States and the Russian Federation, supported by the U.N. military observer mission and the peacekeeping forces of the Commonwealth of Independent States. In Bosnia and Herzegovina, the military implementation of the Dayton Agreement is entrusted to the North Atlantic Treaty Organization (NATO) multinational force, while the return of refugees and displaced persons is entrusted to UNHCR, the electoral and human rights related mission to the Organization for Security and Cooperation in Europe (OSCE) and other civilian and political matters to the European Union (EU) High Representative.

As the problems with which the United Nations deals become more complex, the U.N. system needs to reform itself to become more efficient, effective, flexible, and operational. There have been many discussions among the member states on reforming the U.N. organs such as the Security Council, as well as making the Secretariat and other organizations more cost-effective. Some initiatives are also under way to reform the U.N. system itself. As it enters the 21st century, the U.N. must become more solution-oriented to meet the needs of member states and more effective in preventing conflicts in partnership with other regional organizations.

Who should seek careers in the new, changing United Nations? One should always remember that the U.N. is a forum of international politics, where nation-states debate issues of contention through the prism of their own national interests. While the U.N. Secretariat and organizations, as well as specialized agencies, do have a large degree of autonomy in their activities, ultimately political direction is given by the member states. Therefore, the best international public servants are "idealistic realists," who passionately believe that working toward the achievement of peace, justice, and human rights is in the national interest of all member states. They believe the world today is too interconnected to permit us to ignore problems in any one part of it.

As the U.N. is involved more frequently in complex operations, people with initiative, good analytical minds, and negotiating and managerial skills are more in demand. A good international public servant must be a quick learner, able to adjust to unpredictable situations. He or she must be willing to relocate, often to hardship-duty stations. The ability to work in a multicultural environment is crucial; indeed, the multicultural working environment in different duty stations is one of the things that make careers with international organizations more interesting by widening one's perspective in life.

One of the difficulties in seeking employment with the U.N. system, as in any international organization, is that there is no fixed central recruitment mechanism. Although a range of job categories exist in the U.N., including areas such as political, economic, and social affairs; administration; finance; information systems; and public relations, a job seeker should apply for a vacant post in his or her relevant disciplinary field. Information on vacant posts is available at the recruitment section of the Secretariat, each U.N. agency, and often at the Ministry of Foreign Affairs of member states. Some governments also have junior professional officer (JPO) programs, through which entry-level (P1 or P2 level) professional staff are recruited by U.N. organizations for a fixed period of time (normally two years) at the expense of their respective governments.

I would like to give those who wish to seek careers with the United Nations a piece of advice that Ambassador Donald McHenry gave to me when I was starting with UNHCR: "Start your career in the field." As in any bureaucracy, the headquarters is often too big and one could easily lose sight of what the organization really is doing. It is also easier for junior-level staff to get greater responsibility in field offices. Had I not started my career with UNHCR in Turkey, I would have never had the opportunity to work closely with U.S. General John Shalikashvili, then Commander of Multinational Forces for Operation Provide Comfort, during the Kurdish refugee crisis in 1991 while on my assignment to the military base in southern Turkey as the UNHCR liaison officer. Field assignments provide prime opportunities to learn how multinational and multidimensional operations are set up and to acquire negotiation and middle-management skills. A subsequent headquarters assignment can then be very important in order to comprehend how the system works from a global point of view, i.e., how an international organization makes priorities among many pressing problems. It can also be useful for networking in the organization.

It is sometimes said that in the U.N. people with connections, and not necessarily competence, will always get what they want. I have seen enough to know this is not true. What is important in careers in international careers is the same as in any other career: a responsible attitude, a high degree of professionalism, a teamwork orientation, the willingness and ability to learn, and a belief in and commitment to the principles and future of international organizations.

U.S. citizens should also check the U.S. Department of State entry for the Bureau of International Organization Affairs in the chapter on the U.S. government.

Asian Development Bank

The Asian Development Bank (ADB), headquartered in Manila, Philippines, is an international financial organization created in 1966 to help in the planning and financing of high-priority projects in the developing countries of Asia and the South Pacific. Its stockholders are the governments of 56 countries of North America, Western Europe, and Asian Pacific region. The bank is not an organization within the United Nations system.

The ADB's young professionals program is designed to recruit people under the age of 30 who have superior academic credentials but lack substantive experience. Candidates must be citizens of a member country. They should have advanced training in economics, finance, management, administration, or other related fields and have either a master's degree, its equivalent, or a bachelor's degree combined with two years' work experience.

Proficiency in oral and written English is required. Preferred work experience would be in banking, project analysis, investment planning and analysis, budgets, accounting, and country or sectoral planning.

> Manager, Human Resources Division
> Asian Development Bank
> P.O. Box 789
> 1099 Manila
> PHILIPPINES

Caribbean Development Bank

The Caribbean Development Bank (CDB) serves to contribute to the harmonious economic growth and development of its member countries and promote economic cooperation and integration among them. Its mandate also includes paying "special and urgent regard to the needs of the less developed members of the region." CDB promotes the orderly expansion of international trade, provides technical assistance to members, and assists efforts to promote financial institutions and regional markets for capital, credit, and savings.

The bank has 20 regional members including Anguilla, Antigua and Barbuda, Bahamas, Barbados, Belize, British Virgin Islands, Cayman Islands, Colombia, Dominica, Grenada, Guyana, Jamaica, Mexico, Montserrat, St. Kitts and Nevis, St. Lucia, St. Vincent and the Grenadines, Trinidad and Tobago, Turks and Caicos Islands, and Venezuela. Five nonregional states also are members including Canada, France, Germany, Italy, and the United Kingdom.

The bank has approximately 78 professional staff positions. Approximately 5 to 10 openings occur annually. CDB seeks new recruits with a good bachelor's degree (first or second honors), a relevant higher degree, and usually a minimum of five years' experience. A limited number of young professional positions exist.

> Caribbean Development Bank   tel. 809/431-1600
> P.O. Box 408
> Wildey
> St. Michael
> BARBADOS

Consultative Group on International Agricultural Research

The World Bank, Food and Agricultural Organization, and United Nations Development Program co-sponsor the Consultative Group on International

Agricultural Research (CGIAR). The CGIAR stimulates research that enhances agricultural development in the tropics and subtropics. It provides and coordinates funding for a network of 13 research centers. The United States has traditionally contributed about one-fifth of the group's annual budget.

Each of the agricultural research centers acts independently within the group, recruiting its own staff. Centers primarily employ persons with a Ph.D. or equivalent advanced academic degree, several years of experience in the field, and fluency in at least two languages. Any person interested in employment should write directly to the institution or institutions that are of specific interest and relevance to them.

Centro Internacional de Agricultura Tropical
Apartado Aereo 6713
Cali, COLOMBIA
Focus: agricultural improvement in the lowland tropics of
Latin America.

Centro Internacional de Mejoramiento de Maiz y Trigo
P.O. Box 6641
Mexico 06600, D.F. MEXICO
Focus: improvement of maize, wheat, barley, and triticale crops.

Centro Internacional de la Papa
Apartado 5969
Lima, PERU
Focus: potato and sweet potato improvement.

International Board for Plant Genetic Resources
Food and Agricultural Organization
Via delle Terme di Caracalla
00 100 Rome, ITALY
Focus: onserving gene pools of current and potential crops and forages.

International Center for Agricultural Research in Dry Areas
P.O. Box 5466
Aleppo, SYRIA
Focus: improving farming systems for North Africa and West Asia.

International Crops Research Institute for the Semi-Arid Tropics
ICRISAT Patancheru
P.O. 502 324
Andhra Pradesh, INDIA
Focus: crop improvement and cropping systems.

International Food Policy Research Institute
1200 17th Street, N.W.
Washington, D.C. 20036
tel. 202/862-5600
Focus: strategies and plans to meet world food needs.

International Institute of Tropical Agriculture
PMB 5320
Ibadan, NIGERIA
Focus: crop improvement and land management in humid and
subhumid tropics.

International Laboratory for Research on Animal Diseases
P.O. Box 30709
Nairobi, KENYA
Focus: control of major livestock diseases in sub-Saharan Africa.

International Livestock Center for Africa
P.O. Box 5689
Addis Ababa, ETHIOPIA
Focus: livestock production and marketing constraints in
sub-Saharan Africa.

International Rice Research Institute
P.O. Box 933
Manila, PHILIPPINES
Focus: global rice improvement.

International Service for National Agricultural Research
P.O. Box 93375
2509 AJ
The Hague, NETHERLANDS
Focus: strengthening and developing national agricultural
research systems.

West Africa Rice Development Association
01 B.P. 2551
Bouake 01, COTE D'IVOIRE
Focus: rice improvement in West Africa.

European Bank for Reconstruction and Development

The European Bank for Reconstruction and Development (EBRD) was established in 1991 to foster the transition toward open-market-oriented economies and to promote private and entrepreneurial initiative in the central and

eastern European countries committed to and applying the principles of multiparty democracy, pluralism, and market economies. The bank's headquarters are in London and it currently has offices in 13 countries of operations. The EBRD seeks to help its countries of operations to implement structural and sectoral economic reforms, including demonopolization, decentralization, and privatization, taking into account the particular needs of countries at different stages of transition. Its activities include the promotion of private sector activity, the strengthening of financial institutions and legal systems, and the development of the infrastructure needed to support the private sector. The bank applies sound banking and investment principles in all of its operations. In fulfilling its role as a catalyst of change, the bank encourages cofinancing and foreign direct investment from the private and public sectors, helps to mobilize domestic capital and provides technical cooperation in relevant areas. It works in close cooperation with international financial institutions and other international organizations. In all of its activities, the bank promotes environmentally sound and sustainable development.

Personnel Department
European Bank for Reconstruction and Development
One Exchange Square
London EC2A 2EH
UNITED KINGDOM

European Free Trade Association

The European Free Trade Association (EFTA) is a group of small European countries working for the removal of import duties, quotas, and other obstacles to trade in Europe and the upholding of liberal, nondiscriminatory practices in world trade. The EFTA Council keeps a watch on developments that could restrict or distort trade flows and ensures the observance of EFTA's rules for fair competition in matters such as the use of subsidies and other forms of government to industry and the purchasing policies of public authorities. Within Europe, EFTA works to strengthen and develop its special relationship with the European Union. In world trade, EFTA works with larger organizations such as the Organization for Economic Cooperation and Development (OECD) and the World Trade Organization (WTO).

The EFTA Secretariat employs a staff of under 100 professionals. It offers preparation and servicing of all EFTA and EFTA-EU meetings. The staff provides appropriate research and analysis of all questions dealt with by the association. The working language of the secretariat is English.

European Free Trade Association   tel. (+41) (22) 749-1111
9–11, rue de Varembe
CH–1211 Geneva 20
SWITZERLAND

European Union

The European Union (EU), formerly known as the European Community, was created after World War II by six western European countries. Today the EU has 15 member states: Austria, Belgium, Denmark, Finland, France, Germany, Greece, Ireland, Italy, Luxembourg, the Netherlands, Portugal, Spain, Sweden, and the United Kingdom. The EU continues the integration of Europe that began in the 1950s with the creation of the European Coal and Steel Community (ECSC) in 1951, followed by the establishment of the European Economic Community (EEC) and the European Atomic Energy Community (Euratom) in 1957.

The European Commission is represented in the United States by a delegation in Washington, D.C. Its Office of Press and Public Affairs is responsible for providing information on the activities, policies, and publications of the European Union. It does not have information on specific job opportunities or prospective employers in Europe. General information on EU personnel rules and competitive exams are available from:

Office of Press and Public Affairs   tel. 202/862-9500
European Commission
2300 M Street, N.W.
Washington, D.C. 20037

Employment with the European Union is limited to the nationals of its member states on the basis of a competitive examination. Each institution organizes its own competitions. A general entrance examination for professional staff is given approximately once a year by the European Commission. Competitions for professionals with special qualifications may appear at any time. Competitions are advertised in newspapers and magazines published in member states. The full details and application forms are published in the official journal, C Section. An annual subscription to *Notifications of Open Competitions* can be placed with EU sales agents. The agent in the U.S. is:

UNIPUB   tel. 800/274-4888
4611–F Assembly Drive   fax 301/459-0056
Lanham, MD 20706–4888

EU member state nationals should contact the recruitment division at the individual institutions.

European Parliament   tel. (+352) 43001
Centre europeen   fax (+352) 4300-4842
Plateau de Kirchberg
L–2929 LUXEMBOURG

Council of the European Union Rue de la Loi 170 B–1048 Brussels BELGIUM	tel. (+32) (2) 285-6111 fax (+32) (2) 285-7397
European Commission Rue de la Loi 200 B–1049 Brussels BELGIUM	tel. (+32) (2) 299-1111 fax (+32) (2) 295-0138
Court of Justice Boulevard Konrad Adenauer Plateau de Kirchberg L–2925 LUXEMBOURG	tel. (+352) 43031 fax (+352) 4303-2600
Court of Auditors 12 rue de Alcide de Gasperi L–1615 LUXEMBOURG	tel. (+352) 43981 fax (+352) 439-342
Economic and Social Committee rue Ravenstein 2 B–1000 Brussels BELGIUM	tel. (+32) (2) 546-2155 fax (+32) (2) 546-2085
Committee of the Regions rue Ravenstein 2 B–1000 Brussels BELGIUM	tel. (+32) (2) 546-2155 fax (+32) (2) 546-2085
European Investment Bank 100 Boulevard Konrad Adenauer L–2950 LUXEMBOURG	tel. (+352) 4379-3142 fax (+352) 4377-04

Food and Agricultural Organization

The Food and Agricultural Organization (FAO) was established in 1945 to raise levels of nutrition and standards of living, to improve the efficiency of production and distribution of food and agricultural products and to better the conditions of rural populations. Accordingly, it collects and disseminates technical information relating nutritional needs and improved agricultural techniques; it promotes and recommends national and international action. In addition, it furnishes technical assistance upon request, and organizes and coordinates fulfillment of obligations incurred by members' acceptance of the U.N. Conference on Food and Agriculture recommendations.

Vacancies in the FAO staff generally are concentrated in technically specialized fields. All positions are international and the organization regularly hires between 500 and 1,000 professionals per year for projects of varying length. New hires usually have an advanced degree in one of the agricultural sciences (e.g., agricultural economics, rural planning and engineering, economic development, nutrition) and at least seven years' experience in their respective fields. Overseas living and work experience and foreign language proficiency are preferred.

FAO Liaison Office for
   North America
1001 22nd Street, N.W.
Washington, D.C. 20437

tel. 202/653-2398
http://www.fao.org

Inter-American Development Bank

The Inter-American Development Bank (IDB), established in 1959 to promote the economic and social development of Latin America and the Caribbean, is a major source of external public financing for member countries in Latin America. IDB also functions as a catalyst for mobilizing external private capital for development projects in the region by borrowing in international financial markets and promoting cofinancing arrangements with other financial institutions. The bank seeks to foster a more equitable distribution of development benefits by financing social and economic projects designed to improve living conditions among low-income groups in Latin America. The IDB headquarters are located in Washington, D.C., with field offices in each regional member country (except Canada) and offices in Paris and London.

Most applicants for professional positions at the IDB possess at least eight years' relevant work experience in addition to a graduate degree in such fields as economics, engineering, agriculture, administration, and environmental sciences. Most positions require fluency in at least two of the official languages of the bank, which are English, Spanish, French, and Portuguese.

The bank operates a summer internship program for students who are under 30 years old, enrolled in a graduate-level program, and fluent in two of the official languages.

Employment Section
Inter-American Development
   Bank
1300 New York Avenue, N.W.
Washington, D.C. 20577

tel. 202/623-1000

International Atomic Energy Agency

The International Atomic Energy Agency (IAEA) serves as the world's central intergovernmental forum for scientific and technical cooperation in the nuclear field, and as the international inspectorate for the application of nuclear safeguards and verification measures covering civilian nuclear programs. A specialized agency within the United Nations system, the IAEA came into being in 1957, a few years after U.S. President Dwight D. Eisenhower proposed the creation of an international atomic energy agency in his historic Atoms for Peace speech before the United Nations General Assembly. Today a wide range of IAEA products, services, and programs incorporate the cooperative efforts and interests of the agency's 123 member states.

The global role of the IAEA is basically twofold: One, to help interested countries put peaceful nuclear technologies to work for beneficial applications in fields such as electricity production, health care, agricultural development, and industry; and two, to monitor civil nuclear activities at the request of a state to verify that safeguarded nuclear materials are not diverted to military purposes. This dual role has many dimensions. The IAEA's technical cooperation program comprises nearly 1,400 projects in about 90 developing countries, at a value of about U.S. $50 million. In addition, some 150 IAEA-supported research programs are in some phase of operation around the world. Nearly 3,000 experts are sent each year to developing countries to run training courses, for example, and more than 1,000 scientific fellows and visiting scientists receive hands-on experience each year at national or regional institutes or at one of the IAEA's three research centers and laboratories.

At the end of 1994, the secretariat had a total staff of 2,248, of which 1,671 were in regular authorized posts. Of these, 861 were in the professional and higher categories, representing 87 nationalities. The other 1,387 staff members came under the general service category—clerical, secretarial, administrative, and other support staff—and were generally recruited locally. In addition to the 1,671 regular staff members, the secretariat also employed 577 other staff on temporary assignments or as cost-free experts and staff funded from extrabudgetary sources. For recruitment purposes, the IAEA's Division of Personnel sends vacancy notices to governmental bodies and organizations in member states, and perspective applicants are advised to maintain contact with them. The IAEA's regular distribution of vacancy notices includes ministries of foreign affairs or their national counterparts; national energy and/or atomic energy commissions; universities; permanent missions accredited to the IAEA; the Word Bank; and the following organs of the United Nations: the U.N. Secretariat; U.N. regional commissions; U.N. specialized agencies; offices of the United Nations Development Program (UNDP); and U.N. information centers. In general, posts at the IAEA are for a fixed term of three years. Fluency in English is an essential requirement and often knowledge of other official languages, such as French, Spanish, Russian, Chinese, and Arabic, is desirable.

Division of Personnel   http://www.iaea.or.at
International Atomic Energy Agency
P.O. Box 100
A–1400 Vienna
AUSTRIA

International Civil Aviation Organization

The International Civil Aviation Organization (ICAO), a United Nations special agency, channels, coordinates, and guides aeronautical services of 161 member states and sets standards and recommended practices for world aviation in the technical, economic, and legal fields. ICAO works to develop the principles and techniques of international air navigation; foster the planning and development of international air transport so as to ensure the safe and orderly growth of civil aviation throughout the world; encourage the development of airways, airports, and facilities for international civil aviation; meet the needs of peoples of the world for safe, regular, efficient, and economical air transport; ensure that the rights of contracting states are fully respected so that they have a fair opportunity to operate international airlines; and promote safety of flight in international air navigation. The secretariat, headed by a secretary general, is divided into five main divisions: the Air Navigation Bureau, the Air Transport Bureau, the Technical Cooperation Bureau, the Legal Bureau, and the Bureau of Administration and Services. ICAO works in close cooperation with other members of the United Nations family such as the World Meteorological Organization, the International Telecommunication Union, the Universal Postal Union, the World Health Organization, and the International Maritime Organization. Nongovernmental organizations that also participate in ICAO's work include the International Air Transport Association, the Airports Council International, the International Federation of Air Line Pilots' Associations, and the International Council of Aircraft Owner and Pilot Associations.

In order that the work of the secretariat reflects a truly international approach, professional staff at ICAO are recruited on a broad geographical basis. ICAO normally hires about 25 people per year with experience and education related to aviation in the mechanical, electrical, aeronautical, and chemical engineering fields. A minimum of 10 years' experience in a related technical discipline is required. Proficiency in one or more foreign languages is suggested but not required. Vacancies at the professional level are announced to the contracting states of the organization and are regularly advertised in the ICAO bulletin. The organization also recruits experts for the Technical Assistance Programme; vacancies are not published in the bulletin; U.S. citizens should apply through the U.S. Federal Aviation Administration (see U.S. government chapter).

Public Information Office
International Civil Aviation
   Organization
1000 Sherbrooke Street West
Montreal, Quebec H3A 2R2
CANADA

tel. 514/285-8219
fax 514/288-4772
e-mail: icaohq@icao.org
http://www.cam.org/~icao

International Fund for Agricultural Development

The International Fund for Agricultural Development (IFAD), a specialized agency of the United Nations, was launched in December 1977 as an international financial institution with the mandate of assisting exclusively the rural poor by mobilizing financial resources for agricultural development projects, primarily for the improvement of food production in developing countries. The fund operates through a governing council made up of the entire membership, currently composed of three categories of membership: developed donor countries, developing donor countries, and other developing countries. In line with the fund's special focus on the alleviation of rural poverty in developing countries, the bulk of its resources are made available to low-income countries (those with a GNP per capita of US$805 or less in 1992 prices or classified by the World Bank as International Development Association [IDA]-only countries) on highly concessional terms. The projects and programs financed by the fund are geared to enhancing food production systems and to strengthening related policies and institutions within each country's national policy framework as they relate to poor rural people. Specific objectives are food security through increased agricultural production, the improvement of nutritional levels and the incomes of the poorest rural populations, the landless, marginal farmers, pastoralists, fisherfolk, indigenous peoples, and, across all groups, poor rural women.

IFAD invites both female and male candidates; qualified women are strongly encouraged to apply. Applicants should note that IFAD staff members are international civil servants subject to the authority of the President of IFAD and may be assigned by him to any of the activities of IFAD. The ability to work on one's own initiative with high degree of professionalism and to work with multinational colleagues, officials, and representatives of international organizations is desired. Any application or questions about IFAD recruitment should be marked "Attention Personnel Division" and sent to the e-mail address below. All applicants should complete two copies of the IFAD or any United Nations agency application form or send two detailed curriculum vitae if the form is not available to the address below.

Personnel Division
107, Via del Serafico
International Fund for
  Agricultural Development
Rome 00142
ITALY

e-mail: IFAD@IFAD.ORG
http://www.unicc.org/ifad/
  home.html

International Labor Office

The International Labor Office (ILO), established in 1919 and now a specialized agency associated with the United Nations, works with government, worker, and employer representatives of the world toward peace through improved labor conditions and living standards.

Personnel Department (Room 4–71)
International Labor Office
4 route des Morillons
CH–1211 Geneva 22
SWITZERLAND

Recruitment Officer
International Labor Office
Washington Branch
1828 L Street, N.W.
Washington, D.C. 20036

tel. 202/653-7652
fax 202/653-7687

International Maritime Organization

The International Maritime Organization (IMO) is a specialized organization concerned with the safety of international shipping and the prevention of marine pollution from ships. It provides a mechanism for cooperation in establishing international standards for construction and equipment of ships, navigation, pollution prevention, and the facilitation of maritime trade. The IMO's 125 member states have adopted more than 27 conventions and protocols on maritime affairs.

Considerable experience and expertise in international trade and shipping is required for appointment to the IMO staff. Recruitment for the very limited vacancies, in the case of U.S. citizens, is carried out directly via the United Nations system and through the Department of State.

International Maritime Organization
4 Albert Embankment
London, SE1 7SR
UNITED KINGDOM

International Monetary Fund

The International Monetary Fund (IMF), created at the Bretton Woods Conference in 1944, promotes international monetary cooperation, facilitates the expansion and balanced growth of international trade, provides for exchange stability, establishes a multilateral system of payments, and gives confidence to members by making the fund's resources available only under adequate safeguards. Nearly all staff members are based in Washington, although the fund also maintains small offices in Paris and Geneva. A few staff members also are stationed for varying periods in member countries as resident representatives.

IMF has a professional staff of about 1,200, three-fourths of whom are economic staff. Direct appointments to the staff are only granted to candidates who are well advanced in a career related to international finance and economics. The remainder of the professional staff includes accountants, administrators, computer systems officers, language specialists, and lawyers.

Through its Economists Program, IMF also seeks to recruit highly qualified people under the age of 33 whose academic record, personal qualities, and in some cases work experience suggest they have the potential for successful careers at the fund. Almost all successful applicants have a Ph.D. in economics or finance and many have several years of experience as well. The number selected for participation in this two-year program normally is limited to 30 per year. Individuals appointed directly to the regular staff or on a fixed-term basis usually have significant prior experience in a government department or a financial or academic institution.

The fund maintains a small summer intern program for graduate students who have completed a minimum of one year of academic work in economics. Although permanent positions are not guaranteed to follow, the program is designed to attract potential candidates who will qualify for appointment to IMF staff upon completion of their graduate studies. Applications for this program should be submitted by the end of January.

Recruitment Division   tel. 202/477-7000
International Monetary Fund
700 19th Street, N.W.
Washington, D.C. 20431

International Organization for Migration

The International Organization for Migration (IOM) was established after World War II to move refugees and displaced persons from Europe to countries offering final resettlement and to assist in migration development. Over the years, the organization has become active in resettlement and refugee relief programs on a global scale. IOM has handled resettlement of refugees from Southeast Asia, Eastern Europe, and other areas on behalf of the United States and many other governments. Through its surveys and technical cooperation with governments, IOM seeks to identify the specific needs of both sending and receiving countries and to promote economic and social development and technology transfer through international migration.

IOM has a membership of 55 countries that contribute to its administrative and operational budgets. Observer status is held by 41 other governments. IOM also receives special funding from and works in coordination with other international partners to implement special programs for international migration. The regular contribution from the United States to IOM's total administrative budget is about 30 percent. Headquarters for the organization are in Geneva, Switzerland.

Competition for the various research, management, public relations, and operations executive positions on the permanent headquarters staff of about 150 is stiff. A postgraduate degree, fluency in English and French or Spanish, and considerable relevant experience usually are required. Also, an informal quota system based on national and regional distribution is applied to the recruitment process. The worldwide staff in 60 countries includes about 1,100 international officials and local employees. During emergencies, IOM also employs many temporary, special contract staff in the areas affected by refugee or migrant problems. Although much of this work involves routine clerical and administrative tasks, IOM stresses that it seeks only highly motivated applicants with some college or graduate education and, preferably, work experience in a related field.

IOM Washington Mission   tel. 202/862-1826
1750 K Street, N.W.   fax 202/862-1879
Suite 1110
Washington, D.C. 20006

International Telecommunication Union

The International Telecommunication Union (ITU) is the only telecommunication organization in which virtually all countries of the world are members. As of January 1995, the Union comprises 184 member states and 363 members, including scientific and industrial companies, public and private operators, broadcasters, and regional and international organizations. ITU is designed to maintain and extend cooperation between member states and other members in the use of telecommunications; offer technical assistance to developing countries in the field of telecommunications; promote, at the international level, the adoption of a broader approach to the issues of telecommunications in the global information economy and society; promote the extension of the benefits of the new telecommunication technologies to all the world's inhabitants; and harmonize the actions of members in the attainment of those ends. Headquartered in Geneva, ITU's permanent bureaus are the Radio Communication Bureau (BE), the Telecommunication Standardization Bureau (T.B.), and the Telecommunications Development Bureau (BDT).

Candidates for professional posts are required to have a university degree or its equivalent in one or more of the following fields: engineering, telecommunications, electronics, physical sciences, computer science, mathematics, statistics, languages, or business administration. In addition, 2 to 15 years of progressively responsible work experience in a field related to the post in question is requested. Sixteen posts in the professional category were advertised in the past year. Applications for vacant posts may be submitted through the telecommunication administration of the country of which the candidate is a national or directly to ITU. Vacancy notices are posted on the Union's World Wide Web site.

International Telecommunication Union
Place des Nations
CH–1211 Geneva 20
SWITZERLAND

tel. (+41) (22) 730-5111
e-mail: itumail@itu.ch
http://www.itu.ch

International Trade Centre UNCTAD/GATT

The International Trade Centre UNCTAD/GATT (ITC) is the focal point in the United Nations system for technical cooperation with developing countries in trade promotion. ITC was created by the General Agreement on Tariffs and Trade (GATT) in 1964 and since 1968 has been operated jointly by GATT and the U.N. (through the United Nations Conference on Trade and Development [UNCTAD]). ITC is directly responsible for implementing U.N. Development Programme-financed projects in developing countries and economies in transition related to trade promotion.

ITC works with developing countries and economies in transition to set up effective trade promotion programs for expanding their exports and improving their import relations in six key areas: product and market development, development of trade support services, trade information, human resources development, international purchasing and supply management, and needs assessment and program design for trade promotion. ITC's technical cooperation projects are carried out in all developing areas at the national, subregional, regional, and interregional levels and are undertaken at the request of the countries concerned.

Recruitment for regular professional positions at ITC is carried out by the personnel administration section at headquarters in Geneva. The academic background required for professional positions is generally a university degree in economics or business administration. In addition, relevant experience is required. For lower-level positions, two to four years are necessary. More than 15 years' experience are required for upper-level professional positions.

International Trade Centre   tel. (+41) (22) 730-0111
   UNCTAD/GATT (ITC)   fax (+41) (22) 733-4439
Palais des Nations
1211 Geneva 10
SWITZERLAND

North Atlantic Treaty Organization

The North Atlantic Treaty Organization (NATO) is a defensive alliance consisting of 16 sovereign nations in Europe and North America. Its objectives, as stated in the Washington Treaty of 1949, are to safeguard the freedom, common heritage, and civilization of their peoples, based on democracy, individual liberty, and rule of law; promote stability in the North Atlantic area; unite efforts for collective defense; and preserve peace and security. To this end NATO draws up collective defense plans, establishes required infrastructure and logistical support for those plans, and arranges joint training and military exercises. NATO also pursues closer cooperation in the political, social, economic, cultural, and scientific fields. Since 1992 and 1994 respectively, the North Atlantic Cooperation Council and the Partnership for Peace Program at NATO headquarters primarily seek to increase cooperation and consultation between NATO and the democratic states to our east.

NATO staff positions are open only to citizens of an alliance nation; positions for U.S. citizens are usually filled by the Department of State by seconding U.S. government personnel to the organization, or by direct hire with concurrence of the U.S. government. A useful publication is the NATO handbook available from the U.S. Liaison Office.

North Atlantic Treaty Organization   http://www.nato.int
1110 Brussels
BELGIUM

U.S. Liaison Office
U.S. NATO
PSC 81
Box 200
APO AE 09724

Organization for Economic Cooperation and Development

The Organization for Economic Cooperation and Development (OECD) is the successor to the Organization for European Economic Cooperation (OEEC) that was created in 1948 to implement the Marshall Plan. Formally, the OECD exists to promote economic growth, employment, and stability in member countries while maintaining financial stability; to contribute to sound economic development in member and nonmember countries; and to contribute to the expansion of world trade on a multilateral and nondiscriminatory basis. Since the establishment of the International Energy Agency in 1974, the OECD also has been heavily involved in international energy issues. The organization has served as a caucus of industrialized countries within the framework of the north-south dialog. The United States average contribution to the OECD budget is 25 percent before various credit adjustments.

For successful appointment to the OECD staff of some 700 professionals, a candidate must be a national of one of the 25 member countries of the OECD and demonstrate considerable accomplishment in a specialized discipline such as economics, finance, or energy. A graduate degree, several years of experience, and proficiency in both French and English (fluent knowledge of one and fair knowledge of the other) also is required. Application should be made directly to OECD headquarters in Paris.

Personnel Division
OECD
2 Rue Andre-Pascal
75775 Paris, Cedex 16
FRANCE

Organization for Security and Cooperation in Europe

The Organization for Security and Cooperation in Europe (OSCE) was created in the early 1970s under the name of the Conference on Security and Cooperation in Europe (CSCE) as a multilateral forum for dialog and negotiation between East and West. Until 1990, the CSCE functioned as a continuous conference with periodic formal meetings. Developments in the security situation in Europe since then have led to a fundamental change and to a strengthening of its role. The 1994 Budapest Summit changed the name of the conference to the OSCE.

Summits of heads of state or government of OSCE-participating states set priorities and provide orientation at the highest political level. The Ministerial Council is the central decision-making and governing body of the OSCE. Foreign ministers of participating states meet at least once a year. The Senior Council is responsible for the supervision, management, and coordination of OSCE activities, and the Permanent Council, based in Vienna, is responsible for the day-to-day operational work. The Permanent Council is the regular body for political consultation and decision-making. All activities are financed by contributions by the participating states. Not included in this funding arrangement are the salaries of the seconded personnel, which remain the responsibility of the seconding national administrations.

Jobs are extremely limited at the OSCE, but it is possible to be seconded from one's government. There are also occasional openings on special projects. Language ability is particularly valuable.

Organization for Security and Cooperation in Europe Secretariat Department for Chairman-in-Office Support Kärntner Ring 5–7 1010 Vienna AUSTRIA	tel. (+43) (1) 514-360 fax (+43) (1) 514-3699

Organization of American States

Established in 1890, the Organization of American States (OAS) is much older than the United Nations, although the purpose and structure of the two organizations are similar. Through its eight permanent committees and five specialized agencies, the OAS concerns itself with hemispheric problems ranging from regional security and the settlement of political disputes to economic, social, educational, scientific, and cultural relations among its 34 member states. Its economic development activities have recently changed from the monitoring and regulation of multinational corporation behavior toward the broader issues of promotion of democracy, telecommunications, human rights, drug abuse, trade, investment, and the transfer of technology. The OAS functions primarily as a forum for negotiation of inter-American collective agreements in these areas.

The OAS is headquartered in Washington, D.C., with national offices in each of the active member states. OAS employs about 600 people in professional positions with about 50 openings annually. Professional staff needs generally are concentrated in law, economics, finance, trade, business, education, science, culture, and similar fields. Fluency in at least two of the official languages of the OAS (Spanish, Portuguese, French, and English) is important.

The **Inter-American Institute for Cooperation on Agriculture (IICA)**, an autonomous agency within the OAS, works to encourage, promote, and support the efforts of member states to achieve agricultural development and rural welfare. IICA and several Central American nations have established the Tropical Agricultural Research and Training Center (CATIE), a nonprofit civil association for the promotion of scientific research and education.

IICA employs more than 325 people in national and international professional staff positions. It also contracts with large numbers of short-term consultants. Applicants for professional positions should have a degree in agricultural sciences, development, or other related disciplines. Candidates should also have at least five years of relevant work experience and be proficient in at least two of the IICA official languages (English, Spanish, French, and Portuguese).

Department of Human Resources   tel. 202/458-3285
General Secretariat of the
    Organization of American States
17th Street and
    Constitution Avenue, N.W.
Washington, D.C. 20006

IICA   tel. 202/789-3767
Suite 840
1889 F Street, N.W.
Washington, D.C. 20006

Instituto Interamericano de Cooparacion para la Agricultura
Direccion General
Apartado 55
2200 Coronado
San Jose
COSTA RICA

Pan American Health Organization

The Pan American Health Organization (PAHO), founded in 1902 as an independent, inter-American organization, works to promote and protect the health of the peoples of the Western hemisphere. In 1949, PAHO became the regional office for the World Health Organization (WHO) in the Americas. Together, PAHO and five other WHO regional offices plan and coordinate health activities on a global basis. Projects include implementation of health programs in member states, strengthening of health services, and training of health workers. WHO and PAHO also promote medical research and the exchange of scientific health-care information, cooperate in issuing health regulations on international travel, and coordinate numerous other health-related activities on the global level.

PAHO continually seeks physicians, nurses, sanitary engineers, and health administrators. Medical officers and technicians serve as advisors to governments, as professors in universities, or in teams combating specific public health problems. PAHO/WHO needs staff competent in epidemiological analysis; policy analysis and priority determination; program planning and management; resources mobilization; management information systems; health systems research; international communications; and public information.

Approximately 50 positions are open annually in the field of international public health. Requirements vary depending on the position sought but an advanced degree in public health is highly valued as is at least seven years of experience at the national level and at least two years of participation in technical cooperation programs and activities, preferably in the Americas. Knowledge of Spanish and English is required; Portuguese and French are highly desired.

Pan American Health Organization   tel. 202/861-3200
523 23rd Street, N.W.   http://www.paho.org
Washington, D.C. 20037

United Nations Conference on Trade and Development

The United Nations Conference on Trade and Development (UNCTAD) is a subsidiary organ of the United Nations General Assembly and forms part of the United Nations Secretariat. UNCTAD was created at the request of the developing countries for the establishment of a forum in which they would have a larger voice and which would consider international economic issues with particular attention to the impact on those countries and upon the development process.

Posts at the junior professional level are filled through examinations open only to nationals of member states inadequately represented on the staff of the United Nations Secretariat. Posts above the junior professional levels usually are advertised worldwide. Given equal qualifications, candidates from under-represented member states and women are given preference. There are about 250 professional posts at UNCTAD, most of which require advanced training and experience in economics and a few that require a legal background. Journeymen candidates usually have a Ph.D. or the equivalent and up to five years' relevant experience. Recruits typically are drawn from advanced university research programs or government positions in an appropriate field.

United Nations Conference on
   Trade and Development
Palais des Nations
CH–1211 Geneva 10
SWITZERLAND

http://gatekeeper.unicc.org/
unctad

United Nations Children's Fund

The United Nations Children's Fund (UNICEF) is the only United Nations agency devoted exclusively to the promotion of the needs of children and their families. The organization also plays an important role in the promotion of the basic rights of children embodied in the Convention on the Rights of the Child and in the achievement of the goals set at the 1990 World Summit for Children. UNICEF was created in 1946 as the United Nations International Children's Emergency Fund to help the children of war-devastated Europe. In the early 1950s its mandate was expanded by the General Assembly to address the problems of children in both the industrialized and developing world. UNICEF is a semiautonomous agency of the United Nations.

UNICEF has a diverse workforce of almost 7,500 staff from 153 different nationalities. About 49 percent of the UNICEF staff are located in sub-Saharan Africa; 23 percent in South Asia, East Asia, and the Pacific; 10 percent in Latin America and the Caribbean; and 9 percent in the Middle East and North Africa. The remaining serve in New York, Geneva, Copenhagen, Florence, or in recently created offices in Central and Eastern Europe and the Baltic States.

About 2,000 UNICEF staff are in the professional category, both international and national. Candidates interested in this category must have a first university degree and postgraduate degree in development-related disciplines such as public health, nutrition, primary education, economics, social welfare, sociology, accounting, civil engineering, public administration, or information systems. Candidates are also expected to have several years of professional work experience in a developing country and fluency in English and French, Spanish, or Arabic.

UNICEF
3 United Nations Plaza
New York, NY 10017

tel. 212/326-7000
http://www.unicef.org

United Nations Development Programme

The United Nations Development Programme (UNDP) is the world's largest multilateral source of grant funding for development cooperation. It was created in 1965 through a merger of two predecessor programs for United Nations technical cooperation. Funds come from the voluntary contributions of member states of the United Nations and its affiliated agencies, which provide approximately US$1 billion yearly to UNDP's central resources. UNDP has three overriding goals: to help the United Nations become a powerful and cohesive force for sustainable human development; to focus its own resources on a series of objectives central to sustainable human development (poverty elimination, environmental regeneration, job creation, and advancement of women); to strengthen international cooperation for sustainable human development and serve as a major substantive resource on how to achieve it. Through a network of 132 offices worldwide, UNDP works with 174 governments to build developing countries' capacities for sustainable human development. To execute the projects and programs it supports, it draws upon developing countries' national technical capacities, as well as the expertise of over 30 international and regional agencies and nongovernmental organizations.

People are at the center of all UNDP activities, which focus on six priority themes: poverty elimination and grassroots development, environment and natural resources, management development, technical cooperation among developing countries, transfer and adaptation of technology, and women in development. Entrepreneurship is promoted as a means of creating jobs and reducing poverty. Requests for assistance in areas of good governance and human rights are increasing. Global and interregional programs address worldwide problems, including food security and HIV/AIDS. A UNDP human development report, published yearly since 1990, assists the international community in developing new, practical, and pragmatic concepts, measures, and policy instruments for promoting more people-oriented development. UNDP normally also plays the chief coordinating role for operational development activities undertaken by the whole United Nations system. With the World Bank and the United Nations Environmental Program, UNDP is one of the managing partners of the Global Environment Facility (GEF), through which it is helping countries translate global concerns about ozone layer depletion, biodiversity loss, international water pollution, and global warming into local action plans. In emergency situations UNDP works closely with other U.N. agencies to ensure a relief-to-development continuum.

UNDP recruiting is conducted worldwide on a highly selective basis. A limited number of highly qualified candidates are accepted onto the staff every year. Application is made directly to UNDP and recruitment is done on a strictly competitive basis; no sponsorship is required. As international civil servants, staff members may be assigned to any of UNDP's field offices where they can expect to spend the greatest part of their careers; a four-year tour of duty in any one office is normal. UNDP's professional staff performs a wide variety of functions that normally revolve around the design, monitoring, and administration of projects. A strong postgraduate academic background with an emphasis on international development, several years of relevant experience in a developing country, fluency in at least two of the U.N.'s official languages, a strong commitment to the ideals of the United Nations, and other relevant interpersonal and work skills are essential. The UNDP Junior Professional Officer Program offers young professionals the opportunity to gain experience in international development assistance. Candidates must demonstrate the previously mentioned qualities and skills and be sponsored by their national governments. A select number of summer internships also exist for highly motivated students pursuing graduate degrees.

United Nations Development
   Program
One United Nations Plaza
New York, NY 10017

tel. 212/906-5000
fax 212/906-5001
http://www.undp.org

Consulting Services Unit
UNDP/Office for Project Services
220 East 42nd Street
New York, NY 10017

United Nations Educational, Scientific, and Cultural Organization

The United Nations Educational, Scientific, and Cultural Organization (UNESCO) promotes collaboration among member states in the fields of education, science, and culture. Its programs are organized into five major departments: education, science, social sciences/humanities, culture, and communication. In addition to its own activities in these fields, UNESCO frequently acts as an executor for UNDP and World Bank projects, often cooperating with UNICEF and other U.N. agencies.

Competition for permanent, professional positions on UNESCO's staff is very fierce and subject to considerations of geographical distribution. Because the United States is not a member of UNESCO, the chances of employment for U.S. citizens are very limited. Most candidates must have a Ph.D. and extensive professional experience in one of UNESCO's fields of expertise. Fluency in either English or French is mandatory; field posts may require additional languages. Employment opportunities also exist for short-term contract work with UNESCO. Citizens of member states should apply through the national commission for UNESCO in their country's capital.

UNESCO Office for Liaison
  with the United Nations
2 United Nations Plaza
Room DC2–0934
New York, NY 10017

tel. 212/963-5995
http://www.education.unesco.org

Bureau of Personnel
UNESCO
7 Place de Fontenoy
75700 Paris
FRANCE

United Nations Environment Program

The United Nations Environmental Program (UNEP) seeks to foster the enhancement of the total human habitat and further the study of environmental problems. In developing and carrying out programs geared to these objectives, UNEP relies to the maximum extent possible on the resources of other international, regional, and national organizations. UNEP monitors the environment and incorporates environmental impact considerations into the projects of other U.N. organizations.

Candidates for permanent employment with UNEP should have a graduate degree in environmental studies, populations studies, planning and management, resources, or other related fields and be fluent in two official U.N. languages. Priority is given to those with the highest academic achievements coupled with several years of practical experience at national or international levels. UNEP's activities do not include the direct implementation of projects; consequently, the staff is small and employment opportunities are limited.

United Nations Environment
  Program
Regional Office for North America
2 U.N. Plaza, Rm. DC2–8
New York, NY 10017

tel. 212/963-8138
http://www.unep.unep.no

United Nations Environment Program
P.O. Box 30552
Nairobi
KENYA

United Nations High Commissioner for Refugees

The United Nations High Commissioner for Refugees (UNHCR) is charged with providing international protection for all refugees (defined as persons who have left their native country because of "well founded fears of persecution for reasons of race, religion, nationality or membership in a political or social group") and facilitating their voluntary repatriation. Although the organization's responsibilities include the provision of interim care for displaced persons and the search for permanent solutions for refugee problems, it generally is occupied with the provision of legal services as regards, for example, difficulties with the granting of asylum or forced repatriation.

Much of the demand is for people with backgrounds in protection law, social sciences/community services, health, logistics, security, water and sanitation, finance, and administration. Applicants should preferably have a master's degree and at least three years' post–graduate experience with emphasis in humanitarian work. Preference will be given to women applicants and to applicants who are proficient at a minimum in English and one other United Nations language (French, Spanish, Russian, or Chinese).

A high degree of mobility is required in accordance with UNHCR's mandatory rotation policy. Initial recruitment often takes place during emergency operations, which require a willingness to take up assignments at short notice and for short duration in hardship and nonfamily duty stations located in remote areas where living conditions are often difficult.

Roster Unit
CD00
Recruitment & Career Management Section
UN High Commissioner for Refugees
CH–1211 Geneva 2 Depot
SWITZERLAND

United Nations Industrial Development Organization

The United Nations Industrial Development Organization (UNIDO) functions to promote industrial development in developing countries and to increase the developing countries' share of world industrial production. In support of these goals, UNIDO provides a liaison between public and private groups in the developing and industrialized countries, promotes the transfer of technology and industrial cooperation, trains personnel, assists in the financing of industrial projects in the developing world, and develops industrial projects in all fields of industry in developing countries.

UNIDO has approximately 500 professional staff members worldwide. Posts at UNIDO headquarters are subject to geographical distribution. Candidates for permanent positions with UNIDO must possess a graduate degree in engineering, preferably with a specialization in industrial subsectors like chemicals, metallurgics, or agriculture; business administration; economics; econometrics; or a similar discipline. Proficiency in English or French and several years of relevant work experience are also required. The applications of qualified candidates are entered in the UNIDO computerized roster of applicants. This database is UNIDO's main resource for the identification of suitable candidates for vacant posts. At present, permanent employment opportunities are limited.

The Chief   http://www.unido.org
Secretariat Recruitment Section
Room E05442
United Nations Industrial
   Development Organization
P.O. Box 300
A–1011 Vienna
AUSTRIA

United Nations Institute for Training and Research

The United Nations Institute for Training and Research (UNITAR) was established by the secretary-general pursuant to General Assembly resolution 1934 (XVIII) of 11 December 1963 as a United Nations Agency, an autonomous institution within the framework of the U.N. In April 1993, the General Assembly decided to move UNITAR's headquarters to Geneva, where most training programs are designed and conducted. A liaison office is kept in New York to coordinate training activities. UNITAR's mandate is to enhance the effectiveness of the United Nations in achieving the major objectives of the organization, in particular the maintenance of peace and security and the promotion of economic and social development.

UNITAR has, as its name implies, two main functions: training and research. Recently, however, the main focus has been shifted to training; basic research is only conducted if extrabudgetary funds are provided. The research activities currently undertaken concentrate on training. Training is, according to UNITAR's statute, provided at various levels to persons, particularly from developing countries, for assignments with the U.N. or its specialized agencies and for assignments in their national services connected to the work of the U.N., the organizations related to it, or other organizations operating in related fields. UNITAR's training programs comprise courses on multilateral diplomacy and international affairs management, economic and social development programs as well as fellowship programs in international law and peacemaking and preventative diplomacy.

UNITAR employs a professional Geneva-based staff of about 20. In addition, a number of senior fellows and consultants contribute to the completion of the institute's tasks. Many training activities also call upon senior staff of the U.N. Secretariat and specialized agencies.

United Nations Institute for Training and Research
Palais des Nations
CH–1221 Geneva 10
SWITZERLAND

United Nations Population Fund

The United Nations Population Fund, also known as the United Nations Fund for Population Activities (UNFPA), is the largest internationally funded source of assistance to population programs in developing countries. UNFPA promotes awareness of population problems and provides assistance to developing countries.

UNFPA has a professional staff of about 200, a majority of whom are stationed in New York. The largest number of positions outside headquarters are in Africa and Asia. Candidates for permanent employment with UNFPA must have a graduate degree in economics, demography, sociology, public health, or a related field. Additional requirements include several years of relevant experience, preferably in a developing country, and fluency in English and another of the U.N.'s working languages. Employment opportunities at present are extremely limited. Unpaid internships are often available to those pursuing a graduate degree in a related field.

Personnel   tel. 212/297-5023
United Nations Population Fund
220 East 42nd Street
New York, NY 10017

United Nations Relief and Works Agency

Established in 1949 to assist refugees from the 1948 Arab-Israeli conflict, the United Nations Relief and Works Agency (UNRWA) provides education, health, and welfare services to over three million registered Palestinian refugees living in Jordan, Lebanon, Syria, the West Bank, and the Gaza Strip. UNRWA has 644 elementary and preparatory schools, 8 vocational and teacher training centers, and 123 health centers. UNRWA relies on voluntary contributions, mainly from governments, for its funding. The largest contributor is the United States, providing more than a third of the funds, followed by the European Union and its member governments.

UNRWA employs more than 20,000 people, almost all Palestinian refugees. There are about 170 international positions in the areas of finance, administration, data processing, law, personnel, public relations, and supply. Since 1988, UNRWA has been running emergency operations in the occupied West Bank and Gaza Strip, as well as in Lebanon. These operations account for some of the international positions. Sixty-eight of the international positions are at UNRWA's Vienna, Austria, headquarters; the remainder are at a headquarters unit in Amman, Jordan, Gaza, or in five field offices.

UNRWA had 28 professional vacancies in the past year. Applicants are normally considered only if they have a minimum of three years' work experience in addition to the related educational qualifications.

Chief, Recruitment and Staff Development Division
UNRWA Headquarters
Vienna International Centre
P.O. Box 700
A–1400 Vienna
AUSTRIA

United Nations Volunteers

The United Nations Volunteers (UNV) program is the fourth largest multilateral volunteer program in the world. It is an associated program under the administration of the United Nations Development Programme. Since the inception of the program, men and women from both developed and developing countries alike have provided their professional and technical skills within United Nations projects around the world. At present, volunteers from more than 80 countries are involved in development work in over 100 countries.

Approximately 1,970 volunteers currently hold field positions with the UNV program, ranging from agronomists to dentists to engineers to medical specialists to humanitarian and emergency relief workers. Requirements for these positions include the knowledge of one foreign language (English mandatory), a master's degree, and at least three to five years' work experience. This emphasis on experience, coupled with the high degree of commitment and motivation inherent in volunteer service, produce an extremely efficient agency for development on an international level.

United Nations Volunteers
United Nations Development
   Programme
1775 K Street, N.W .
Suite 420
Washington, D.C. 20006

tel. 202/331-9130
http://suna.unv.ch

United Nations Secretariat

The United Nations Secretariat coordinates the activities of the United Nations. Candidates for employment with the U.N. Secretariat should be specialists in economics, administration, information, or political affairs. In filling professional vacancies, the secretariat is mandated by the General Assembly to achieve and maintain geographical balance within its staff. Junior professional posts are, as a rule, filled through competitive examinations, given in countries that, at the time, are unrepresented or under-represented in the secretariat. A candidate eligible to take the examination must be less than 32 years old, hold a first-level university degree, and be fluent in English or French, the two official U.N. languages. Middle- and upper-level candidates generally are required to hold a graduate degree and to have attained recognized standing in their fields.

The U.N. Secretariat staff numbers around 3,000 but is expected to shrink in the coming years. Employment opportunities are rather limited for the foreseeable future. The secretariat occasionally arranges internships for graduate students specializing in a field related to the work of the U.N. Request for information regarding this and other employment opportunities should be directed either to the Department of State Office of U.N. System Recruitment (for U.S. citizens) or directly to the address below.

Recruitment and Placement
  Division
Office of Human Resources
  Management
United Nations Secretariat
New York, NY 10017

http://www.un.org

United Nations University

The United Nations University is not a university in the traditional sense. Designed to offer a multidisciplinary approach to specific issues, it has no students in the usual sense, no faculty, and no central campus. The university's work is carried out through research and postgraduate training networks in both the developed and developing countries. Current research, training, and dissemination activities are focused on five program areas: peace, development, and democracy; the global economy; global life-support systems; alternative rural-urban configurations; and science, technology, and global learning. In addition to teaching credentials, applicants for a teaching position should have considerable experience in relevant fields and disciplines, especially within the developing world. Knowledge of relevant languages and fluency in Japanese also are important.

United Nations University
Liaison Office for North America
2 UN Plaza
New York, NY 10017

United Nations University   tel. (+81) (03) 499-2811
Toho Seimei Building
15–1, Shibuya-ku
Tokyo 150
JAPAN

Universal Postal Union

The Universal Postal Union (UPU), a specialized agency of the United Nations tracing its origins back to the Berne Treaty of 1875, promotes freedom of transit, the diffusion of technical cooperation between the administrations of UPU member countries, and the improvement of the organization and efficiency of the international postal system. Over 180 countries currently abide by the union's acts.

The union is organized into a congress, an executive council, a consultative council for postal studies, and an international bureau. The congress, composed of representatives of all member countries, is the supreme authority of the union. The executive council is composed of 40 members elected by congress with regard to equitable geographic distribution. This council ensures the continuity of the union's work and is responsible for promoting, supervising, and coordinating all aspects of postal technical assistance. The Consultative Council for Postal Studies (CCPS) is composed of 35 members and is responsible for carrying out studies of major problems affecting postal administrations in all UPU member countries. The central office of the union, headquartered in Berne, is responsible for the coordination, publication, and dissemination of information regarding UPU and the international postal service. It also handles administrative matters of the union and acts as a clearinghouse for settlement of debts between postal administrations relating to transit charges, terminal dues, and international reply coupons.

UPU has about 140 professional positions. Because of the technical nature of the work done by professional category staff of the international bureau, only career officials from postal administrations having a number of years of experience are recruited to that category. Applications must be submitted by the postal administration of a candidate's country of origin.

Universal Postal Union
Weltpoststrasse 4
CH–3000 Berne 15
SWITZERLAND

World Bank Group

The World Bank Group works to help developing countries reduce poverty and promote sustainable development. Unlike many international aid programs, however, the bank does not make grants but rather lends money to developing countries which must repay the loans. The World Bank Group comprises five organizations. The **International Bank for Reconstruction and Development**, commonly referred to as simply the World Bank, is the oldest and largest international organization devoted to promoting development through direct loans, technical assistance, and policy advice. The bank lends to developing countries with relatively high per capita incomes. The money IBRD lends is used to pay for development projects, such as building highways, schools, and hospitals and for programs to help governments change the ways they manage their economies.

The **International Development Agency (IDA)**, known as the "concessional loan window" of the bank, shares staff with the World Bank but differs in terms of the financing it provides. IDA provides assistance on concessional terms to the poorest developing countries that cannot afford to borrow from IBRD.

The **International Finance Corporation** (IFC) encourages private growth enterprises in developing countries through its financial services and the provision of its expertise in legal and technical aspects of private business. IFC lends directly to the private sector; it does not seek or accept government guarantees. IFC, one of the few international development organizations that makes equity investments as well as providing loans, aids the private sector by providing long-term loans, equity investments, guarantees and "stand-by" financing, risk management, and "quasi-equity instruments" like subordinated loans, preferred stock, and income notes.

The **Multilateral Investment Guarantee Agency (MIGA)**, the newest member of the World Bank Group, promotes foreign investment for economic development by providing investors with guarantees against noncommercial risk like expropriation and war. MIGA also provides advisory and consultative services to member countries to assist in creating a responsive investment climate and an information base to guide and encourage the flow of capital.

The **International Centre for Settlement of Disputes (ICSID)** promotes increased flows of international investment by providing facilities for the conciliation and arbitration of disputes between governments and foreign investors. ICSID also provides advice, carries out research, and produces publications in the area of foreign investment law.

In addition to technical expertise, the World Bank seeks candidates with the breadth of education and experience to take a comprehensive view of the development issues with which it is concerned. The majority of successful candidates for employment with the bank have many years of experience in the field and normally join the bank between the ages of 35 and 50.

Through its Young Professionals Program (YPP), however, the bank does seek younger candidates who show potential for building a successful career in international development. Current and former young professionals comprise about 18 percent of all professional staff in the World Bank Group. To be eligible for consideration, YPP applicants must not have reached their 32nd birthdays as of July 1 of the selection year; have a master's degree (or equivalent) in economics, finance, or a related field; and have either a minimum of two years' relevant work experience or continued academic study at the Ph.D. level. Fluency in English is required, and speaking proficiency in one or more of the bank's other working languages (i.e., Arabic, Chinese, French, Portuguese, and Spanish) is beneficial. Work experience in a developing country also is desirable. Competition for the program is strong. Each year the program receives thousands of applications for 20 to 30 positions. Interested and qualified persons should submit a self-addressed envelope requesting application forms for the program by early fall.

In addition to regular staff positions, there are a small number of temporary research and summer positions available at the World Bank.

Recruitment Division   tel. 202/477-1234
Personnel Department   http://www.worldbank.org
World Bank
1818 H Street, N.W.
Washington, D.C. 20433

World Food Council

The World Food Council (WFC), a policy organ of the United Nations, deals with world food problems. Established in 1974, WFC is made up of 36 member states elected for a three-year period from the U.N. General Assembly. Together with the Food and Agriculture Organization (FAO) and the World Food Programme (WFP), WFC monitors progress in dealing with food and hunger problems, suggests remedial action, mobilizes support, and coordinates assistance efforts. Headquartered in Rome, the WFC employs a small staff consisting of approximately 12 experts in economics and the social sciences. An advanced university degree and several years of professional experience are minimum requirements for most posts. Employment opportunities are extremely limited.

World Food Council   tel. (+39) (6) 57971
Viale delle Terme di Caracalla
00100 Rome
ITALY

World Intellectual Property Organization

The World Intellectual Property Organization (WIPO), one of the 16 specialized agencies of the United Nations system, promotes the protection of intellectual property in the world through cooperation among states. Intellectual property comprises industrial property (inventions, trademarks, and industrial designs) and copyright and neighboring rights. WIPO staff conduct studies; publish reports, books, and newsletters; and provide services to member states, especially to developing countries.

The organization employs a permanent staff of over 500 from over 55 countries. Vacancies for professional posts are generally advertised through the appropriate administrations of WIPO member states and in WIPO periodicals. Most professional posts require staff with a legal background and considerable experience in the field of intellectual property. For most posts, staff must have at least a very good knowledge of English and French.

World Intellectual Property
  Organization
34 chemin des Colombettes
CH–1211 Geneva 20
SWITZERLAND

tel. (+41) (22) 730-9111
fax (+41) (22) 733-5428

World Meteorological Organization

The World Meteorological Organization (WMO) is a specialized agency of the United Nations with a membership of 181 states and territories. WMO was created to facilitate worldwide cooperation in the establishment of networks in the making of meteorological, climatological, hydrological, and related geophysical observations, as well as their exchange, processing, and standardization. WMO also promotes training, research, and technology transfer. The organization fosters collaboration between meteorological and hydrological services and furthers the application of meteorology to aviation, shipping, water resources management, agriculture, other human activities, and sustainable development.

The total number of professional positions in WMO is 141. The organization advertises professional post vacancies infrequently. Professional staff are expected to have a university degree, often a Ph.D, and 5 to 10 years' related experience. The best opportunities for Americans have been and will continue to be for those with considerable experience in the fields of meteorology, hydrology, physical sciences, environmental chemistry, electrical engineering, business administration, or similar disciplines depending on the specifications for the position advertised. Employment opportunities are distributed to the permanent representatives of members of WMO. Thus, they are always available in the national meteorological services of member countries. In the United States, information is available from the U.S. National Weather Services of the National Oceanic and Atmospheric Administration (NOAA) in Silver Spring, Maryland (see the chapter on U.S. government). It is also available from the American Meteorological Society, 45 Beacon Street, Boston, Massachusetts 02108. The WMO only accepts applications for specific vacancies.

World Meteorological Organization   http://www.wmo.org
41, Avenue Giuseppe Motta
Case Postale No. 2300
CH–1211 Geneva 2
SWITZERLAND

World Trade Organization

The World Trade Organization (WTO), the successor organization to the General Agreement on Tariffs and Trade (GATT), seeks to liberalize and expand world trade. Over 130 member countries now belong to WTO; together, they account for almost 90 percent of world trade.

The World Trade Organization has a small professional staff of about 170 in Geneva. Five to 10 new officials generally are hired annually. Recruitment standards are very high. Potential candidates need strong academic backgrounds, work experience in economics and international trade policy, and proficiency in French.

Director, Personnel Division   fax (+41) (22) 739-5772
World Trade Organization   http://www.unicc.org/wto
Centre William Rappard
154 rue de Lausanne
CH–1211 Geneva 21
SWITZERLAND

4

Banking

Martin Rust *

My interest in banking flowered while an exchange student in Florence in 1980. I discovered the power of foreign exchange by seeing the dollar soar from 750 to 1,200 lira in eight short months, triggered largely by the 1980 election of Ronald Reagan. Our program funds where "unhedged," i.e., funded with a set amount of dollars at the outset, so we benefited greatly when the dollar sharply strengthened by spring. When asked by our director how we wished to use the windfall, chants of "party, party, party" grew into a crescendo, resulting in a trip ending only when the money ran out. After rounding Sicily, we made it all the way to Athens. All of this due to simple currency movements.

This episode taught me the powerful link between politics and economics; a political event, like a presidential election, could have a direct, profound, and very real economic impact. Having always been interested in politics, history, and economics, I thought banking might be the career that tied them all together. I was right.

This chapter focuses on jobs in commercial banks, specifically in the large or multinational corporate arena. Because commercial banking is a complex field rattled by dramatic change, it is helpful to review some recent history to better comprehend what a bank is today, where the good jobs might be, and why.

---

* Martin Rust, a 1986 graduate of Georgetown University's Master of Science in Foreign Service program, is Senior Vice President, Corporate Banking, for First Union Corporation, covering large corporations in Richmond. Previously, he worked for six years at Fuji Bank and before that for two years at Chemical Bank, both in New York City, in the same capacity. He also serves as an adjunct professor at The College of William and Mary, where he teaches a course entitled Multinational Corporate Banking in the Graduate Business School.

Commercial banks and investment banks have traditionally been separated by the 1933 Banking Act known also as Glass-Steagall. This formal and legal division was designed to prevent a recurrence of what many felt were bank abuses at the public's expense leading up to the 1929 Stock Market Crash. Namely, that Wall Street banks used "widows and orphans" deposit money to irresponsibly speculate in the booming stock market of the 1920s. By protecting the general public's money (customer bank deposits) from sophisticated investor funds with Glass-Steagall, legislators sought to ensure that Wall Street could never again harm the public (voters) with its arcane and risky practices. Federal Deposit Insurance Commission insurance was created for commercial banks as an added safeguard to boost public confidence that hard-earned savings would be protected.

Commercial banks, then, are in the core business of lending, or using their balance sheets, to produce profits. Investment banks, however, sell mainly services, such as merger and acquisition (M&A) advice, equity and debt underwriting, and selling and trading of securities. Until recently, their respective cultures were as different as their core businesses. Commercial bankers tended to draw good but not rich salaries, work long but not endless hours, and view their jobs as highly secure as they worked their way up the corporate ladder. Investment bankers, however, tended to have good salaries with higher potential for rich bonuses based on production, work very long hours in an intense environment, and recognize their jobs and pay were vulnerable to cycles and individual performance. Much of this has changed in recent years, with many commercial banks now resembling investment banks.

Turbulence of the Banking Industry—Under Attack

Upon graduation from college, my notion of a banker was a bit of a blend between grand financier and diplomat; well compensated, intellectually challenging, professional career path requiring high verbal and math skills. That was essentially correct. What I had not counted on was the turbulence that hit the industry, touched by the economy's ebb and flow (business cycle), compounded by added risk from interest rate volatility. I hit one of the troughs in May 1982 while looking for a bank job right out of college. There was deep economic "stagflation," and Mexico had just announced suspension of debt payments, kicking off what later was called the "Latin Debt Crisis."

The 1980s were a bad time for U.S. banks as they wrestled with the several threats to the traditional business of banking. Large banks struggled with nonperforming Latin debt, which led to large loan losses. The core of bank lending, corporate loans, was being eroded by borrower preference for the cheaper and deeper public markets, exploding with growth in credit media like Commercial Paper (CP), Medium-Term Notes (MTNs), and bonds. While on the deposit side, consumers were showing a strong preference for mutual funds over low yielding bank savings vehicles. A commercial bank by definition is in the business of taking deposits and making loans, producing net interest income. Because large loans and customer deposits were being lost to new competitors at an alarming rate and existing Latin and real estate loans were souring, this was a lousy period for banks and for bank jobs.

Partial hope arrived by the mid-1980s with the Wall Street boom, strong economic growth, and high consumer confidence, but they masked the structural flaws still embedded in the industry. In addition to bad Latin debt and competition from nonbanks, there was simply an oversupply of banks, about 15,000. (For perspective, Japan and Germany have one-fifteenth that amount in economies whose Gross Domestic Product (GDP) is more than one-half of the U.S.) Also casting a pall was the fact banks were culturally ill-prepared for competition and deregulation due to relatively bureaucratic and plodding procedures, the heritage of FDIC subsidies, heavy regulation, and a self-perceived specialness. Moreover, as real estate loans began to sour due to the excesses of the economic boom, bank regulators sharply tightened their grip, shaking an already unsteady banking industry. Credit ratings at most of the big U.S. banks fell ominously, raising costs and further exposing them to competition. Finally, the threat of competition from foreign lenders, especially huge, aggressive, and well-capitalized Japanese banks in search of market share, loomed dark on the horizon.

With the October stock market crash and final round of Latin debt loss reserves in late 1987, the outlook for big U.S. banks was bleak. There were frequent rumors of some of the nation's largest banks going bust.

Recovery and Turnaround

Yet, in the late 1980s, helped by an easing of credit by the Fed, a surprisingly resilient U.S. economy, creative bank balance sheet management, sharp cost controls, and past investment in technology beginning to pay off, U.S. banks were poised for a healthy recovery. In contrast, the Japanese banks were wounded by falling real estate and stock prices at home, forcing capital to retreat to Japan were it was needed. Credit ratings for those banks, tarnished by growing bad assets, thinning capital, and questionable management practices, plunged just as U.S. bank ratings were recovering. European and Canadian banks, never as extended nor aggressive as the Japanese, retreated slightly but staked out profitable market niches here.

Finally, the very forces that caused so much pain for the banking industry—overpopulation, high costs, deregulation, and intense competition—were now forcing a tonic for its ills: consolidation. Weaker banks are being bought out by stronger ones with stock, due to an accounting convention that penalizes cash purchases. That means stock prices are the key determinant of who survives and who is bought. Since a bank's stock prices are so important, and earnings are its key driver, there is a new and almost ruthless focus on bank profitability by management. It holds the key not only to shareholder returns, but management's very existence. There are only two ways to boost profitability: cut costs or increase revenue. Both have had a real impact on banking jobs.

General Employment Trends

Cutting costs has meant fewer, but generally better, jobs. Banks now number roughly 10,000. It is estimated by the time the industry is fully consolidated, the U.S. will have but 10–15 very large banks that will serve large-scale wholesale and retail banking needs, while hundreds of local, much smaller banks will be left to serve outlying fragments. So expense control means a "rationalization," or trimming of jobs. But it also means controlling cost, which can be better achieved by tying costs to results or linking compensation to performance. By reducing fixed costs (salaries) and increasing variable costs (bonuses based on results), commercial banking is more resembling investment banking, with attendant cultural changes, including longer hours, rich pay for top performers, and a greater move toward more risk/more return.

Boosting revenue has meant giving customers what they want, and few corporate customers still need loans. What they do need are sophisticated products and services delivered in a crisply professional and highly responsible way. To that end, most big banks have developed what are known generically as capital market groups, and have reengineered the bank to make bankers think of themselves more as sales professionals, more responsive to the market and the customer, and less as bankers.

So Where Are the Jobs and What Are the Employers Looking For?

Banks are still hiring, and they still offer some of the best jobs around. Before interviewing, recognize today's big bank is a restless, dynamic, and profit-driven business shaped by the outlined factors. It bears little resemblance to the banks of old. Unlike the past, where banks had a niche for international bankers, today's overseas positions are filled mainly by local nationals. Experience has suggested hiring locally is preferred since it is lower-cost and lower-risk, has less transition involved, and is politically smart. Therefore, the bank jobs available today are mainly in the U.S. and with the top banks, most of which are headquartered in New York (with the notable exceptions of NationsBank and First Union in Charlotte, North Carolina, and Bank of America in San Francisco, California).

Both commercial and investment banks are looking for smart, articulate professionals who are analytically or sales driven and committed to a career in finance. The first questions to ask yourself are: Which do I prefer, analysis or sales, and would I like to work in finance?

Because banks typically provide their own training, it is not critical to have an M.B.A., but you must show strong evidence of business or finance focus. That means courses in economics, accounting, finance, investments, or banking are a big plus. Because each bank is so different, and has been through so much wrenching change this past decade, make sure you study the culture of the bank. You can get good insights from annual reports and news articles, but there is no substitute for talking with a person who works there. Questions to ask include: Is the bank aggressive or cautious? Is it financially strong, well positioned, and focused? What areas does it specialize in? What is management like? How is employee compensation determined? Where is it located? What do its competitors think of it? And most important, do I think it is a good fit for me?

Banks have account officers, who work with credit underwriters to deliver credit products (loans, lines of credit) to customers. Many banks now call those officers relationship managers or RMs, a recognition one person must have overall responsibility for the client (no longer customer) relationship with the bank, which may encompass many products from areas throughout the bank. The RM is the fulcrum upon which balances the relationship, the link to the bank, and responsible for winning, maintaining, and growing the account. The RM is credit-trained, meaning he or she has formal bank credit training and has spent time as an analyst prior to being put in a line role with client responsibility. Skills required for this generalist, high-profile job include credit (provided by the bank), general finance, sales, and diplomacy. This is a non-entry-level position.

A variety of capital markets specialists work with RMs to market and deliver products and services. This is where the bulk of new hiring is occurring. Those positions, like the RM, require prior experience, typically some type of apprenticeship. Below is a brief overview of such jobs, varying from bank to bank. All these activities occur here or abroad, in dollar or foreign currency, but the bulk occur in U.S. dollar, domestic.

- *Syndications*—Selling bank credit exposures to other banks. Syndication allows banks to step up to larger deals, since they will sell off much of the risk and generate underwriting fees to boost the return on their position. Traditionally, large buyers of syndicated deals are foreign banks, especially Japanese. It is a hot growth area for banks. Credit and especially sales skills are required.

- *Private Placements*—Placing generally long-term (greater than seven years) fixed rate loans with private (insurance company) investors. This too is a hot area, since it generates solely fee income for the bank, involves no credit exposure, just underwriting risk, and raises needed money for the client at good rates from a diverse (nonbank) source. Credit and especially sales skills are required.

- *Derivatives/Foreign Exchange (FX)*—This group generates fee income by selling products to hedge both interest rate and FX risks resulting from client operational and balance sheet exposures. It too is a hot growth area and, if one is successful, pays quite well. Skills required would be more esoteric and intellectually demanding, but certainly nothing beyond the learning bounds of the average MSFS student. Understanding financial markets and what drives interest and foreign exchange rates would be key skills associated with this job. This job requires heavy sales and financial skills. The FX area might be one of the more intellectually appealing areas for students of international affairs.

- *Asset Backed Finance (ABF)*—This area generates fee income by "securitizing" or "monetizing" assets with sufficient economic scale and statistically reliable cash flows. They package these assets as a group and resell them to third-party investors, typically commercial paper holders, at a discount and on a recurring basis and forward the proceeds, less fees, to the client. This job requires strong sales and credit skills, as well as strong technical expertise (which again, can be learned).

• *Leasing*—This area generates fee income for the bank by arranging and often investing bank money in equity or debt in leases for clients. Any asset that can be leased, such as planes, rolling stock of any kind, computers, plant and equipment, would be a candidate for this group. This requires similar skills to those for ABF.

• *Project Finance*—Similar to ABF and leasing, this is typically nonrecourse (to the client) finance secured by the project's assets and contracts and relies specifically on project cash flow for repayment. Lately this area has been very hot internationally, as developing countries privatize assets such as utilities, and players utilize project finance to fund their investments. This would require strong technical, credit, and sales skills.

Foreign (Non-U.S.) Banks

The same positions generally can be found at most of the big non-U.S. banks too. These banks, all big, all relatively strong, tend to hire in cycles that reflect underlying domestic economies and changing management focus. The U.S. market, because of its depth, breadth, and relative market freedom, remains an attractive and rich place to operate. As with all job searches, the burden is on the seeker to ferret out information on each bank, but it's safe to assume that foreign banks are permanent fixtures on the corporate banking landscape, with fluctuating degrees of importance.

Key questions to ask yourself when interviewing with a non-U.S. bank include: How do you think you would fare in a foreign-culture bank? Is it sufficiently committed to your market? Do you have long-term career aspirations there, and if so, will the fact that you are not from the home country affect you meaningfully? Here, as with U.S. banks, understanding the culture, drive, and history of the bank is vital.

Investment Banks

Jobs with investment banks are the toughest to win, and to have, period. This is due mainly to the cyclical and risk-oriented nature of the business, resulting in a culture that richly rewards top performers while weeding out nonperformers. This can mean long hours, sometimes grueling travel, and constant pressure for the investment banker. These jobs can be highly rewarding, however, both financially and intellectually. Major investment banks are almost all located in New York City (Wall Street). In general, the major job types fall under trader or investment banker, whose deals can sometimes take months, or even years, to complete. The analyst supports the banker or trader, or follows stocks and/or bonds underwritten by the bank.

Again, you should determine if investment banking is right for you, and if so, which bank and in which function. As the old saying goes, commercial bankers depend on other people's money, while investment bankers depend on their wits. As mentioned earlier, trends today are blurring the lines that distinguish commercial from investment banking. In fact, a handful of commercial banks like J.P. Morgan are enjoying good success in investment banking. This trend should be expected to continue as commercial banks use their greater size, growing experience, and a crumbling Glass-Steagall to their advantage.

In short, then, banks still have good jobs and plenty of them. But you should think long and hard about which bank and which area is right for you. Generally, that which you find most enjoyable is that in which you will excel. More good news is that once inside a bank, there are several career paths available if time and circumstances change your interests. Be aggressive, flexible, and creative in your job search. Good banks and good jobs are always at a premium. Don't assume like the bankers of old that customers will come to you. You must go to them.

American Bankers Association

The American Bankers Association (ABA) acts as a consensus-building and lobbying organization for influencing government policy affecting the banking sector. It represents 90 percent of the U.S. banking industry's assets. Every year the association sponsors an annual convention and numerous schools, conferences, and workshops. Through its American Institute of Banking, it conducts more than 1,000 courses and other educational activities each year. ABA publishes several periodicals concerning compliance with government regulation, current banking practices, and public information. ABA is the secretariat for the annual International Monetary Conference.

The association has a staff of more than 350 professionals of whom 4 work in its international division. Its annual budget is about $50 million.

American Bankers Association   tel. 202/663-5000
1120 Connecticut Avenue, N.W.
Washington, D.C. 20036

Bank of Montreal

The Bank of Montreal is a leading North American financial institution that operates in the North American (United States, Canada, Mexico) and international markets. The bank has had an international presence since the establishment of offices in New York and London in 1818. Today, the bank is a major player in the world's increasingly unified financial markets.

Individuals interested in professional employment at Bank of Montreal take part in one or two of the bank's structured training programs. The Associate Development Program (ADP) leads to careers as relationship managers in the Corporate and Institutional Financial Services (CIFS) pillar of Bank of Montreal, servicing the bank's large corporate portfolio. The Treasury Development Program (TDP) leads to careers in the Treasury's sales and trading unit in CIFS. These programs are designed to produce high-potential, qualified employees capable of contributing to the bank's overall profitability. Formal classroom training, provided at Bank of Montreal's Institute for Learning, combined with on-the-job training and specific product rotations, enables the ADP or TDP participant to develop core banking skills required for the specific portfolio to which they are assigned.

Candidates for the ADP program should have two to four years of related (financially oriented) work experience and a master's degree in business or equivalent professional designation. Well-developed skills in judgment, negotiation, financial analysis, financial modeling, professional selling, and interpersonal skills are mandatory.

Director, ADP Program   tel. 212/605-1429
Bank of Montreal
430 Park Avenue
New York, NY 10022

Director, TDP Program   tel. 416/867-2780
Bank of Montreal
One First Canadian Place, 19th Floor
100 King Street West
Toronto, Ontario M5X 1A12
CANADA

Bank of New York

The Bank of New York, founded in 1784 by Alexander Hamilton and the nation's oldest bank operating under its original name, is the 16th-largest bank holding company in the U.S. The bank provides a complete range of banking and other financial services to corporations and individuals worldwide through its core businesses: securities and other processing, credit cards, corporate banking, retail banking, trust, investment management and private banking, and financial market services. The Bank of New York is an important lender to major U.S. and multinational corporations and is the leading retail bank in suburban New York. The bank is also the largest provider of securities-processing services to the market and a respected trust and investment manager.

The Bank of New York hires master's degree graduates with a concentration in finance, strong writing skills, and one to three years' previous financial analysis experience for corporate banking associate positions and as corporate credit analysts. As associates, new hires work closely in support of the more experienced corporate finance professionals. In addition to financial modeling and credit analysis, associates participate in all aspects of business development and relationship management. They work closely with and gain knowledge of key product groups throughout the bank, including loan syndications, capital markets, securities processing, and cash management. Analysts work with relationship managers, senior credit analysts, and loan syndicators to analyze and structure credit transactions.

The Bank of New York	tel. 212/635-7717
13th Floor	
One Wall Street	
New York, NY 10286	

Banque Indosuez

Banque Indosuez is the wholly owned subsidiary of Compagnie de Suez, one of Europe's largest financial holding groups. The bank was responsible for the construction of the Suez Canal during the last century and accordingly takes its name from the canal. The bank is international in its scope. Its head office is in Paris, and it has branches and affiliates in 65 countries around the world, including all the major financial centers.

During the past decade, the bank has developed its investment banking business, in addition to wholesale commercial lending services available to corporations, financial institutions, governments, and high net-worth individuals. To meet this challenge an international recruitment strategy has been put in place that targets talented graduates with master's and M.B.A. degrees who can have initial placement in Paris, as well as locally. Such recruitment is managed directly or indirectly by the head office.

The business of the bank is managed by eight divisions of the bank: commercial (domestic and international), financial markets (including important activities in the most recent products), stockbroking, equity underwriting, asset management, private banking, asset finance, and mergers and acquisitions. Limited opportunities are available in most of these areas, as well as in back office and more specialized functions.

Recruitment criteria include intellectual capacity, but just as important are interpersonal skills, adaptability to different cultures and working practices, as well as common sense and a sense of humor. Recruits are expected to have an international outlook and mobility. A working knowledge of French is not essential but is useful. The bank's training institution is based in England and provides a level of education that is professional and career oriented.

Director of Recruitment   tel. (+33) (1) 44 20 28 29
Human Resources Department
Banque Indosuez
96, Boulevard Haussmann
75008 Paris
FRANCE

Brown Brothers Harriman

Founded in 1818, the investment firm Brown Brothers Harriman serves its clients as commercial bankers, portfolio managers, securities brokers and custodians, and mergers and acquisitions advisors. Investment services are supplied to foreign financial institutions through offices in London, Paris, Tokyo, and Zurich.

Brown Brothers Harriman has a small officer training program. Graduates are placed in various domestic and international banking and investment departments. Recipients of B.A., M.A., and M.B.A. degrees are accepted for the training program. Following the training program, some trainees are assigned to account manager positions in New York or locations abroad. From their base in New York, account managers in international private banking market the firm's banking and investment services to investors in Europe, Latin America, and the Far East. Account managers in the International Institutional Sales Group work at offices in London, Paris, Zurich, or Tokyo providing advisory services to overseas institutional clients. Candidates for overseas assignments must have appropriate language skills and meet residency requirements.

Brown Brothers Harriman   tel. 212/483-1818
59 Wall Street   http://www.bbh.com
New York, NY 10005

Chase Manhattan Bank

Chase Manhattan Bank, the result of the 1996 merger of Chemical Bank and Chase Manhattan, is the largest bank in the United States. It offers a full range of financing, risk management, and advisory services to corporate and institutional clients worldwide. It also serves domestic mid-size and small businesses. Chase has over 50 foreign branches, representative offices, subsidiaries, and affiliates operating in 40 countries throughout Asia, Europe, Canada, the Middle East, Latin America, and Africa. The Banking and Corporate Finance Group offers commercial lending and investment banking products to large corporations and government entities both domestically and internationally. The Global Securities and Foreign Exchange Trading Group is responsible not only for trading and sales activities in securities and foreign exchange but also for funding and trading in the international money markets, international corporate finance, and worldwide institutional asset management. Most overseas operations are restricted to trading and distribution capabilities within international financial markets. Hiring for overseas operations primarily takes place in the foreign countries where operations are located. At senior levels, promotions are made from within the bank.

For undergraduates, entry-level programs are offered in areas such as consumer banking, general management, consumer services and sales, corporate finance, private and middle-market banking, and auditing. For an M.B.A., career tracks within consumer banking are offered including general management, marketing, and business planning.

Vice President, University Relations   tel. 212/622-0514
Chase Manhattan Bank
140 East 45th Street
New York, NY 10017

Citibank/Citicorp

Citibank/Citicorp is a premier global financial services organization. With a network linking over 90 countries, Citibank is the only international bank with a significant presence in so many markets. For the consumer or institutional, corporate, or private investor, this means worldwide access to Citibank's products and services, supported by the diversity of the Citibankers' experience, skills, and talent.

All members of the management associates (MA) program begin with an orientation program designed to integrate them into the Citibank culture and educate them on Citibank's product range, customer base, and regional and corporate strategies and objectives. On-the-job learning throughout the program consists either of rotational training through different units within a business or intensive training within the same unit. The program lasts between 12 and 24 months and will vary depending on the assigned country and performance. Preferred fields of study for candidates include finance, business, marketing, computer science, and related subjects. All applicants must have demonstrated language fluency and be presently authorized to work on a full-time basis in the country to which they are applying.

Global MA Programs   tel. 212/559-4360
Floor 12 / Zone 3   fax 212/793-6432
Citibank
575 Lexington Avenue
New York, NY 10043

Credit Suisse

Founded in 1856 in Zurich, Credit Suisse is the oldest of the three big Swiss banks. In Switzerland, Credit Suisse is one of the leading full-service banks with a range of services geared to the needs of all customer segments. In partnership with Swiss Volksbank it has one of the most extensive branch networks in Switzerland. Outside Switzerland, it concentrates mainly on business with major corporate and private customers and correspondent banks. With over 90 branch and representative offices worldwide, Credit Suisse has a presence in all major financial centers, leading industrial nations, and markets with high growth potential. Credit Suisse is a group company of CS Holding, one of the leading financial services groups in the world. Operating from some 500 offices worldwide and employing more than 50,000 people, CS Holding is active on all five continents and in all of the world's principal financial centers. The investment banking firm CS First Boston is also a group company of CS Holding.

Candidates for positions with Credit Suisse should be quick, energetic, flexible, team-oriented, and enthusiastic self-starters with strong communication, quantitative, computer, and problem-solving skills along with a desire to succeed.

Credit Suisse   tel. 212/238-2000
P.O. Box 3700
Church Street Station
New York, NY 10008–3700

Deutsche Bank

Deutsche Bank, the largest bank in Germany, is one of the leading banking institutions in the world. Through its extensive network of domestic and foreign branches and subsidiaries, the bank—a universal bank under German law, which means it can provide both commercial and investment banking products and services—provides a broad range of financial services including retail and corporate lending; project finance; trade finance; leasing; foreign exchange trading; primary securities issuance; secondary market trading; corporate finance; mergers and acquisitions advice; asset management; derivatives; and real estate, financial, and economic research. Deutsche Bank employs over 55,000 people worldwide, almost one-fifth of whom are non-German nationals. A great emphasis is placed on promotion from with the bank.

Candidates for positions with Deutsche Bank should have an M.B.A. or a master's degree in international affairs or a related discipline and proficiency in German and be willing to relocate internationally. Previous experience in financial services is preferred.

University Relations	tel. 212/474-8000
Deutsche Bank	http://www.deutsche-bank.de
31 West 52nd Street	
New York, NY 10019	

Dresdner Bank

Headquartered in Germany, Dresdner Bank is one of the world's major banks. U.S. branches of Dresdner North America are located in New York City, Chicago, and Los Angeles. Since Dresdner does not have a formal credit training program, all applicants must have knowledge of finance and fluency in German. Those who possess a bachelor's of business administration are most frequently hired. The bank's training program covers organizations, operations, international banking, and credit training at a money center bank.

Opportunities for American nationals are almost exclusively with the bank's American branches. U.S. citizens may apply, however, to any other office provided they are able to obtain all necessary work permits.

Human Resources Department	tel. 212/574-0100
Dresdner Bank AG	
75 Wall Street	
New York, NY 10005–2889	

Fuji Bank

Established in 1880, Fuji Bank holds a leading position in both the Japanese domestic and international financial markets and is one of the largest financial institutions in the world. In the United States, Fuji Bank and Trust, based in New York, is oriented primarily toward commercial lending but also performs well in various types of structured finance including real estate, aircraft, and project finance. U.S. branches are located in Chicago and New York with agencies and representative offices in Atlanta, Houston, Los Angeles, San Francisco, and Seattle. Other U.S. subsidiaries include Heller Financial in Chicago, primarily a factoring company and lender to middle-market companies, and Fuji Wolfensohn International in New York, a vehicle for cross-border mergers and acquisitions.

In Europe, Fuji Bank has a high profile in aircraft financing and has been actively participating in syndicated loans and promoting sovereign risk loans. The bank also is focusing on network expansion in the EC region. A noteworthy operation is Fuji Capital Markets, based in London and designed to engage in capital market transactions in both the U.S. and European markets. Fuji Bank also is active in Asia and Australasia with emphasis on network expansion and the syndicated loan market.

Overseas offices of Fuji Bank have autonomy in hiring local staff. Hiring for head offices in Tokyo is conducted in Tokyo with interviews sometimes conducted by staff at overseas offices. Candidates for positions in Japan must be fluent in Japanese. Internationally oriented positions include credit analysis, planning, and information development. In addition to Japanese language, prerequisites include an academic background in economics, accounting, or finance and an understanding of the Japanese corporate structure.

Planning Officer   tel. (+81) (3) 201-6303
The Fuji Bank, Limited
International Planning Division
1–5–5, Otemachi, Chiyoda-ku
Tokyo 100
JAPAN

Human Resources   tel. 212/898-2400
The Fuji Bank, Limited
2 World Trade Center
New York, NY 10048

GE Capital

With a AAA rating, assets totaling nearly $145 billion, and an average annual net income growth of 20 percent over the last 10 years, GE Capital is one of the largest and most diversified corporations in the global finance market. Its 24 distinct businesses fall into five major categories: specialized financing, mid-market financing, consumer services, equipment management, and specialty insurance. Possessing a global presence in a majority of its businesses,

GE Capital intends to continue meeting its goal of being number one or number two in each of its markets.

The Global Leadership Development Program is an intensive 12- to 18-month training process designed to quickly develop talented individuals from around the world and to prepare them for a global career in financial services within GE Capital's worldwide operations. The program typically consists of several real-world work experiences within specific businesses coupled with professional training courses in business practices and leadership development.

Most program members hold an M.B.A. coupled with significant work experience and/or educational experience abroad, preferably in financial services, and fluency in business English and the language of the placement country. A competitive candidate will possess superior academic performance, a career focus, high levels of initiative, a minimum of three to five years' relevant work experience, persuasive communications skills, demonstrated leadership abilities, and a global mindset.

Director, Global Program Recruiting   fax 203/357-3960
GE Capital
260 Long Ridge Road
Stamford, CT 06927

Goldman, Sachs

Goldman, Sachs is a full-service global investment banking and securities firm. Its clients include corporations, governments, institutions, and individuals worldwide.

Founded in 1869, it is among the oldest and most strongly capitalized firms in the financial services industry and one of the few major financial organizations that continues as a private partnership. Goldman, Sachs is a leader in virtually every field of investment, finance, and research as well as mergers and acquisitions. Goldman, Sachs is headquartered in New York; has regional headquarters in London, Tokyo, and Hong Kong; and has offices throughout the Americas, Europe, and the Asia-Pacific region. The firm serves its clients through teams of professionals who provide state-of-the-art services and products in local markets and have distinctive capabilities to help them capitalize on opportunities worldwide.

Goldman, Sachs & Co.   tel. 212/902-1000
85 Broad Street   www.gsco.com
New York, NY 10004

Hambrecht & Quist

Headquartered in San Francisco, Hambrecht & Quist (H&Q), with 11 offices in six countries, has been a leading investment banker for emerging growth companies for over 25 years. Founded in 1968 on the belief that companies and investors in high-growth industries require specialized industry expertise and financial services from an investment banking partner, H&Q has established itself as a leading investment bank by building long-term relationships with many of the world's most successful growth companies and growth stock investors. H&Q achieves and maintains its specialization in technology, life sciences, branded consumer, and information services sectors by limiting its client base to high-quality companies and investors that are within its industry focus areas. H&Q also offers its corporate clients a full range of financial services, from venture capital to large-scale underwriting and M&A advisory. Hambrecht & Quist's executive financial services, institutional sales, and trading groups have specialized expertise in the firm's focused areas of coverage. The venture capital group includes investment professionals and a number of consultants who offer a diversified blend of expertise in the firm's targeted industries and extensive experience in growing entrepreneurial companies.

Most candidates for employment with Hambrecht & Quist are top students from leading graduate schools. Many have technical backgrounds and specific expertise in one of H&Q's areas of specialization.

Hambrecht & Quist   tel. 415/576-3300
One Bush Street   http://www.hamquist.com
San Francisco, CA 94104

J.P. Morgan

J.P. Morgan is a global financial services firm that serves governments, corporations, institutions, individuals, and privately held firms with complex financial needs through an integrated range of advisory, financing, trading, investment, and related capabilities. Investment banking provides advisory and financing services to multinational corporations, privately held companies, and sovereign governments. Equity research creates industry-based research and gives investment recommendations to portfolio managers. Municipal finance offers advice and financing for public sector clients, including state and local governments.

Analysts for each group research and synthesize information using public or client sources, prepare financial models and analyses, and assist experienced professionals in preparing and delivering client presentations and research reports. Assignments are similar for all three groups; differences exist in their business activities and the clients served. Qualifications for two- and three-year analyst positions include quantitative and analytical skills; the ability to think critically, especially with regard to the broader implications of quantitative data; and high energy and motivation to work in a demanding environment.

J.P. Morgan   tel. 212/483-2323
23 Wall Street   http://www.jpmorgan.com
New York, NY 10260

Merrill Lynch

Merrill Lynch is a leading financial management and advisory company committed to providing unsurpassed advice, guidance, execution, and a full range of integrated financial services for its clients worldwide. Through its Corporate and Institutional Client Group, Merrill Lynch serves corporate, government, and institutional clients in every major market sector. Merrill Lynch's Private Client Group serves individual and small- to medium-size businesses. Merrill Lynch holds leadership positions in strategic advisory services, underwriting, distribution, and research.

Merrill Lynch's Global Markets serves individuals, institutions, large corporations, and governments in every region of the world. Merrill Lynch helps issuers efficiently access capital globally, funds the development of companies in emerging markets, provides merger and acquisition advice worldwide, and assists investors in identifying appropriate investments through an international network of 12,500 financial consultants and an institutional sales force of more than 670. The Private Client Group includes more than 500 domestic offices and 50 international offices in 35 countries.

Looking ahead, Merrill Lynch foresees greater growth in investment banking advisory services and in foreign investing for its U.S. and international clients. Most international positions are in Hong Kong, London, or Tokyo, but opportunities often arise in New York, Toronto, Los Angeles, and Singapore. Candidates should possess superior academic achievement, evidence of leadership ability, comfort with technology, and the language of modern finance. The ability to speak a second language is increasingly important. A degree in a financial field is not necessary.

Recruiter   http://www.ml.com
Corporate and Institutional Client Group
Merrill Lynch
World Financial Center—North Tower
250 Vesey Street
New York, NY 10281–1323

Montgomery Securities

Montgomery Securities is a nationally recognized investment banking firm that focuses on high-quality growth companies in five industry sectors: consumer products/services, financial services, health care, technology, and real estate/home building. Montgomery has pursued a consistent strategy since it was founded in 1969: to provide the highest caliber investment banking and brokerage services to growth companies in selected dynamic industry sectors. Montgomery has approximately 800 employees.

The Montgomery analyst program provides the Wall Street investment banking experience in San Francisco. Montgomery analysts spend one to two years working as corporate finance generalists with experienced investment banking professionals in all five industry sectors. Client teams at Montgomery tend to be smaller than at other investment banks, giving analysts greater direct exposure to clients, the opportunity to earn added responsibility, and closer interaction with experienced bankers.

Montgomery is looking for candidates with outstanding academic and extracurricular achievements. While no specific major is required, familiarity with financial concepts and strong quantitative skills are important. In addition, high energy, a desire to excel, personal integrity, and strong communication skills are important.

Montgomery Securities   tel. 415/627-2000
600 Montgomery Street
San Francisco, CA 94111

Morgan Stanley International

Morgan Stanley is a major international securities firm providing services on a worldwide basis to a large and diversified group of clients and customers including multinational corporations, governments, emerging growth companies, financial institutions, and individual investors. Its businesses include securities underwriting; distribution and trading; merger, acquisition, restructuring, and other corporate finance activities, including merchant banking, stock brokerage, and research services; asset management; trading of futures, options, foreign exchange, and commodities; corporate real estate advice; and global custody, securities clearance services, and securities lending. Morgan Stanley operates worldwide through six divisions: investment banking; equity; fixed income; asset management; merchant banking; and finance, administration, and operations.

Each division at Morgan Stanley hires approximately 75 to 100 individuals as financial analysts or in other capacities each year. There is a two-year training program designed for college graduates who have outstanding academic records, demonstrated leadership capabilities, and good interpersonal skills. While no specific majors are required, individuals must be comfortable with numbers and mathematical concepts.

> Human Resources   http://www.ms.com
> Morgan Stanley International
> 25 Cabot Square
> Canary Wharf
> London E14 4QA
> UNITED KINGDOM

NationsBank

The largest bank in the American South, Southwest, and Mid-Atlantic regions and one of the largest banking companies in the United States, NationsBank covers 27 percent of the U.S. population. It is among the largest and most capable providers of corporate finance, trust, leasing, factoring, and cash management services to corporate clients throughout the nation. The institutional bank includes corporate banking, investment banking, and global trading and distribution activities for NationsBank. Successful integration of these three areas enables NationsBank professionals to provide financial expertise to their clients in the origination, structuring, and distribution of a variety of transactions. By coordinating the efforts of lenders, product specialists, and securities and trading specialists, the institutional bank seeks to meet the entire spectrum of financial needs of its clients. Relationship building is the dominant focus of the group.

In the training program for corporate relationship managers, new hires receive a combination of production work and classroom training in either Charlotte or Dallas. Advancement throughout the training program is based on individual performance. The investment bank focuses on structuring and arranging financial transactions and providing advice on mergers, acquisitions, divestitures, and other strategic business issues. Investment bank analysts go through a two-year program open to both business and liberal arts graduates. The program is designed to help analysts develop a broad understanding of financial instruments and techniques ranging from private placements of long-term debt to interest rate protection. New analysts are assigned to different areas and work on specific transactions as part of a team, supporting senior professionals by researching industry trends, organizing data, providing quantitative analyses, structuring transactions, preparing company valuations, and writing description memoranda.

The NationsBank Global Trading and Distribution area works closely with both the corporate and investment bankers, and professionals in this division are responsible for the sales and trading of securities and the marketing and trading of foreign exchange services.

College Recruiting Manager   tel. 704/388-3429
NationsBank Corporation
NationsBank Plaza, T24–8
Charlotte, NC 28255

Salomon Brothers

A leading global investment bank with offices around the world, Salomon Brothers is known in particular for its securities underwriting as well as a variety of financial research operations. International career opportunities at Salomon Brothers exist in investment banking and sales and trading.

The investment banking department consists of four main sections: U.S. corporate finance, which services major U.S. and foreign clients with offices in New York, Chicago, San Francisco, and Los Angeles; capital markets, with centers in New York, London, Hong Kong, and Tokyo; financial institutions, which provides complete investment banking services to a broad range of financial institutions; and international investment banking. Salomon's investment banking activities in Asia include offices and affiliates in over eight countries, in addition to professionals in the New York office dedicated to serving Asian clients in the U.S. In Europe, the investment banking group in London is staffed primarily by European nationals and is supported by offices in Frankfurt and Madrid. The Latin American coverage group, based in New York with an office in Mexico City, is staffed by professionals with cultural and general investment banking experience in all the major countries of Latin America. Salomon does not require candidates to choose a specific functional specialty during the interview process; most associates who join investment banking enter a one-year generalist program where they have the opportunity to work with many products and franchise groups. Financial analysts join the firm in a two-year training program and should possess an undergraduate degree with distinguished academic achievement.

Salomon Brothers provides sales and trading services to a wide variety of customers from around the world and conducts proprietary trading activities in many financial instruments. Sales and trading trainees spend the first four months at the firm in Salomon's in-house training program. Candidates for positions with Salomon Brothers should possess a university degree with high academic standing. Candidates interested in non-U.S. opportunities should contact the appropriate individual in New York.

Human Resources Department   tel. 212/747-7000
Salomon Brothers
Seven World Trade Center
New York, NY 10048

Socimer International Group

Socimer International Group was founded in 1976 as part of Transafrica Holding, A Spanish conglomerate, jointly owned by the Salama family and André & Cie, a Swiss-bases diversified commodities trading firm. Socimer International specializes in providing financial services in emerging markets. Its main areas of activities are corporate financial advisory, capital markets, asset management services, and consulting services to governments and institutions such as the World Bank, USAID, United Nations Development Programme, and the Inter-American Development Bank.

Over the years, Socimer has established a local presence in seven major financial centers in Latin America, such as Santiago, Mexico City, and Saõ Paulo. This broad network is complemented by European offices in Geneva and Madrid, and in the United States by Socimer International in New York and Socimer Securities. The group employs about 150 professional worldwide.

Recruitment is based mainly on international financial experience, a master's degree in a relevant area, and fluency in Spanish and English.

Socimer International Corporation   tel. 212/446-2777
12th Floor   fax 212/832-5939
450 Park Avenue   http://www.socimer.com
New York, NY 10022

Socimer Securities Corporation   tel. 305/371-4848
Suite 1110   fax 305/371-5348
1401 Buckell Avenue
Miami, FL 33131

Standard & Poor's (S&P)

Standard & Poor's Rating Group (S&P), based in New York with 15 offices in 12 countries, is one of the world's leading financial rating agencies. It is a McGraw-Hill company. S&P's points of financial focus range from public finance to derivative securities, from the asset-backed bonds of structured finance issues to insurance company stability or mutual fund volatility. S&P does not engage in trading or underwriting activities.

S&P analysts interact with the world's leading financial intermediaries, banks, corporations, governments, and other capital market participants. They visit the institutions they analyze. For example, they inspect the real estate used as collateral for mortgage-backed bonds and meet with government leaders. S&P analysts work closely in teams that encourage collaborative efforts to arrive at a quality rating. As developed and emerging market countries all over the world seek capital for their industrial and infrastructure growth, they increasingly turn to the U.S. capital markets, the most liquid in the world, as a guidepost for developing their own systems.

Candidates for positions with S&P should be energetic team players with a demonstrated record of academic achievement, usually in fields such as business, finance, economics, or mathematics, and possess strong analytical capabilities.

Manager, Staff Development
Standard & Poor's Rating Group
25 Broadway
New York, NY 10004

Standard Chartered Bank

Standard Chartered Bank (SCB) is an international banking group founded in 1853 and headquartered in London. It has a network of more than 600 offices in more than 40 countries and employs a staff of more than 25,000 people. The firm's strategy is to build and grow its strong businesses in East and Southeast Asia, enhance its historical position in the Middle East and South Asia, and develop its African businesses in a focused way. SCB concentrates its operations in Organization for Economic Cooperation and Development (OECD) countries on those activities that support its franchise in newly industrialized and developing markets.

SCB hires undergraduate and graduate students in a variety of disciplines to work in treasury, corporate, personal banking, and standard chartered markets. The firm offers a six-week professional induction course and a three-month international line assignment; a new employee's first appointment in his or her country or region of origin. SCB predominantly recruits international students studying in the U.S. and U.K. The number of recruits depends on the firm's anticipated business requirements for the forthcoming year. Last year SBC recruited for Botswana, China, Ghana, Hong Kong, Indonesia, Kenya, Malaysia, Mexico, Singapore, Thailand, U.A.E., U.K., U.S., Zambia, and Zimbabwe.

V.P., International Graduate Recruitment
Standard Chartered Bank
707 Wilshire Blvd. W5–15
Los Angeles, CA 90017

Wells Fargo Bank

Wells Fargo Bank has provided a variety of financial services since 1852. With operations primarily in California and over 660 branches, it is particularly strong in the retail and business banking sector. Recently merged with First Interstate Bank, its operations are primarily domestic, but it does provide financial products and services to meet the international banking needs of the bank's domestic customers. An alliance between Wells Fargo and the Hong Kong and Shanghai Banking Corporation (HSBS) provides access for customers to HSBC's worldwide network of 1,400 offices in more than 50 countries.

Competition for employment with Wells Fargo is highly competitive. While most positions dealing with international matters are filled by those with previous experience in international or commercial banking, some entry-level professional positions do exist. Candidates with a bachelor's degree and master's degree candidates should have a solid grounding in finance, accounting, economics, or international relations.

University Relations   tel. 415/477-1000
Wells Fargo Bank   http://wellsfargo.com
475 Sansome Street
San Francisco, CA 94163

5

Business

KATHERINE R. TAYLOR*

As we near the end of the 20th century, international business is both simpler and more complex than it has ever been before. Simpler, in that globalization and competition are renewing companies' focus on core competencies, while communications and travel are shrinking the planet. More complex, in that the very nature of doing business transnationally in an increasingly interlinked world requires executives to be familiar with an ever-greater range of factors, interconnections, and local customs and laws.

At the same time, the rate of global information creation is increasing at an exponential rate—some say the amount of information in the world has doubled in the last 18 months. Businesses are having to adapt to these changes in an ever-more-rapid fashion in order to continue to compete. And, no doubt, to the international business world of 2010 and whatever new technological wonders it may bring, the late 1990s will seem as leisurely as the pre-PC, preinternet, and faxless world of a few years ago appears to us today.

This growing complexity can provide opportunities for graduates in international affairs who are able to combine a business mind-set and know-how with international skills and experience. As a job candidate, it is a plus to be perceived as global, or as a regional expert, particularly when fluent in one or more languages. And being able to interact successfully in different cultures, with a diversity of people, is a useful management talent—one increasingly recognized by hiring managers and human resource specialists.

---

* Katherine R. Taylor, a 1992 graduate of Georgetown University's Master of Science in Foreign Service program and an International Business Diplomacy honors certificate holder, is marketing and sales manager for GE Transportation Systems for South and Central America. She has also served as GE Mexico's business development manager in Mexico and in Ralston-Purina International's marketing department in Mexico. Ms. Taylor has a B.A. in political science from Yale University and a certificate of political studies from the Institut d'Etudes Politiques de Paris.

Nevertheless, those of us who cherish the international arena, who have at times fallen in love with cultures or languages other than our own, need to remind ourselves of a simple truth: The business of business is creating shareholder value. Businesses become global in order to continue to add value. This is an important truth, because in corporations today you will rarely be considered vital simply because you are an internationalist. Rather, it is functional or other business acumen that is most highly prized, with languages and other talents providing additional value. An international business career can be very exciting and stimulating, but it also tends to be extremely competitive.

Another reality of international business today and in the future is the virtual office. With global paging devices, voice-mail, e-mail, faxes, and other advances in information technology, the boundaries of time and space are being blurred. This has enormous impact both on our effectiveness and on how we work. Work becomes fully transportable and can often be done at any time of the day or night—we may often rue the day we accepted an Asian posting, as we are forced to respond to urgent faxes at 3:00 a.m. Hong Kong time. In my own case, for example, this essay was begun in São Paulo, Brazil, worked on in Belo Horizonte, amended in Erie, PA, and completed in Washington, D.C.—all thanks to my handy IBM Thinkpad.

It is important to master these virtual tools. But they are just aids in answering fundamental questions that cut across cultural or geographic boundaries, such as: Does the organization understand its objectives and priorities? Do your employees understand what they need to do and do they know where to get any support they may require? Have you instituted proper controls while empowering employees?

In the lean, agile corporations of today, where a quarter of the people are often generating twice the revenue, and working harder than ever before, sensitivity to culture and diversity can become a winning managerial characteristic, in both domestic and transnational work environments. No doubt this will vary relative to size and nationality, industry, and the individual culture of the organization in which you work, as different companies place different premiums on particular management styles. But a clear trend in U.S. business today is the move away from hierarchical, top-down, multilayered organizations to flatter, simpler structures in which leadership among your peers is a must for getting things done.

Moreover, U.S. corporations can no longer provide job security in the traditional sense. Security can come only from continuing to generate value for the shareholders and from continuing to satisfy customers. Business is alive in that it must constantly adapt and shift to survive and is always requiring more effort from its employees.

Joining a corporation itself is an exercise in learning a "foreign" culture: each usually has its own language and symbolism, its rituals and standard operating procedures, its expectations and timing. It is important to consider carefully your own values before accepting a job with a particular organization; research them both in the media and with current employees and match that against your own needs and aspirations.

As already mentioned, one way to succeed in a corporation is to provide clear and definable value-added, usually categorized as functional expertise. This often entails having to earn your spurs in a functional role in a domestic location before being assigned to an international office. The traditional international career track of the nomadic foreign service employee or expatriate is becoming rare indeed. The increased tax and benefit expenses make it virtually prohibitive for all but recognized high-potential employees. Unless they have had prior business experience, it is unusual to find a recent graduate as a new hire in an international operating position abroad.

In the United States, departments labeled exclusively "international" have been mostly dismantled, as staff levels have been reduced and positions today tend to be global in nature, undifferentiated by national boundaries. One remaining functional approach in the international arena, however, is that of the trade or international policy specialist. This role has been tightened somewhat by corporations' reengineering and restructuring efforts but is key for many businesses and industries.

This, perhaps more than any other, is the most recognizably international of business functions, in that its focus is still the interactions among nations, their respective export policies and financing arms, and trade or other international negotiations and agreements. It spans a broad range of industries and issues, from intellectual property rights for the entertainment industry, to the financing of large infrastructure investments in power and telecommunications in developing countries, to export controls on certain technologies with national security implications.

It is important to recognize, however, that trade is usually considered a "staff" function, an often justified but ongoing cost of doing business that can be somewhat removed from the business's operational functions. This is so, too, if you are working on these and related issues in an industry or trade association: You can provide support for corporations, but are further away from their core functions.

The most obvious and recognized international skill is speaking another language fluently and being familiar with the cultural and regional knowledge that accompanies it. This is something that hiring managers can get their arms around as a clearly defined skill. And it often proves invaluable in practice. For example, when dealing with so-called "high-context" cultures—those in which societal or organizational position, body language, and situation shape the way a communication is perceived and interpreted—it is essential to be able to understand the elements of that context. Miscommunications can effect negotiations and lose deals, affecting a corporation's ability to generate revenue.

Similarly, an understanding of cross-border issues can provide depth to the structuring of a negotiation or profitability analysis. Even something as simple as considering the exchange rate risk of a certain transaction can potentially be very costly if those involved do not consider its implications. I have certainly found this to be the case in my personal experience.

I have worked almost exclusively for large American multinationals and this essay is a reflection of my experiences with small- to medium-sized businesses as clients or suppliers. Still, the corporate giants are trying to absorb more and more of a small business mentality—becoming faster and more efficient, improving customer service, and using benchmarking to allow businesses to share best practices across industries and borders.

For some, the excitement of a nomadic international lifestyle is the dream of a lifetime while others prefer the stability of a core U.S. location with international travel. What cannot be denied is that the choice of an international assignment or career entails relocation. It is worth thinking carefully about your needs for personal and career balance before embarking on an international assignment. My own experience, although I have been very fortunate, is that I am often so eager to get the job that I may not allow myself enough time to think through all of the ramifications for my personal life.

In closing, let me emphasize that no one will manage your career for you. Rather, we each have a personal responsibility to manage our own moves and progression. Your career will be the result of a series of choices—not right or wrong, but yours.

ABB Asea Brown Boveri

ABB Asea Brown Boveri, headquartered in Zurich, Switzerland, is a $29.7 billion company serving electric power generation, transmission and distribution, industrial and building systems, and rail transportation customers. More than half of ABB's sales are in Europe; one-quarter are in Australia, Asia, and Africa; and one-fifth are in the Americas. Worldwide employment with ABB numbers over 200,000. ABB U.S. employs over 25,000 people at 50 manufacturing plants and 300 sales and service centers. ABB's activities are highly decentralized, as in all hiring. ABB is looking for candidates in a wide variety of academic disciplines.

ABB   tel. 203/750-2200
501 Merritt 7
P.O. Box 5308
Norwalk, CT 06856–5308

Amoco

Amoco is one of the world's largest publicly traded producers of crude oil and natural gas in the world. In business since 1889, Amoco is the 13th largest industrial corporation in the United States and has about 43,000 employees worldwide. Amoco is divided into three main sectors: exploration and production, petroleum products, and chemicals. It also has several smaller, specialized operations. The company has major oil and natural gas facilities in the Middle East, South America, North America, and the North Sea.

Amoco has entry-level positions encompassing professional disciplines ranging from technical degrees to pure sciences and from business through liberal arts. Candidates with finance backgrounds are needed for one of Amoco's finance departments or in the planning and economics department. Hiring is decentralized.

University Relations—MC 3608   tel. 312/856-5111
Amoco Corporation
200 East Randolph Drive
Chicago, IL 60601

American International Group

American International Group is the leading U.S. international insurance and financial services organization and the largest underwriter of commercial and industrial insurance in the United States. Its member companies write property, casualty, marine, life, and financial services insurance in more than

130 countries and jurisdictions. The company was founded in 1919 by Cornelius Vander Starr in Shanghai, China, and thereafter expanded to the United States, Latin America, Europe, and the Middle East. Through these and other offices, strong ties have been built between American International and government financial officials in many countries.

The company employs more than 30,000 employees worldwide. It seeks students who have an interest in international business and who are willing to tackle the problems associated with today's changing environment. Between 15 and 30 trainees are hired each year.

Manager, College Relations   tel. 212/770-7000
American International Group, Inc.
72 Wall Street, 6th floor
New York, NY 10270

Apple Computer

Apple Computer develops, manufactures, and markets an extensive line of personal computers, communications products, peripherals, and system software designed to address the needs of individuals, businesses, educational and scientific institutions, and governments. The company is engaged actively in more than 120 countries and employs about 12,000 people worldwide. Five major divisions make up the Apple organization: Apple USA, Apple Pacific, and Apple Europe (involved in marketing); Apple Products (focused on research and development); and Apple Manufacturing (concerned with producing the company's products).

Hiring is decentralized with positions being filled on an office-by-office basis. Requirements also differ widely between divisions and even within divisions depending on the office and its location. More information may be obtained by contacting the address below. The human resources department also can provide information.

Apple Computer   tel. 408/996-1010
College Relations Department
20525 Mariani Avenue
Cupertino, CA 95014

Chesapeake Corporation

Chesapeake Corporation is a Fortune 1000 packaging and paper company. Chesapeake's primary businesses are packaging, kraft, and tissue paper products. Founded in 1918 and based in Richmond, Virginia, Chesapeake serves markets mainly in North America and Europe from 40 locations in 13 states across the United States. The company owns approximately 350,000 acres of forestland and employs more than 5,400 people. Chesapeake utilizes a decentralized operating philosophy to encourage creative decision-making at the business level and to promote an entrepreneurial management style. The operating philosophy embraces the use of incentive-based pay for performance and employee involvement. The company recognizes a responsibility to conduct its affairs with an appreciation for environmental awareness.

Candidates for international positions with Chesapeake should possess an advanced degree (M.B.A. or equivalent), at least two years' work experience (preferably internationally), foreign language ability, and solid market research skills.

Manager of Employee Services   tel. 804/697-1147
Chesapeake Corporation   fax 804/697-1199
P.O. Box 2350
Richmond, VA 23218–2350

C. Itoh

C. Itoh & Co. (America) Inc. is a diversified multibusiness corporation with global capabilities serving more than 5,000 major clients. Established in 1858 as a textile wholesaling concern, C. Itoh has evolved into a broad-based international organization. The 11 operating groups handle more than 50,000 products and commodities from textiles to machinery, electronics, chemicals, metals, produce, energy, and general merchandise. C. Itoh America's research, management, financial, and technical skills have been servicing industry and commerce in the United States for more than 30 years. Specialists throughout the United States work with the worldwide resources of the parent company, C.Itoh & Co., Ltd. New business is generated for American and foreign clients by developing new markets and processes, coordinating the movement of resources through distribution channels, managing domestic and international business projects, and investing in and guiding joint ventures. As the flagship subsidiary of a leading Japanese *sogo shosha* (general trading company), C. Itoh America offers the business community broad access to world trade.

Human Resources   tel. 212/818-8001
C. Itoh & Co. (America) Inc.
335 Madison Avenue
New York, NY 10017

DuPont

Headquartered in Wilmington, Delaware, DuPont is a research- and technology-based global chemistry and energy company offering high-performance products in chemicals, polymers, fibers, and petroleum. Founded in 1802 to manufacture black powder, the company is today one of the largest and most diversified industrial corporations in the world. With more than 110,000 employees and 200 manufacturing and processing plants in more than 40 countries on six continents, more than 50 percent of $40 billion in annual sales is outside the United States. DuPont serves worldwide markets in the aerospace, apparel, automotive, agriculture, construction, packaging, refining, and transportation industries.

DuPont promotes almost exclusively from within and most employees start in entry-level positions. Most DuPont managers are transferred outside the Wilmington headquarters. DuPont has an extensive college recruiting program for entry-level engineers and computer and financial systems people in the United States.

DuPont Human Resources	tel. 800/774-2271
Nemours Building	fax 800/631-2206
1007 Market Street	
Wilmington, DE 19898	

General Mills

General Mills is a major marketer of consumer foods and a leader in the full-service dinner house restaurant business. Headquartered in Minneapolis, Minnesota, the company is one of the largest corporations in the United States with more than 97,000 employees and operations in almost every state. The company has about 60 Red Lobster restaurants in Japan and is involved in the cookie and confection business in Western Europe. Cereal Partners Worldwide, the company's joint venture with Nestlé Foods to produce and market General Mills in Europe, Latin America, and the ASEAN markets of the southwestern Pacific, is the world's number two cereal company outside North America.

Career opportunities for B.A.s and M.B.A.s exist in marketing, marketing research, finance, human resources, manufacturing, engineering, strategic planning, and analysis.

Director, Recruitment &	tel. 612/540-2311
College Relations	
General Mills	
P.O. Box 1113	
Minneapolis, MN 55440	

Hakuhodo

Established in 1895, Hakuhodo is one of Japan's oldest marketing, advertising, and public relations agencies. Hakuhodo provides market research, media relations, strategy, and concept planning services. The company also sponsors the Hakuhodo Institute of Life and Living, which studies the consumption behavior and social orientation of the Japanese people by examining individuals' day-to-day thoughts and feelings, emotional and intellectual needs, aspirations, concerns, and worries through questionnaires and interviews. Headquartered in Tokyo, the firm's office network spans 48 countries. Hakuhodo has about 3,500 employees worldwide. About 40 people are employed in its U.S. offices in New York, Atlanta, and Los Angeles. U.S. hiring is handled through the New York office; other positions are filled through the Tokyo office.

Hakuhodo Advertising America   tel. 212/684-7000
18th Floor
475 Park Avenue South
New York, NY 10016

Hakuhodo
22, Kanda-Nishikicho 3-chome
Chiyoda-ku
Tokyo 101
JAPAN

International Language and Culture Center

International Language and Culture Center (ILCC) was established in 1976 as a small translation house and has since grown to a registered staff of more than 400 from eight countries. ILCC has expanded to serve international business and culture through communication services, coordination of major events, public relations, and commercial publications. The company's clients include multinational manufacturers, financial institutions, international advertising and human resources companies, and Japanese government agencies.

ILCC seeks bright, articulate people to work in Japan as interpreters, translators, English editors, and rewriters. Bilingual Japanese who are studying overseas and highly proficient, bilingual non-Japanese who plan to reside in Japan are urged to apply. ILCC is especially interested in energetic people with backgrounds in liberal arts, Asian studies, international relations, languages, English, business, marketing, and human relations to work in Japan on a freelance basis. Major study in specific fields will be considered secondary to language proficiency.

International Language &   tel. (+81)(3) 5562-3661
   Culture Center   fax (+81)(3) 5562-3666
2–17–44, Akasaka Minato-ku   e-mail: mft@ilcc.com
Tokyo 107
JAPAN

Johnson & Higgins

Johnson and Higgins serves as international insurance brokers and employee benefit consultants and actuaries. The firm is a global leader in its field with 53 U.S. offices, 120 foreign offices, and more than 100 correspondent offices abroad.

Johnson & Higgins' continuing global focus provides opportunities for candidates with academic backgrounds in international affairs. Most new recruits hold bachelor's degrees and are hired into apprenticeship positions, but for those interested in insurance as a career the company provides special training and educational programs. Recruiters look first and foremost for a breadth of background and a good scholastic record.

Human Resources Department   tel. 212/574-7000
Johnson & Higgins   fax 212/574-7190
Third Floor
125 Broad Street
New York, NY 10004

MCI

MCI is one of the world's largest and fastest-growing diversified communications companies. MCI offers consumers and businesses a broad portfolio of services including long distance, wireless, local access, paging, internet software and access, on-line information services, business software, and global telecommunications services.

Since its founding 27 years ago, MCI has grown to a $13 billion company. Through a number of key strategic ventures and alliances, with companies such as BT, News Corp., and Banacci, MCI is providing new services to its customers around the world.

Today, there are some 40,000 "MCIers", working in hundreds of offices around the world from the headquarters in Washington, D.C., to business centers such as London, Paris, Frankfurt, Tokyo, Beijing, Moscow, Mexico City, and Sao Paulo.

MCI is looking for recent graduates with degrees in such fields as computer science, engineering, finance, business, and international relations.

Human Resources   tel. 202/872-1600
MCI   http://www.mci.com
1801 Pennsylvania Avenue, N.W.
Washington, D.C. 20006

Microsoft

Founded in 1975, Microsoft designs, develops, markets, and supports a wide range of personal computer software systems, applications, development tools and languages, hardware peripherals, and books. The company offers a family of operating system products to satisfy any level of customer need; Microsoft Windows, introduced in 1990, is regarded as the standard operating system for personal computers worldwide. In addition to its offices in the United States, Microsoft has 48 international subsidiary offices worldwide and international manufacturing and distribution facilities in Ireland and Puerto Rico. Microsoft software is sold in more than 50 countries in over 30 languages. The Microsoft Network on-line service, designed to provide access to the expanding world of electronic information, represents Microsoft's next step toward the realization of its vision of the future.

Microsoft employs over 17,000 people worldwide. Career opportunities with Microsoft exist in software and consumer product (multimedia) design and development, product marketing and sales, technical support, and consulting. For most positions, a bachelor's degree in computer science, computer engineering, or another technical discipline is needed.

Recruiting
Microsoft Corporation
Dept. P8001–9596
One Microsoft Way, STE 303
Redmond, WA 98052

tel. 206/882-8080
tel. 800/892-3181
e-mail: jobinfo@microsoft.com
http://www.microsoft.com

Nestlé

Nestlé is one of the world's leading food companies, with sales almost exclusively in branded products. Nestlé is a global company: 45 percent of its business is in Europe and more than 35 percent in the Americas; almost 20 percent of its sales are generated in the other regions of the world. Nestlé does more than 98 percent of its business outside of Switzerland, its home country, and has over 490 factories in more than 70 countries.

Nestlé is looking for recent college graduates in a wide variety of disciplines, including business, accounting, finance, marketing, international affairs, and computer science.

College Recruitment Office
Nestlé USA
800 North Brand Boulevard
Glendale, CA 91203

tel. 815/549-6000

Nestlé S.A.
Avenue Nestlé
1800 Vevey
SWITZERLAND

tel. (+41) (21) 924-2111

Proctor & Gamble

Proctor & Gamble (P&G) is one of the world's largest consumer products companies. P&G's international operations have grown into a vast network in over 56 countries worldwide. Company locations include Latin America, Europe, Asia, the Middle East, and North America. Positions filled commonly fall under the following categories: advertising/brand management, sales management, finance and accounting, management systems, product development, and manufacturing.

Procter & Gamble employs over 50,000 people overseas. For international positions, the company seeks mostly foreign nationals who will return to their home countries to begin careers. Anyone with foreign language fluency and significant international experience, however, will be considered. There are few starting positions available in or outside of the United States. Due to a strict policy of promotion from within, the company has beginning-level positions only for individuals with bachelor's and master's degrees. Procter & Gamble is constantly looking for good people because of the company's rapid growth.

Manager, International Recruiting   tel. 513/562-1100
Procter & Gamble International
P.O. Box 599
Cincinnati, OH 45202

Reuters Holdings

Reuters Holdings employs over 11,000 people in 180 offices in 80 countries, with 3,000 people in London alone. Other large offices are in Amsterdam, Switzerland, Japan, Hong Kong, and the United States. Reuters is familiar as a supplier of TV programs and news, but it also supplies financial information to banks and investment houses. Reuters also develops software packages for using their information products. Reuters has four graduate training schemes (programs): journalism, marketing, accountancy, and technical. The training schemes are extremely competitive. The training lasts for two years and many trainees go on to become regular staff members. In addition to the training schemes, many countries hire staff on an ad hoc basis. Reuters looks for people with an international outlook, an innovative mind, complete mobility, and an ability to get along with people of all cultures and backgrounds.

Reuters Holdings   tel. (+44) (71) 250-1122
John Carpenter House
John Carpenter Street
London EC4P 4AJ
UNITED KINGDOM

Rockwell International

Rockwell International is a major global, diversified, high-technology company with two-thirds of its sales coming from commercial and international markets. This international company is applying advanced technology to a wide range of products in its aerospace, electronics, automotive, and graphics businesses. Rockwell produces a broad spectrum of products from newspaper printing presses to the space shuttle. The company's role as a defense and aerospace contractor, although diminished in volume, remains a very important part of the company. More than a third of all Rockwell employees now work outside the United States, where Europe is their major market.

Rockwell's international activities are coordinated out of its corporate office in Arlington, Virginia. There are approximately 10 professional positions in the office filled through internal or external searches. Requirements for these positions are a bachelor's or advanced degree in accounting, engineering, management, or trade, all preferably international in scope. In addition, Rockwell seeks individuals with international relations, area studies, or similar degrees and relevant experience in sales, accounting, marketing, or statistics. Prior experience in a related field, either with Rockwell or elsewhere, is required for positions in Rockwell's international functions.

Corporate College Relations   tel. 412/565-2000
Rockwell International
P.O. Box 4250
Seal Beach, CA 90740–8250

Texaco

Texaco is one of the world's largest integrated oil companies. Its worldwide operations comprise several major activities: exploration, production, refining, marketing, transportation, and research. Offices and operating facilities are maintained at various locations throughout the world. The largest employee centers are in Texas, New York, Louisiana, and California.

Career opportunities with Texaco are primarily in the fields of engineering (chemical, petroleum, mechanical, electrical, civil, metallurgical), geology, geophysics, computer science, accounting, chemistry, mathematics, physics, liberal arts, business administration, marketing, and petroleum land management. Texaco also has high-potential opportunities in a number of specialized areas such as law, economics, finance, employee relations, and public relations.

While Texaco's operations are worldwide, new recruits usually are assigned to domestic locations, at least for the first several years. Texaco and its subsidiaries and affiliates abroad are staffed largely by nationals of the countries where they operate. Opportunities for overseas assignments at entry level do not occur often since most assignments call for highly experienced people in specialized fields such as geology, geophysics, engineering, accounting or marketing. Fluency in a foreign language, especially French, Italian, German, Spanish, or Portuguese, is often a requirement for overseas assignments.

Manager, Professional Employment
Texaco, Inc.
TEXACO Heritage Plaza
1111 Baby Street
Houston, TX 77002

Texaco Europe and/or Texaco   tel. 914/253-4000
   Middle East/Far East
Manager, Human Resources
2000 Westchester Avenue
White Plains, NY 10650

Texaco Latin America/West Africa
Manager, Human Resources
150 Alhambra Circle
Coral Gables, FL 33134

USX

USX, headquartered in Pittsburgh, Pennsylvania, comprises three major industry segments: energy, steel, and diversified businesses. Its energy segment consists of Marathon Oil Company and its subsidiaries involved in worldwide crude oil and natural gas exploration and production, and Texas Oil & Gas Corp. and its subsidiaries primarily engaged in domestic oil and gas exploration and production. USX's steel segment, known as USS, is the largest domestic integrated steel producer in the United States. It is involved in the production and sale of a wide range of steel mill products as well as ownership and operation of domestic iron ore properties. USX's diversified businesses include multiple business units with operations in foreign manufacturing, engineering and consulting services, domestic transportation, agricultural chemicals, fencing projects, real estate, and mineral resources management. Employment opportunities exist in a range of fields and disciplines.

USX Corporation   tel. 412/433-1121
Suite 727
600 Grant Street
Pittsburgh, PA 15219

BUSINESS-RELATED ORGANIZATIONS

American Electronics Association

The American Electronics Association (AEA) is a 3,000 member group committed to protecting the interests and increasing the competitiveness of the American electronics and technology industry. Based in Washington, D.C., with a staff of 100, AEA also has offices in Tokyo, Brussels, and Beijing. AEA's focus is international—the organization operates on the premise that half of its revenue should come from overseas. It is the vehicle for grassroots action on key industry issues and effective legislative advocacy at all levels of government and serves as a channel for access to important, up-to-the-minute technology business information. AEA also functions as a network for U.S. technology companies, with forums for alliance building, creativity connections, and technology context education.

Ideal candidates for positions with AEA should be fluent in a foreign language and have excellent writing skills. A master's degree in a discipline like political science, international affairs, business, or economics is usually preferred.

American Electronics Association   tel. 202/682-9110
International Trade Affairs   http://www.aeanet.com
1225 I Street, N.W.
Washington, D.C. 20005

American Forest & Paper Association

The American Forest & Paper Association (AF&PA) is the single national trade association of the forest, pulp, paper, paperboard, and wood products industry. AF&PA represents over 400 member companies and related trade associations (whose memberships are in the thousands) that grow, harvest, and process wood and wood fiber; manufacture pulp, paper, and paperboard products from both virgin and recovered fiber; and produce engineered and traditional wood products.

AF&PA's international activities include influencing trade policy at the federal level; monitoring international trade developments; collecting, analyzing, and disseminating statistics on the international forest products trade; and promoting exports of U.S. forest products. AF&PA's international staff members have varied backgrounds, with experience in economics, environment, trade policy, and/or languages.

American Forest & Paper Association   tel. 202/463-2700
Suite 800
1111 19th Street, N.W.
Washington, D.C. 20036

American Iron and Steel Institute

The American Iron and Steel Institute (AISI) is a nonprofit association of North American companies engaged in the iron and steel industry. It comprises 50 producer member countries, including integrated, electric furnace, and reconstituted mills, and more than 100 associate member companies who are suppliers to, or customers of, the industry. Member companies account for more than two-thirds of the raw steel produced in the United States, most of the steel manufactured in Canada, and nearly two-thirds of the flat-rolled steel products in Mexico.

The International Trade section monitors legislative and executive actions in import and export trade in steel, organizes research and symposia on North American and global trade law and steel trade practices, maintains contact with government officials concerned with international trade, makes recommendations for action to the institute's governing bodies, and engages in public advocacy of AISI's positions.

American Iron and Steel Institute   tel. 202/452-7100
Suite 1300
1101 17th Street, N.W.
Washington, D.C. 20036

American Petroleum Institute

The American Petroleum Institute (API), founded in 1919, is the U.S. petroleum industry's primary trade association. Its membership includes more than 300 companies representing a broad cross section of petroleum and allied industries in exploration, production, transportation, refining, and marketing. API provides public policy development, advocacy, research, and technical services in support of its membership.

API is headquartered in Washington, D.C., and has offices in New York City and 33 state capitals east of the Rocky Mountains. In the Southwest, Rocky Mountain area, West Coast, and Alaska API works in conjunction with regional and state oil and natural gas associations. The institute staff consists of approximately 500 professionals with a broad variety of backgrounds.

American Petroleum Institute   tel. 202/682-8000
1220 L Street, N.W.
Washington, D.C. 20005

Council of the Americas

The Council of the Americas, an affiliate of the Americas Society, Inc., is a U.S. business association dedicated to advocacy of the interests of its nearly

200 international corporate members doing business in Latin America. The Council, broadly representative of total U.S. investment in the region, is the private sector vehicle for promoting positive change and future development led by the private sector in the hemisphere. Its various member constituencies include industrial, financial, and service companies. Consensus and viewpoints are communicated to Latin American government officials and U.S. policymakers as well as to the domestic Latin American private sector.

The council has 18 staff members, 10 in New York and 8 in Washington, D.C. Applicants should have undergraduate or graduate degrees in international relations, international business, economics, finance, or related fields. Language capabilities also are encouraged.

Council of the Americas   tel. 212/628-3200
680 Park Avenue
New York, NY 10021

Council of the Americas   tel. 202/639-0724
1310 G Street, N.W.
Washington, D.C. 20005

Council on Competitiveness

The Council on Competitiveness was founded in 1986 to serve as a focal point for leadership efforts aimed at improving the competitive position of the United States in global markets. The council's core agenda is built around four interrelated and interdependent issues: capital formation and investment policies, science and technology, international economics and trade, and human resources. To address public policy issues, the council publishes reports and position statements developed with the assistance of council members, staff, and expert advisers. To promote public awareness, the council publishes a monthly newsletter that chronicles major trends, policies, and people affecting competitiveness; a Competitiveness Index comparing U.S. performance to that of other nations is released annually.

At its peak, the council has 14 staff members. New graduates usually enter at the position of council associate, which is comparable to that of a research assistant. For its council associates, the council seeks master's degree candidates with a concentration in international trade, business, economics, public policy, and/or technology. Work experience in other associations or think tanks specializing in these issues or experience on Capitol Hill is preferred.

Council on Competitiveness   tel. 202/682-4292
Suite 650   fax 202/682-5150
1401 H Street
Washington, D.C. 20005

Electronic Industries Association

The Electronic Industries Association organizes and promotes the interests of about 1,200 companies involved in the manufacture of electronic components, equipment, and systems with consumer, industrial, and government applications. It sponsors trade shows, develops engineering standards, cooperates with the government in ensuring national security objectives, and lobbies on behalf of its members in Congress and the executive branch.

The staff of almost 200 supports the work of an extensive system of special divisions and councils.

Electronic Industries Association
2500 Wilson Boulevard
Arlington, VA 22201

tel. 703/907-7500
e-mail: pmcquire@eia.org

Environmental Export Council

The Environmental Export Council (EEC) is the only nationwide, nonprofit business association helping to forge a partnership between the environmental industry and government to promote the export of U.S. environmental goods and services. Its 140 members principally include both large and small corporations from all sectors of the environmental business market, as well as from several national laboratories, universities, and trade associations. EEC maintains a strong, private sector, business-oriented focus with the aim of increasing its members' export market share. It also conducts study tours, trade and reverse-trade missions, conferences, seminars, and workshops. It keeps member organizations in the forefront of the global industry by providing information on global environmental business opportunities.

EEC has a staff of eight full-time professionals. EEC also uses contractors and provides opportunities for internships. Staff members have a variety of technical backgrounds with some business/marketing experience as well as cross-cultural skills.

Environmental Export Council
Suite 805
1835 K Street, N.W.
Washington, D.C. 20006

tel. 202/8466-6933
fax 202/789-1623

Health Industry Manufacturers Association

The Health Industry Manufacturers Association represents the interests of manufacturers of medical devices. Its members control about half of the world market share. Association members work on regulatory and reimbursement issues. The association works with both the U.S. and foreign governments in the develop of public policy on issues of interest to its members.

Most hiring is done out of the ranks of government employees. Although it favors people with policy degrees and experience, the association is not likely to hire recent graduates unless they have considerable experience in the health-care industry. The hiring process for the association is informal. The qualifications the association looks for in new hires include analytical skills, experience working in health care (especially in reimbursement systems or managed care), a public policy background, health-care economics, and general analytical skills. Member companies occasionally contact the association when looking to fill specific needs—usually these are efforts to fill "hardship" posts. In general, people looking to work overseas have to work in the industry for a period of time.

Health Industry Manufacturers   tel. 202/783-8700
   Association   fax 202/783-8751
1200 G Street, N.W.
Washington, D.C. 20005

National Association of Manufacturers

The National Association of Manufacturers (NAM) is a broad-based national business group exclusively representing manufacturers, advocating a pro-growth, pro-manufacturing policy agenda. The NAM reinforces the legislative and regulatory activities of its member firms, delivering member services through a professional staff of 175 in Washington, D.C., and 10 regional offices across the country. Currently, NAM consists of approximately 13,000 companies and their subsidiaries, more than 80 percent of whom are small manufacturers, representing in excess of 18 million employees. NAM's member firms produce 85 percent of the manufactured goods and services in the United States and represent nearly every sector of the U.S. economy.

Candidates for position with NAM should have a master's degree in a field related to the organization's activity, including business and international affairs. Skills required included good analytical and writing abilities and the ability to work independently.

National Association of   tel. 202/637-3000
   Manufacturers   fax 202/637-3182
1331 Pennsylvania Avenue, N.W.
Suite 1500—North Tower
Washington, D.C. 20004–1790

National Cargo Bureau

The National Cargo Bureau (NCB) is a nationwide, nonprofit membership organization dedicated to the safe stowage, securing, and unloading of cargo on all types of vessels. It formulates recommendations to governmental agencies on safe stowage of dangerous goods, grain and other cargoes and offers low-cost loading inspection surveys. NCB has a long-standing relationship with the U.S. Coast Guard whereby NCB professionals serve as advisors or delegation representatives to the International Maritime Organization on behalf of the United States.

The individuals selected for these duties all have extensive professional backgrounds in the marine industry. NCB rarely recruits for professional and international positions outside the bureau; rather, it relies on its own senior personnel.

National Cargo Bureau   tel. 212/571-5000
30 Vesey Street   fax 212/571-5005
New York, NY 10007

Port Authority of New York & New Jersey

The Port Authority of New York & New Jersey is a public agency whose purpose is to develop and operate transportation, terminals, and other facilities of commerce in the New York-New Jersey port area and to enhance the economic growth of the region. It operates as a financially self-supporting entity; project capital must be raised from revenues produced by its facilities and by borrowing money on its own credit. Among its operations are three airports—John F. Kennedy International, LaGuardia, and Newark International; two vehicular tunnels—Holland and Lincoln; four bridges—George Washington, Bayonne, the Goethals, and the Outerbridge Crossing; a rapid transit rail system—PATH; bus and marine terminals; and the promotion of international trade for the bistate region through the World Trade Center.

Individuals interested in applying for the Management Training Program should have a master's degree in public or business administration, management, or a related field.

The Management Training Program
The Port Authority of NY & NJ
One World Trade Center—44N
New York, NY 10048

U.S.-China Business Council

Established in 1973, the U.S.-China Business Council is a private, nonprofit membership association of about 790 American firms engaged in trade and investment with the People's Republic of China. Its primary objective is the promotion and facilitation of bilateral economic relations, and its activities include general seminars, committee meetings, specialized tailored briefings, and market research. The council publishes a bimonthly magazine, a monthly newsletter and occasional papers.

The Council's present staff of 20 includes professionals with backgrounds in Chinese, East Asian studies, business administration, and government. Opportunities for employment are infrequent, but internships are available.

> The U.S.-China Business Council tel. 202/429-0340
> 1818 N Street, N.W.
> Suite 500
> Washington, D.C. 20036

United States Council for International Business

The United States Council for International Business represents American business positions in the major international economic institutions and before the executive and legislative branches of the U.S. government. Its primary objective is to promote an open system of world trade, finance, and investment. The council is the American affiliate of the International Chambers of Commerce, the Business Industry Advisory Committee (BIAC) to the OECD, and the International Organization of Employers (IOE).

The Council hires entry-level program managers for whom it seeks master's degree recipients, usually in international affairs or international economics. Work experience is desirable, but not always essential, for entry-level managers. Applicants should, however, have a solid background in one or more of the following issue areas with which the Council is concerned: air transportation; arbitration; banking technique and practice; competition law and policy; environment; European Union; financial services; industrial relations; insurance; intellectual property; international information and telecommunications policy; marketing, advertising, and distribution; multinational enterprises and investment; sea transportation; taxation; and trade policy.

> United States Council for tel. 212/354-4480
> International Business
> 1212 Avenue of the Americas
> New York, NY 10036

6

Consulting

MARK BUENING *

The consulting profession continues to thrive and grow as the pace of change in business and government increases. There appears to be no end in sight for technological, economic, and political change. All this ensures the ongoing need and role for consultants to help businesses and governments adapt. Consultants are increasingly being called upon to help solve wide-ranging and complex problems in every area of business or government activity, including (but not limited to) strategy, operations improvement, organizational design, change management, information systems design and implementation, marketing and public relations, performance measurement and management, benefits and compensation planning, balance sheet restructuring, and litigation support.

The consultants' task is to assist their clients in solving problems or seizing advantages—related to business, competition, or technology—when clients need or want to augment their own internal resources. Providing clients with the best, most appropriate advice on the problem or opportunity at hand is of utmost importance. Clients can be domestic or foreign government agencies, international organizations, corporations, or public institutions. Most consulting work is done on a fee basis and consulting success depends in large part upon the client

* Mark Buening, a 1986 graduate of Georgetown University's Master of Science in Foreign Service program and an International Business Diplomacy honors certificate holder, is a Senior Manager in Ernst & Young LLP's National Office in New York. He is part of their National Planning Group, an internal strategic planning group serving the firmwide, industry, functional, and geographic business leaders of this integrated professional services firm. He now focuses on strategic and organizational issues of importance to the Ernst & Young International organization worldwide. Prior to joining Ernst & Young LLP, Mr. Buening was an associate with McKinsey & Company, Inc. in their Cleveland, Ohio, and São Paulo, Brazil, offices. He graduated with honors from DePauw University in 1980 with a B.A. in political science.

receiving value in excess of the consulting fees paid.

Clients look to consultants for an objective viewpoint, specialized knowledge or expertise, and the ability to focus on a problem or opportunity in a way and with a time commitment that the client themselves cannot, given their need to manage the many varied activities of their businesses. Because of experience gained while serving other clients, consultants bring an ever-broader understanding and perspective of potential solutions to each case. Often, they have dealt with the same issues in several organizations and have firsthand knowledge and experience in state-of-the-art approaches and methodologies. A career in consulting is fast-paced, challenging, and varied. Such a career offers the opportunity to see the world and to address important strategic, operational, and organizational issues facing business and government leaders.

The expectation that a consultant will address particular problems or opportunities for their clients has generally meant that consulting work is project based. In most cases, a project team of consultants is assembled to address the particular client problem or opportunity, and consideration of the specific skills and talents of individual consultants are often vital in determining the makeup of the team. Team sizes depend upon the complexity of the issues involved, the scope of the project, and the time allotted for completion. In most large consulting firms, the team includes one or more partners who oversee the client relationship, a project manager who monitors day-to-day project activities, and a few associates or analysts who do data gathering, analysis, and hypothesis testing. In other situations, especially in smaller firms, one consultant may work independently. Even when part of a team, however, consultants often work independently on assigned areas of analysis or research.

Consulting firms exist in a wide variety of sizes and flavors. They range from sole practitioners to organizations of several thousand consultants working worldwide. There are even in-house consulting groups or departments that serve the rest of their own company as clients. Some consulting firms focus solely on providing consulting services; others offer an integrated package of business advisory services including consulting, audit, accounting, tax, and other services. Some focus on particular areas of expertise in certain industry or business activities while others strive to be "one-stop shops" that offer services across a variety of industries and activities. The general consulting classifications are:

- management and strategy consulting (performance improvement);

- information systems consulting; and

- economic development or public policy consulting.

Thus, the nature of consulting advice can cover international business and finance, trade and investment, marketing and promotion, project feasibility and design, acquisition or divestiture planning and implementation, economic analysis and forecasting, public policy, international affairs, process design, information systems design and/or development, and competitive analysis.

Individual consultants can be generalists or specialists, and each category is essential in particular situations. Generalists usually act as diagnosticians or problem-solvers focusing on broad-ranging and integrated management issues. They probe the inner workings of an organization or do external research to define the scope of a problem or opportunity by using a range of analytic tools and frameworks to shape a solution and design an action plan. Most generalist consultants have some in-depth knowledge of a particular industry and/or functional area, but they normally use insights and experiences across companies or industries to address client-specific situations. Specialists, on the other hand, bring a greater degree of technical knowledge of particular industry or function to a project. Specialists supply the details necessary to customize generalist solutions for cases where specific content is important to the implementation of the solution.

Like its client industries, the consulting profession itself is undergoing and reacting to more rapid environmental change than it has experienced in the past. The industry is increasingly competitive as companies maneuver to define their competitive advantage. Older firms are facing new competitors as some firms expand their services from either management, information systems, or development consulting into the other areas. Particularly illustrative of this trend has been the historic movement of computer manufacturers into information systems design and implementation consulting and more recently also into management consulting. Likewise, several management consulting firms have also acquired information systems firms to develop capabilities in that area of the market.

Despite the increased competitiveness and changing consulting landscape, consulting as a whole has experienced impressive growth rates. This is often attributed to the increasing pace of change and the fact that certain consulting services will be important whatever the current state of the business cycle (expansion or recession). In a state of expansion, organizations may need consultants to help identify how to best take advantage of growth opportunities; while in a state of recession, organizations will have an increased need for cost reduction, market protection, and other appropriate advice. Given these trends, most analysts expect continued growth and change for the consulting profession.

The international aspects of and opportunities in consulting are many, particularly in the larger international consulting firms or whenever the client is a global or multinational organization. For example, there are always international aspects and considerations involved in the development of a strategy, operations improvement, or organizational redesign for an international organization, such as a Fortune 500 company. Even smaller companies will often use consultants to help them expand into international markets. In the public sector, the role and geographic breadth of the institution being served will often require a heavy international component to the consulting work. Finally, almost any consulting expertise, however narrowly defined, is applicable to other international organizations in the same industry or in the same situation. In my own case, I have worked on consulting projects for several international corporations where a perspective and understanding of international issues was extremely important and I was also assigned to a six-month manufacturing facility consolidation project in Brazil. In my current position, I also consult my company on issues of international strategy and operations and this work requires international travel and expertise. For the internationally minded consultant, most international consulting firms provide ample opportunities for their consultants to work on projects in foreign offices for a short-term, long-term, or even permanent transfer basis.

The skills required to be a successful consultant include strong analytical capabilities, an ability to work independently and within deadline, problem-solving, teamwork, and outstanding written oral communications. Beyond this, a generalist is hired largely for insight while a specialist is sought for unique knowledge. While most consulting firms have in-house training programs designed to build and hone required skills, most training is done on the job.

In hiring, most major consulting firms seek candidates with advanced degrees in business or other specialty areas. In addition, most consultants hired as specialists have years of specific industry or functional experience. In some cases, more experienced consultants with unique expertise are hired on retainer to fulfill a specific contract within a specific time frame instead of being asked to join the firm full-time. For most foreign assignments, previous international experience and language proficiency usually are required. Some firms offer summer positions to students who are obtaining their advanced degree.

Many large firms also offer candidates with undergraduate degrees positions as business analysts or interns. Most such programs last two years, after which the individual usually pursues a graduate degree. In some cases, the firm will offer financial assistance and/or make an offer of employment after successful completion of graduate studies.

The point of entry into a consulting firm will be influenced by the focus of the firm and the nature of the position. Many firms have active recruiting programs to attract candidates from undergraduate and graduate schools for the full-time associate, business analyst, and internship positions. Alternatively, ask a reference librarian for Dun's or other consulting directories that list, geographically and by specialty, the thousands of consulting firms in the United States and abroad to contact them directly. For experienced hires, many of the major consulting firms retain executive search firms that refer candidates to meet specific personnel needs. For consultants on retainer positions, leads on contracts for specialist consulting needs can be found in the Department of Commerce, the Agency for International Development, and the Department of State have publications that list U.S. government contract awards. For other international contracts, the United Nations and World Bank have similar registries of outstanding contracts pending award. In addition, international and trade periodicals like *The Economist*, and *Oil and Gas Digest* frequently advertise government contract bid solicitations.

It is difficult for most consultants to describe succinctly what a typical day is like. There is a high degree of variability from project to project, and this is one aspect of the job most consultants highly value. There is usually also a high degree of ambiguity and uncertainty. There may be frequent and extensive travel requirements and long hours. There are few careers as stimulating, diverse, demanding, and potentially lucrative as consulting. Many find consulting a rewarding experience, whether it be for a few years or a lifetime. If it is for a few years, the experience gained and the skills developed are well-suited and sought after by many organizations for a variety of positions.

Advisory Board

The Advisory Board Company offers a unique blend of strategic research and consulting to many of the world's largest service corporations. Focusing primarily on the financial services and health-care industries, as well as the human resources departments of Fortune 2000 companies, the Advisory Board serves clients in North America, Europe, and the Pacific such as banks, savings and loans, brokerage houses, insurance companies, hospitals, health systems, and pharmaceutical companies.

Candidates for positions with the Advisory Board should be energetic graduates of top universities, preferably with master's degrees in disciplines such as management, finance, accounting, or international affairs with strong analytical and research abilities. Prior experience in one of the areas of the Advisory Board's areas of expertise is beneficial.

Advisory Board Company   tel. 202/672-5600
The Watergate   http://www.advisory.com
600 New Hampshire Avenue, N.W.
Washington, D.C. 20037

Andreae, Vick & Associates

Andreae, Vick & Associates is a government relations consulting firm that specializes in U.S. foreign policy. The firm monitors and analyzes policy developments in both the executive and legislative branches to keep clients abreast of actions that could impact their international trade and investment objectives. Through its understanding of the decision-making process in Washington, the firm provides strategic counsel on how clients' interests can be most effectively supported in Washington. Andreae, Vick & Associates also assists clients in obtaining financial support from Washington-based trade finance institutions and actively works with U.S. government and non-profit organizations to promote the creation of democratic government systems and political parties in developing countries.

Andreae, Vick & Associates was established in 1990 and currently employs five full-time staff people. Two new staff members were hired in the last year. Associate candidates should have a master's degree in a related field such as international relations, international business, government, or public policy. A strong understanding of the U.S. government and other foreign policy actors is required. Capitol Hill experience is strongly preferred.

Andreae, Vick & Associates   tel. 202/466-5601
Suite 606   fax 202/466-3667
1101 17th Street, N.W.
Washington, D.C. 20036

American Management Systems

American Management Systems (AMS) is a business and information technology firm whose business is to partner with clients to achieve breakthrough performance through the intelligent use of information technology. AMS provides a full range of services: business reengineering, change management, systems integrations, and systems development and implementation. The company, which recently completed its 25th consecutive year of growth, is headquartered in Fairfax, Virginia, and has offices in 41 cities throughout North America and Europe.

AMS helps clients achieve their goals through a combination of business consulting grounded in expertise in their clients' industries, a deep understanding of the power and limitations of information technology, and dedication to meeting commitments.

AMS specializes in selected markets including telecommunications, financial institutions, federal government agencies, state and local governments, educational institutions, insurance, health care, and pharmaceutical companies.

American Management Systems tel. 703/267-8000
4050 Legato Road http://www.amsicc.com
Fairfax, VA 22033–4003

Arthur Andersen/Andersen Consulting

The Arthur Andersen worldwide organization, the fastest growing of the "Big 6" accounting and consulting firms, operates 358 offices in 74 countries and employs more than 72,000 people. More than half of these offices and nearly half of the employees are located abroad. The organization serves more than 40,000 clients worldwide through two business units: Arthur Andersen, which provides audit and business advisory, tax, and specialty consulting services, and Andersen Consulting, which offers total business integration, consulting, and information technology solutions.

Each of the Arthur Andersen business units conducts its own recruitment program almost exclusively through campus interviews and working with university career planning and placement offices. In 1990 the firm recruited at about 550 U.S. colleges and universities and hired about 4,100 new graduates. New hires typically have degrees in accounting, business administration, economics, management, engineering, computer science, and information systems, although some liberal arts majors also are hired.

New professional employees typically spend a good deal of their first few years in training, both in the classroom and as part of client engagement teams. Arthur Andersen places significant emphasis on continuing professional education as evidenced by its $300+ million annual investment in training at its full-time campus in St. Charles, Illinois, and through local offices. Andersen employees receive, on average, more than 150 hours of training a year. As employees progress in the firm they assume more and more supervisory and marketing responsibility, and many opportunities are opened up to transfer to other offices in the United States and abroad.

To obtain more information, interested students should contact any Arthur Andersen office or the following address.

Arthur Andersen   tel. 202/862-3100
1666 K Street, N.W., Suite 500 http://www.arthurandersen.com
Washington, D.C. 20006   http://www.ac.com

A. T. Kearney

A. T. Kearney is an international, multidiscliplined general management consulting firm with offices worldwide. The firm has worked for clients in every industry in more than 90 nations, include both mature and newly market-oriented economies. A. T. Kearney has had a continuous presence in North America since 1926, in Europe since 1964, and in Asia since 1972. The firm's mission is to help its clients gain and sustain competitive advantage, now and into the future. A. T. Kearney strives to excel by delivering tangible results, providing a strong process orientation that focuses on implementation, providing service enhancements, and practicing total quality management.

Recruiting takes place primarily for consulting positions and for business associates. Consultants must have a master's degree, which is usually but not necessarily an M.B.A. Business associates must have an undergraduate degree in such areas as engineering, mathematics, economics, business, or management.

Corporate Recruiting Department   tel. 312/648-0111
A. T. Kearney   fax 312/223-6200
222 West Adams
Chicago, IL 60606

Bain & Company

Founded in 1973, Bain & Company is one of the world's leading strategy consulting firms. Bain is dedicated to helping major international corporations improve bottom-line results and achieve significant increases in the market values of their companies. Bain employs nearly 1,200 people in 23 offices worldwide and serves over 500 clients in 60 countries in North and South America, Western Europe, Eastern Europe, Africa, the Middle East, and the Pacific.

Candidates should be top graduates of leading colleges and universities possessing excellent academic credentials, strong analytical skills, and high levels of motivation.

Bain & Company   tel. 617/572-2000
Two Copley Place   fax 617/572-2427
Boston, MA 02117–2000

Booz-Allen Hamilton

Booz-Allen Hamilton, an international management and technology consulting firm with more than 75 offices around the globe, serves most of the largest industrial and service corporations in the world, the departments and agencies of the U.S. federal government, and major institutions and government bodies across the globe. The firm's diverse assignments range from strategic planning and acquisitions to global markets, energy policy design, and technological advancement. Through its Worldwide Commercial Business and Worldwide Technology Business, Booz-Allen provides services in strategy, systems, operations, and technology to clients in more than 75 countries. The firm combines its integrated service base with specialized expertise in more than 20 industry practices.

Booz-Allen employs more than 2,700 professionals. While most of the Booz-Allen professionals have an M.B.A., a wide variety of academic backgrounds and employment experience exists among its staff, including training in international affairs. While professionals hired from industry enter at all levels, M.B.A.s usually join the firm as associates, and recent college graduates are typically hired as consultants.

University Relations   tel. 212/697-1900
Booz-Allen Hamilton   http://www.bah.com
101 Park Avenue
New York, NY 10178

The Boston Consulting Group

The Boston Consulting Group's (BCG) top reputation in management consulting derives from more than 30 years' experience. The firm's mission is to help clients attain success by guiding, developing, facilitating, and enriching the client's strategy development process. BCG's professional expertise spans more than 50 industries, including consumer and industrial, financial, and nonfinancial (including utilities). The majority of BCG's clients rank among the 500 largest companies in each of its three major locations—North America, Europe, and Asia. In addition, the firm works with a number of public and private medium-sized companies and smaller, growing firms. More than 90 percent of BCG's top clients continue to work with the firm from one year to the next.

Founded in 1963, The Boston Consulting Group now has more than 1,200 consultants based in 36 offices worldwide. A majority of consultants with BCG hold M.B.A.s or other advanced degrees from leading business schools; most have held previous managerial positions in a broad spectrum of private and public sector organizations. Most assignments involve one or more teams of three to six BCG professionals, including one or two officers, a project manager, and several consultants, working with a similar group of client staff. The team incorporates a mix of seniority and skills to balance the capabilities needed for the project. Individual assignments can last anywhere from 2 to 12 months or more, depending on the complexity of the challenges and the client's needs. BCG encourages its consultants outside the United States to spend a portion of their careers in the United States and urges its U.S.-based consultants to do the same abroad.

The Boston Consulting Group	tel. 617/973-1200
Exchange Place	fax 617/973-8049
Boston, MA 02109	

Braxton Associates

Braxton Associates is the international strategy consulting division of Deloitte & Touche LLP, one of the world's largest professional service firms. With 10 offices on five continents, Braxton Associates serves a wide range of clients in consumer and industrial sectors, working collaboratively to identify opportunities, set priorities, create organizational momentum, and achieve marketplace results. Braxton's clients come from a wide range of industry sectors, including consumer products, manufacturing, retailing, telecommunications, health care, high technology, and financial services. Braxton's clients include many of the world's most successful blue chip companies, including half of the Fortune 50. Braxton serves its multinational clients from 10 strategically positioned offices on four continents. The firm calls on Deloitte & Touche's wide range of industry skills and worldwide connections while maintaining its own special character.

Business analysts (BAs) work with seasoned consultants and senior executives from client firms to address crucial strategic issues. Unlike peers at many firms, BAs generally work on only one case at a time, allowing full focus on the industry and issues at hand. In addition to the opportunity to work closely with experienced consultants and top executives from client firms, the BA role also provides a significant opportunity to gain exposure to a variety of industries. Candidates for the BA position should be top students with a demonstrated record of success able to work independently toward deadlines and work in a demanding, team-oriented environment.

Braxton Associates	tel. 617/439-7100
200 State Street	fax 617/439-4827
Boston, MA 02109	http://dttus.com/braxton/
	braxbros.com

Braxton Associates	tel. 212/492-3700
1633 Broadway, 4th floor	fax 212/492-3198
New York, NY 10019	

Chemonics International

Founded in 1975, Chemonics International is an international consulting organization focusing on development issues. Initially conceived to provide technical assistance to underdeveloped countries in agriculture, natural resources, and rural development, the firm is now active in a wide variety of activities, including agribusiness, management information systems, finance and banking, investment promotion, biodiversity, environment and eco-tourism, and health delivery systems management. Chemonics manages many projects funded by international organizations such as USAID, the World Bank, the Asian Development Bank, the African Development Bank, and the Inter-American Development Bank. Chemonics also performs advisory services to foreign governments and to private clients.

Much of Chemonics's recruitment is done through the database of experts it maintains. Most professionals are hired to staff specific projects. To be entered in the database, Chemonics generally requires a graduate degree in a discipline related to the particular project, extensive overseas field experience, and fluency in a foreign language, especially French, Spanish, or Arabic.

Chemonics International	tel. 202/466-5340
2000 M Street, N.W.	
Washington, D.C. 20036	

Coopers & Lybrand

Coopers & Lybrand is an international accounting firm with more than 61,000 people in 640 offices in 107 countries. The firm offers services in accounting and auditing; tax; management consulting; and actuarial, benefits, and compensation consulting.

Candidates for positions in accounting and auditing typically have undergraduate or advanced degrees in business administration, engineering, liberal arts, management information systems (MIS), law, or management. A concentration in accounting at either the graduate or undergraduate level is helpful. Candidates for local, state, federal, or international tax practices typically have a law or other advanced degree such as an M.B.A. or a master's degree in taxation. They also may have an undergraduate accounting degree or transfer from the company's audit staff.

Students with a computer science/MIS background often join the Information Technology (IT) Audit Services Group within the Management Consulting Service (MCS) area. Direct assignment to MCS generally requires an M.B.A. combined with industry experience or a relevant degree in areas such as engineering, MIS, finance, or accounting.

Candidates with a background in mathematics and actuarial science are sought for positions within actuarial and employee benefits services. Employment inquiries should include one's general geographical preference. Overseas assignments are occasionally available.

Director, National Recruiting tel. 212/536-2000
Coopers & Lybrand http://www/colybrand.com
1251 Avenue of the Americas
New York, NY 10020

Deloitte & Touche

Deloitte & Touche is one of the nation's leading professional services firms, providing accounting and auditing, tax, and management consulting services throughout the United States. Deloitte & Touche is part of Deloitte Touche Tohmatsu International, a global leader in professional services with 59,000 people in offices in 126 countries. The firm has the resources, knowledge, and experience to serve its clients, who include nearly 20 percent of the world's large businesses, each with sales or assets in excess of $1 billion, as well as thousands of other national and international enterprises, public institutions, and fast-growing companies worldwide. The Management Consulting practice offers a scope of services ranging from strategy development through implementation of total system solutions. Other practices include Financial Management, Business Process Reengineering, Client Server Systems Integration, Financial and HR Applications Implementation, Process Industries, and a variety of information technology services. In addition, the firm sponsors a number of high-visibility conferences, including the World Economic Forum and the Europe Alliance Conference.

Deloitte & Touche has a substantial number of entry-level and more advanced career openings available each year in all parts of its practices. The experience and qualifications requirements for these openings vary widely.

Deloitte & Touche LLP   tel. 212/489-1600
1633 Broadway   fax 212/489-1687
New York, NY 10019–6754   http://www.dttus.com

Delphi International

Delphi International (DI), a nonprofit, nonpartisan organization, offers comprehensive international exchange and business services to U.S. and foreign clients. DI promotes international cooperation and understanding by offering education and training, exchanges, and observational study programs for U.S. and foreign government agencies, private companies with international business interests, and international development institutions. DI also organizes company visits and internships and awards International Communication Certificates.

Through Delphi International Consulting, DI provides customized management and technical training, cross-cultural and organizational development, and other assistance to those in the global marketplace. Through Delphi Travel Unlimited, DI offers travel services to the international professional exchange and business communities. In new hires, Delphi International looks for experience in international program management and for backgrounds in foreign languages and living abroad.

Delphi International   tel. 202/898-0950
Seventh Floor   tel. 800/826-0196
1090 Vermont Avenue, N.W.
Washington, D.C. 20005

Development Associates

Development Associates is a management and government consulting firm specializing in educational, social, and economic development programs in the United States and overseas. The company's international projects largely focus on the fields of education, nutrition/public health, family planning/population, developmental administration, rural development, and urban/regional planning.

Development Associates, with one regional office in San Francisco and offices abroad in the Dominican Republic, El Salvador, Guatemala, Nicaragua, Panama, the Philippines, and Puerto Rico, can draw on a staff of about 250 active consultants and specialists worldwide. More than 75 percent of their staff speaks one or more foreign languages. New recruits usually possess a technical background (such as economics) with two to five years of overseas experience. Candidates with a bachelor's degree generally apply for research analyst positions; those with advanced degrees are considered for professional slots. There are about 150 people involved on a full-time basis in professional, international capacities. For short-term consultancies, up to 120 additional persons are recruited annually.

Development Associates   tel. 703/276-0677
1730 North Lynn Street   fax 703/276-0432
Arlington, VA 22209   e-mail: devassoc@mcimail.com

Environmental Resources Management

Environmental Resources Management (ERM) is a worldwide environmental, health, and safety consulting firm. In business since 1971, ERM works privately with big companies (primarily in the energy and chemical industries) and, less often, publicly with a wide range of central governments. ERM also works with the European Commission. ERM totals 2,500 professional staff—mainly scientists, engineers, and other technical people—250 of whom are in Europe. The United Kingdom practice focuses more on public policy issues than in the United States, with the exception of a small office in Washington, D.C. Economic analysis of public policy is important; 20 policy people are based in London, 6 in Oxford, and a few in Brussels.

ERM has no formal recruitment process. Candidates should be flexible, and overseas experience and proficiency in local languages in developing countries are helpful. ERM does hire some generalists but looks for solid technical skills. ERM often brings individuals in on a temporary consulting basis; in some cases these arrangements may yield a permanent job.

Environmental Resources Management
8 Cavandish Square
London, W1M OER
UNITED KINGDOM

Ernst & Young

Ernst & Young LLP is the U.S. member firm of Ernst & Young International, a leading international professional services firm dedicated to helping companies identify and capitalize on business opportunities throughout the world. Practice areas include accounting and auditing, tax, management consulting, corporate finance, restructuring and reorganization, capital markets, cash management, valuation, benefits and compensation consulting, and outsourcing services. Ernst & Young has over 680 offices in over 125 countries. The firm's professional expertise is engaged by a broad range of organizations, including multinational corporations, owner-managed companies, governments, and nonprofit institutions operating in both developed economies and emerging markets worldwide. Significant international opportunities exist in all practice areas and are enhanced by international residencies and exchange programs.

The mission of Ernst & Young's Management Consulting practice is to contribute to their clients' long-term success and competitive strength. This is accomplished by helping clients to identify solutions that improve performance, assisting in implementing those solutions, and aiding in managing the subsequent change.

The Management Consulting practice offers both performance improvement and information technology services. The overall objective of the performance improvement (PI) practice is to enhance the performance of all or part of a client's business. Improvements are measured by both marketplace criteria and financial results and against operating benchmarks. PI engagements fall into four categories: strategic management, performance measurement, change management, and process improvement. By combining specific approaches, techniques, tools, benchmarks, and information from their most successful engagements, Ernst & Young consultants bring added value to clients whose challenges in the competitive marketplace continue to grow. PI issues include profitability, globalization, customer focus, quality, time, cost competitiveness, innovation of products/services design and delivery, people and organizational capabilities, and postservice and support.

In addition to recruiting for the U.S. firm, coordination is also provided for Ernst & Young offices in other countries. Management consulting candidates must have strong academic performance, first-rate analytical skills, excellent interpersonal abilities, a willingness to travel, and a career goal of helping companies make and implement better business decisions. Management consulting graduate degree candidates should have at least two years of work experience after their bachelor's degree. Preferred are undergraduate degrees in engineering, accounting, finance, information systems, or other strong quantitative or business degrees.

Management Consulting   tel. 410/783-3725
    Director of Campus Recruiting
Ernst & Young LLP
1 North Charles Street
Baltimore, MD 21201

Ernst & Young LLP   tel. 212/773-3000
787 Seventh Avenue   http://www.ey.com/us
New York, NY 10019

European Public Policy Advisers Group

European Public Policy Advisers Group (EPPA) is a leading independent, pan-European public affairs company, offering strategic advice to multinational corporations, medium-sized businesses, trade associations, nonprofit organizations, and national and regional bodies interested in enhancing their respective interests in Europe. EPPA has 14 offices throughout the European Union and beyond, including Central and Eastern Europe.

EPPA's highly qualified, multilingual, and multinational team of 40 consultants is drawn from a variety of vocational backgrounds, including business, economics, law, politics, and public administration. EPPA's consultants work in purpose-built teams drawn from across its national and EU offices to meet specific client needs. EPPA's fields of activity cover all major policy areas, including international trade.

European Public Policy
   Advisers Group
142–144 Avenue de Tervuren
1150 Brussels
BELGIUM

tel. (+32) (2) 735 8230
fax (+32) (2) 735 4412
e-mail: hamilton@marketing.
EPPA.com

The Futures Group

The Futures Group (FUTURES) is a strategic planning, marketing, and management consulting organization that helps clients make critical decisions in the face of future uncertainty. FUTURES's commercial sector portfolio focuses on strategic planning, market analysis, and forecasting in the private sector. The company's private sector client list includes many Fortune 500 companies in a variety of fields, including pharmaceuticals, financial services, communications, transportation, and energy. FUTURES applies many of its private sector skills and techniques to promote international development, its major public policy focus. FUTURES is committed to building sustainable development through the transfer of technology to local experts and institutions through the development of appropriate project designs. FUTURES's public sector portfolio includes contracts in health, population, environment, AIDS, food assistance, and women in development. Clients include USAID, the World Bank, the World Population Society, the African Development Bank, the World Health Organization, and the American Association for Retired Persons. FUTURES has permanent offices in the United States in Glastonbury, Connecticut, Washington, D.C., and Chapel Hill, N.C., and abroad in Cairo, Accra, Nairobi, Rabat, Jakarta, and Mexico City. FUTURES opens additional offices when necessary to implement project activities.

FUTURES currently has a full-time staff of more than 120 employees representing a wide range of disciplines in the natural and social sciences. FUTURES's core staff work with hundreds of consultants employed on a part-time, consulting associate, or retainer basis. Areas of technical expertise include marketing, economics and econometrics, demographics, market research and analysis, advertising, business analysis, statistics, evaluation, communication, training, and cost-benefit analysis. Staff are proficient in all of the major world languages, as well as myriad regional and local languages and dialects.

> The Futures Group
> Suite 1000
> 1050 17th Street, NW
> Washington, D.C. 20036

Gartner Group

Gartner Group is the world's leading independent advisor to business professionals making information technology (IT) decisions. With more than 195 analysts in 53 locations worldwide serving 12,500 individual clients representing 4,150 organizations, the Gartner Group advisory services cover the full range of IT products and services, from applying technology to businesses, to following major trends and directions in IT, to managing and measuring IT infrastructures.

The Research Associate Training Program brings inexperienced yet talented individuals into the organization for 24 months of rotational training in various areas of the company, such as multimedia, personal computing, marketing, and high-performance computing. Candidates should have a record of high academic achievement and possess attributes that enable them to assimilate and analyze information quickly, communicate clearly and concisely, and thrive in the Gartner Group culture.

> Recruiter
> Gartner Group
> 56 Top Gallant Road
> Stamford, CT 06904
>
> tel. 203/975-6672
> fax 203/975-6555
> http://www.gartner.com

Hill and Knowlton

Hill and Knowlton is the world's leading international public relations consultancy with an international network of about 50 offices and some 1,200 employees. In addition, the consultancy works with more than 70 associate companies, many of whom have been Hill and Knowlton's partners for more than 10 years. Hill and Knowlton is part of the WPP Group, the world's largest marketing services company.

Candidates come to Hill and Knowlton from a wide variety of academic and professional backgrounds.

Hill and Knowlton   tel. 212/885-0300
466 Lexington Avenue   fax 212/885-0570
New York, NY 10017

J.E. Austin Associates

J.E. Austin Associates is a strategic management consulting firm specializing in advising the top management of private companies and government agencies in developing countries to implement major strategic changes. J.E. Austin Associates works with private companies, the U.S. Agency for International Development, the World Bank, the Inter-American Development ment Bank, the United Nations, the OECD, and other bilateral donors on private investment and private sector development projects.

Candidates for positions with J.E. Austin Associates should possess an advanced degree with a strong background in economics and/or international relations and excellent analytical, writing, and research skills.

J.E. Austin Associates   tel. 703/841-9841
Suite 306   fax 703/841-9847
1911 North Fort Myer Drive
Arlington, VA 22209

KPMG Peat Marwick

KPMG Peat Marwick is the U.S. member firm of Klynveld Peat Marwick Goerdeler (KPMG), an international professional services firm. KPMG operates more than 1,100 offices in 134 countries. It plays integral roles in nearly every type of financial transaction from financing and corporate restructuring to advice on transactions in securities, real estate, and other assets. The firm's accounting services are especially well-known in the commercial banking, construction and real estate, health care, higher education, high technology, insurance, manufacturing, merchandising (retail and wholesale trade), state and local government, thrifts, and transportation fields. A full range of tax and consulting services are offered as well.

While the majority of overseas positions are filled by local nationals, each overseas office has a number of non-nationals who provide specific skills and knowledge. The firm's international transfer program provides two-year transfer opportunities for professionals with at least three years of experience. The firm's busy season exchange program for audit and tax professionals provide four-month transfer opportunities for professionals with a minimum of two years' experience.

In addition to recruiting on behalf of the U.S. firm, coordination is also provided between foreign nationals studying in the United States and KPMG offices in their home countries. Because of the large influx of Japanese and Korean investments in the United States, KPMG is particularly interested in receiving resumes from nationals of those countries studying accounting, taxation, or other business-related disciplines.

University Relations Manager—GU/IA
KPMG Peat Marwick LLP
Three Chestnut Ridge Road
Montvale, NJ 07645–0435

Kurt Salmon Associates

Kurt Salmon Associates (KSA) is the world's largest management consulting firm specializing in the retail and consumer products industries. Its clients are leading manufacturers and retailers of a wide range of personal, home, and recreational consumer products, such as food, clothing, footwear, housewares, home improvement products, sporting goods, and magazines. KSA provides clients with services in strategic planning, marketing strategy, organization development, business process reengineering, supply chain strategy, Efficient Consumer Response readiness assessment, sourcing strategy, manufacturing operations improvement, productivity enhancement, facilities planning and design, logistics strategy, and information systems.

KSA's international offices are located in the United Kingdom, Germany, Italy, Switzerland, and Hong Kong. The firm has more than 425 professionals worldwide and plans to hire approximately 100 new consultants in the next year. All international offices conduct their recruiting of new consultants independent of the U.S. offices. Individuals with engineering degrees and fluency in both English and Spanish will be considered for manufacturing operations and sourcing assignments in the U.S. and/or Latin America.

Director of Recruiting   tel. 609/452-8700
ATTN: Department 125   fax 609/452-8090
Kurt Salmon Associates
103 Carnegie Center, Suite 205
Princeton, NJ 08540

Louis Berger International

Louis Berger International offers consulting services in engineering, economics, environment, agriculture, architecture, and planning to commercial, industrial, governmental, and private clients in the United States and abroad. Among its many divisions is the Center for Rural Development, which assists clients in planning and implementing integrated rural development projects and programs. *Berger World* is a quarterly publication focusing on a topic of current concern to the company.

Louis Berger employs more than 1,000 people in about 70 different countries. New recruits generally have a minimum of five years' experience in their respective fields, fluency in a foreign language (preferably Spanish or French), and an advanced degree. A few entry-level positions, however, are available each year in the United States to graduates. The majority of recent staff additions have come from the fields of civil engineering, economics, environmental engineering, urban and regional planning, transportation planning, and architecture.

Personnel Director   tel. 201/678-1960
Louis Berger International
100 Halsted Street
P.O. Box 270
East Orange, NJ   07019–0270

McKinsey & Company

McKinsey & Company is an international management consulting firm. Founded in 1926, the firm has maintained continued growth and currently has 65 offices in 35 countries, with more than 3,200 consultants. The firm serves organizations in most industrial nations and in some developing countries on matters of strategy, organization, and operations. The firm's mission is twofold: to help clients make substantial and lasting improvements in their performance and to build a firm able to attract, develop, excite, and retain exceptional people. McKinsey takes an integrated, general management approach to client work, addressing business problems and challenges from the broad perspective of senior management. The firm also devotes considerable time and effort to *pro bono* work for nonprofit organizations worldwide.

Associates join teams of two to five other professionals (partners, associates, business analysts, or specialists) and play an active role in all aspects of the study: fact-gathering, analysis, development of recommendations, and implementation. The associates are normally involved in presentations to and discussions with top management and are expected to raise issues and express opinions throughout a project. The associates must work effectively with client teams, adhere to strict professional standards, put the client's interests and needs first, and be prepared for a demanding lifestyle.

McKinsey & Company seeks candidates with outstanding intellect, leadership, work experience, initiative, and proven ability to work effectively with people at all levels in an organization. The firm looks for individuals with strong records of academic and managerial/professional achievement who have the capacity for continuous development. While most associates hold an M.B.A., others have graduate degrees in economics, engineering, law, medicine, public policy, and other professional fields. New hires usually have three to five years of work experience. Candidates must have citizenship or permanent working papers for the country to which they apply and meet language requirements.

McKinsey & Company   http://www.mckinsey.com
Seventh Floor
1101 Pennsylvania Avenue, N.W.
Washington, D.C. 20004

Mercer Management Consulting

One of the leading international management consulting firms, Mercer Management Consulting helps major corporations around the world address their most critical strategic challenges. Mercer works in partnership with its clients to identify and seize the most attractive opportunities for accelerated growth and strengthened prosperity. Mercer takes an integrated view of the challenges of strategic change and is committed to growing rapidly throughout the world to solidify its leadership position. Recently, Mercer has enhanced its presence in Europe, the Pacific Rim, and Canada and plans to continue its expansion worldwide aggressively over the next five years. While continuing to place its greatest emphasis on promoting and rewarding individual initiative.

Mercer has more than 1,000 consultants working in 13 offices worldwide. The firm interviews and hires candidates primarily from leading graduate schools in North America and Europe. Although many individuals are hired directly from graduate school, virtually all have had from 3 to 10 years of full-time work experience. The firm is a member of Mercer Consulting Group, the global consulting organization of Marsh and McLennan Companies.

Mercer Management Consulting   tel. 202/778-7400
2300 N Street, N.W.   http://www.mercermc.com
Washington, D.C. 20037

Monitor Company

Monitor Company, one of the world's preeminent consulting firms, is headquartered in Cambridge, Massachusetts, and has offices in Amsterdam, Frankfurt, Hong Kong, Johannesburg, London, Los Angeles, Madrid, Milan, New York, Paris, Seoul, Tokyo, and Toronto. Founded in 1982, it has grown from three employees to a global firm of over 500. Monitor has relationships with one-third of the Fortune 500 companies—and many of their international equivalents—in such diverse industries as electronics, telecommunications, aerospace, energy, retailing, and financial services.

Monitor's practice focuses on strategy consulting. Most projects fall into one of the following area: competitive strategies for business units in individual industries; corporate strategies for diversified companies; strategies for entering or acquiring new businesses; and organizational redesign to support continuous strategic action. Monitor increasingly consults with state and national governments about their competitive prospects.

Monitor recognizes that a person's background or educational degree—years on Wall Street or an M.B.A., for example—does not translate into consulting success, so there are no distinctions of title at Monitor. Apart from the form's directors, all members of the consulting staff have the same title: consultant. Candidates should be creative, analytical, and teamwork oriented. Requirements include a superior academic record, a willingness to take initiative and assume responsibility, and a desire to learn.

Recruiting Coordinator
Monitor Company
25 First Street
Cambridge, MA 02141

Nathan Associates

Founded in 1946, Nathan Associates is an experienced and recognized consulting firm in economic policy analysis in the United States and abroad. Nathan Associates has provided technical assistance and advisory services in more than 70 developing countries worldwide. These services have been funded by a variety of international agencies, including the World Bank; the regional development banks of Africa, Asia, South and Central America, and the Caribbean; the United Nations Fund for Development; the UN's Food and Agriculture Organization; and the United States Agency for International Development. Some of Nathan Associates' activities have been financed by the countries themselves or by individuals seeking objective evaluations for their investments.

The permanent staff, including Nathan teams in resident service overseas, represents a wide range of specialties. These include macroeconomic analysis and policy formulation; agricultural economics; urban and infrastructure development; national and regional development planning; taxation and municipal finance; industrial development; management information systems; sectoral studies in agriculture, transportation, and energy; and institutional development.

Overseas and professional staff is supported by persons with graduate level degrees in economics, business administration, or public policy. The firm looks for quantitative skills and work experience in a developing country as well as fluency in a second language.

Nathan Associates, Inc.   tel. 703/516-7700
2 Colonial Place
2101 Wilson Boulevard
Suite 1200
Arlington, VA 22201

PA Consulting Group

PA Consulting Group's business is technology and management consulting. The firm works with clients in business and industry to manage complex change and to create business advantage through technology, with a strong concentration on the development of next-generation products, processes, and technologies. The firm also consults in strategic market planning, technology, due diligence for mergers and acquisitions, and the management of complex technology-driven projects.

London-based PA Consulting Group employs approximately 1,700 professional consultants in more than 80 offices located in 20 countries. The North American headquarters, located just outside Princeton, New Jersey, also house one of the firm's two research and development laboratories; the other is in Cambridge, England. In the United States, PA's efforts are primarily directed at the health care/pharmaceutical, information/telecommunications, and automotive/consumer products sectors. At the international level, PA also consults to the food, retail, aerospace, media, and financial industries as well as government agencies.

PA typically recruits M.B.A. graduates with three to five years' experience in their field.

PA Consulting Group   tel. 609/426-4700
279 Princeton Road
Hightstown, NJ 08520

Planning & Development Collaborative International

Planning & Development Collaborative international, or PADCO as it is more commonly known, is an international collaborative formed to provide governments and private clients in Africa, Asia, Latin America, and the Near East with research, planning, training, and management services for urban and rural development. All professional employees have at least a bachelor's degree, speak more than one language, and have had previous experience in their respective fields. PADCO, however, will allow work with such voluntary agencies as the Peace Corps, as well as living in a developing nation, to satisfy the previous work experience requirement. PADCO typically hires two to four interns a year; five to seven junior or senior level technical positions are filled annually. The academic fields represented by the 20 to 25 professional employees include economics, finance, regional development, engineering, architecture, and urban planning.

PADCO	tel. 202/337-2326
Suite 170	fax 202/944-2350
1025 Thomas Jefferson Street, N.W.	e-mail: 518-0899@mcimail.com
Washington, D.C. 20007–5209	

The Planning Technologies Group

The Planning Technologies Group (PTG) is a specialized strategy consulting firm committed to improving long-term performance by creatively using technology to improve corporate strategies and decision-making. PTG specializes in the areas of strategy consulting, mergers and acquisitions, information systems, decision sciences, and executive environment. PTG combines traditional strategy consulting, with extensive experience from such firms as McKinsey, BCG, and Bain, with cutting edge technology tools to effect change in the client organization. The firm offers an unusual opportunity for associates to develop those capabilities—consulting skills as well as technology—while working with clients. PTG also provides a collegial atmosphere where associates work directly with company partners and principals. Associates will be exposed to a broad range of business problems in multiple industries, including pharmaceutical, high-tech, entertainment, health care, and financial services.

Associate consultants at PTG analyze and model dynamics of client business and/or industry, work with client teams to design and support client and internal software/hardware applications (including network administration), and develop strategy and investment recommendations. Applicants for the associate consultant position should possess strong initiative, high energy, a sense of humor, and a team-oriented attitude. Strong quantitative and analytical skills are required; familiarity with spreadsheets and modeling is a plus. A familiarity with general software/hardware basics is desired, as well as an aptitude for and interest in desktop technology applications. Network applications capabilities are also useful.

Recruiting Coordinator	tel. 617/861-0999
The Planning Technologies Group	fax 617/861-1099
92 Hayden Avenue	
Lexington, MA 02173	

Pragma Corporation

The Pragma Corporation is an international development consulting firm, with a network of offices in the United States, Asia, Eastern Europe, and the Newly Independent States. Headquartered in metropolitan Washington, D.C., Pragma also manages projects in Africa, Latin America, the Caribbean, and the Middle East. With a large international staff of multidisciplinary and multilingual professionals, Pragma addresses the particular needs of clients in capital markets, agriculture and agribusiness, training, municipal development and decentralization, export promotion, environment, health and nutrition, and energy.

Pragma has designed and implemented close to 400 projects for diverse clients in more than 65 countries and continues to expand into new areas of international business and technical assistance. The firm works with U.S. and international private firms; development institutions, including the Agency for International Development, the World Bank, the Asian Development Bank, and the Inter-American Development Bank; nongovernmental and private voluntary organizations; and academic institutions.

Pragma staff and consultants come from or have resided in the various regions of the world where Pragma does its work: Asia, the Middle East, Africa, the Caribbean, Latin America, and the United States.

The Pragma Corporation	tel. 703/237-9303
116 East Broad Street	fax 703/237-9326
Falls Church, VA 22046	e-mail: pragma1@ix.netcom.com

Price Waterhouse

Price Waterhouse, one of the world's largest accounting firms, maintains 300 offices in more than 80 countries. The firm's extensive overseas activities provide excellent opportunities for those seeking careers in international affairs.

Most people begin their careers at Price Waterhouse in auditing. New hires in this division spend three weeks in training where basic auditing techniques are presented through case studies drawn from actual client situations. Computer applications also are introduced. Training then continues on the job, where employees join an engagement team as staff accountants. Job assignments usually focus on audits of cash, accounts payable, payrolls, fixed assets, and prepaid and accrued items. After a year with the firm, auditors take a 40-hour intermediate auditing course as well as courses in advanced audit testing techniques, audit program development, income tax concepts, and writing skills. College graduates frequently are engaged directly for the Management Consulting Services Department that advises clients in financial and operational planning and management, electronic data processing, and information resource management. Those who have had no prior business experience, however, are encouraged to gain initial experience on the audit staff.

Most of Price Waterhouse's tax staff are transfers from the auditing division, although the firm does accept some individuals as direct hires. All new tax professionals receive training in the firm's policies and procedures and standards of systems development. For five days, new hires work on case studies and spend some time building communications skills. They also receive technical training in computer programming, design and documentation, modeling, and installation.

Like most accounting firms, Price Waterhouse requires all professional staff members to take a minimum of 20 hours of classes per year and 120 hours over a three-year period. When employees reach the senior accountant level, usually after two to three years with the firm, they can apply for an overseas assignment. Service tours of up to two-and-a-half years are offered in Britain, Europe, South America, Australia, and the Far East. At the end of the tour, participants may remain in the foreign office or return to the United States.

Many Price Waterhouse offices operate internship programs open to those demonstrating both technical ability and maturity. Standards for selection are high since interns are considered for permanent positions. Interns work on the same types of assignments given to new staff members in conjunction with more experienced professionals. Interested individuals should inquire at a specific Price Waterhouse office about program availability.

Director, National Recruitment   tel. 212/489-8900
Price Waterhouse   http://www.pw.com
1251 Avenue of the Americas
New York, NY 10020

SRI International

Founded in 1946 as the Stanford Research Institute, SRI is one of the world's largest and most respected research and consulting organizations. The institute is an independent, nonprofit corporation serving business and government clients worldwide. The International Policy Center (IPC) is the professional resource within SRI charged with providing top-quality research, analysis, and strategic planning on international economic policy issues, finance, agricultural policies and investment, and export and tourism promotion. IPC staff have conducted in-country assignments in over 80 countries throughout the world. In recent years, IPC clients have included, among others, international banks and insurance companies; multinational business and manufacturing corporations; U.S. government agencies such as the departments of State, Treasury, and Commerce and the Agency for International Development; national governments and central banks; and multilateral financial institutions such as the World Bank and the Asian Development Bank.

SRI has a staff of 3,500 professionals located in 24 offices worldwide, including Europe, East and Southeast Asia, and the Middle East. Professionals at SRI have a wide range of academic backgrounds and experience.

SRI International   tel. 703/524-2053
1611 North Kent Street
Arlington, VA 22209

Towers Perrin

Towers Perrin, one of the world's largest multifaceted management consulting organizations, has more than 70 offices in 66 cities across 19 countries in the United States, Canada, Europe, Asia, Australia, and Latin America. Among its 8,000 clients are some of the largest and most prestigious companies in the world, including more than 70 percent of the Fortune 1000, more than 50 percent of the Canadian Financial Post Top 500 industrial companies, and three-quarters of both the 100 largest life insurance companies and the top 100 property/casualty insurers. Towers Perrin serves its clients how and where their needs dictate, assembling teams of consultants and specialists from different offices to work anywhere in the world. Towers Perrin has three divisions: Towers Perrin Management Consulting, Tillinghast (insurance consulting), and Towers Perrin Reinsurance (reinsurance brokers and intermediaries). The firm has total staff of 5,000, with a professional staff of 2,500.

General management consulting at Towers Perrin is divided into two core areas: strategic human resource and organizational counsel, including human resource strategy, organizational restructuring and work process reengineering, and business strategy counsel at the corporate, business unit and functional levels. Towers Perrin recruits consultants in two ways. Those joining early in their careers generally come directly from an M.B.A. program after having had a few years of work experience, while those joining in mid-career usually have five to ten years of experience in addition to an M.B.A. or other relevant advanced degree. Beginning consultants spend their first two to three years gaining experience on a wide variety of assignments and being trained in the firm's core service areas. After this period of generalization, they must affiliate with one of the core service areas or with an industry group. Associates generally have college degrees and some business experience; they usually work for the firm for two to three years before returning to graduate school or taking positions elsewhere. Those with the appropriate experience and education may be promoted directly to consultant. Associates work in the firm's core service areas and are assigned to client engagements as soon as possible.

Towers Perrin   tel. 914/745-4000
100 Summit Lake Drive   fax 914/745-4100
Valhalla, NY 10595

TransCentury

TransCentury is an international and domestic consulting group made up of the TransCentury Corporation, the New TransCentury Foundation, and Transcentury Development Associates. In its more than 20-year existence, TransCentury has focused on U.S. youth and community development projects as well as international development, investment, and procurement. TransCentury has worked in all 50 U.S. states and in more than 80 countries worldwide in areas such as women in development, agriculture, procurement, labor and migration studies, refugee resettlement, nutrition and health, and numerous other related fields. TransCentury recently has been involved in an enterprise development project in Senegal and procurement of medical supplies in Egypt and Morocco.

In recent years, TransCentury has had between 25 and 100 openings in international positions. These positions require at least three years' overseas work experience, an advanced degree, and knowledge of a foreign language. TransCentury looks for individuals with academic or work experience in such fields as engineering, economics, international development, public health, nutrition, regional planning, environmental sciences, business administration, and education. Assignments are either in the United States or on projects overseas.

New TransCentury Foundation   tel. 351-5500
Suite 1017
1901 North Fort Myer Drive
Arlington, VA 22209

7

Media

In the summer of 1993, at a workshop on computer-assisted journalism, a former White House press aide called print reporters a derisive name: dinosaurs. We reporters didn't take it well. We fired off an e-mail missive that set him straight: "Dinosaurs are extinct, but we still bite." We knew, though, that he was partly right. We ink-stained wretches were just too proud to admit it. The print medium, particularly newspapers, is slowly heading toward extinction—a trend that aspiring reporters should keep in mind as they plan their careers.

It is clear that there will be fewer newspapers published in the future. There has already been a major reduction, from 1,772 dailies in 1950 to 1,538 last year. Those that survive are likely to downsize their staffs. Some of the titans in the field, including Knight-Ridder and Times-Mirror, are currently wielding the axe. But journalism won't disappear. It will simply reemerge in new—that is, electronic—forms. When Microsoft's Bill Gates was asked recently how the print media will be affected by the current rush on-line, he said reporters will still be needed. How, exactly, is unclear. This grim snapshot is not meant to confuse or discourage prospective Woodwards and Bernsteins. Though morale in many newsrooms is low now because of the uncertainty about the future, journalism is still a lot of fun. How many other jobs pay their workers to witness and write about history as it happens, whether it's a fire down the street or U.S. troop deployment in Bosnia?

---

* Wendy Koch, a 1986 graduate of Georgetown University's joint Bachelor/Master of Science in Foreign Service program, *magna cum laude*, covers foreign affairs for Hearst newspapers. Her stories are carried on the New York Times newswire. Previously, she covered Congress for the Gannett News Service and Small Newspaper Group, and European politics and economics for the Voice of America. Ms. Koch has won national and regional awards and serves as secretary of the National Press Club and a term member of the Council on Foreign Relations.

Journalism will always be an exciting field, one that can even be intellectually rewarding at times. It does have two notable drawbacks: long hours and generally low pay. A recent survey of new college graduates indicated that journalists earn the worst average starting salaries, about $20,154. A reporter's pay improves with experience, enabling most to earn at least $30,000. Yet, unless reporters move into management, only those who work at major news organizations can expect to earn more than $60,000 a year—relatively few can break six figures. And yet there is no end of young people eager to enter journalism.

To be a star in this competitive field, you have to be not only talented but also consistent and focused. In short, you need a game plan. Consider the advice the father of a friend once offered him: "Be so good they can't say 'no'." In print media, this means mastering a few skills and getting experience:

1. *Writing.* You can never be a good enough writer. Even if you decide later to leave journalism for another field, you'll always benefit from a stellar style, because so few people have it. The journalists who stand out in a crowd are those who are not only clever reporters but also enticing storytellers. There is appallingly little good writing in newspapers and magazines today. Missing too often is the old-fashioned but simple art of storytelling.

   If you want to brush up on your writing, the time-tested guide, *The Elements of Style* by Strunk and White remains a winner. Also good is *The Art of Feature Writing* by Bill Blundell, the former writing coach of *The Wall Street Journal*—arguably the best-written newspaper in America. On almost any day, the three anchor stories on the *Journal*'s front page serve as fine examples of news writing.

   Young reporters distinguish themselves by showing creativity and originality. The best of them write with attitude or perspective and develop their own narrative voice.

2. *Computer know-how.* While mastering the computer may seem a prosaic skill, it may help your entry into the emerging realms of journalism, many of which will be electronic based. Learn how to dazzle old or even middle-aged editors, many fearful of the new gadgetry, with your ability to surf the Net, download databases, and analyze the figures—all in an instant.

3. *Clips.* You need writing samples. The best bet is writing for your college newspaper. If you're studying abroad, write a colorful piece and offer it to your local newspaper. If you lack clips but still want to apply for a reporting job, send along essays you wrote in college. But don't send anything too long or academic. Journalism is the real world and most editors aren't interested in theoretical polemics.

4. *Internships.* While most journalism internships don't pay, some do, so look hard. Many newspapers offer summer internships that give students a chance to write. Gannett, the largest U.S. chain of dailies, has such a program. Even major newspapers like *The Washington Post* and *The New York Times* have paid training opportunities. The spots are so few and the competition so fierce that you can't count on landing one. You should, however, check them out.

   In my own case, internships were the key. During the school year I interned for PBS, working as a researcher on the *Mac-Neil-Lehrer Newshour*. Later, I interned for Voice of America (VOA), where I wrote stories for broadcast. That internship evolved into a full-time reporting job after graduation.

5. *Persistence.* Since journalism is a competitive industry, you have to pursue jobs with a laser-like intensity. Pick a few newspapers or other publications that you want to work for. Be realistic, though—don't expect to start at *The New York Times*, even if you're brilliantly talented and have wonderful connections, though both would help. Once you've pared your list, send a short, snappy letter to the news editor. Follow up with phone calls, asking for an informational interview or feedback. Don't give up after one try. Bob Woodward landed a job at *The Washington Post* only after he relentlessly hounded Ben Bradlee, who got so tired of the calls he finally hired him!

   Avoid the scattershot approach, the 100-letter mass mailing. You won't have the time to follow up each letter with a call, and personal contact is crucial. Answering ads is a reasonable tactic but don't expect great results. Scores of people respond to a decent ad, many of which are posted only to comply with personnel rules. Often, the company already has a candidate in mind. Besides, the best jobs are rarely posted. So target and pursue— and be prepared to wait. Sometimes luck is what counts most.

As for the debate over whether journalism school is necessary, the jury is still out. Many editors, especially those who attended journalism schools themselves, tend to prefer hiring first-timers who have been schooled in the trade—for good reason. Journalism students are generally given more opportunity to write concise pieces than others who study liberal arts. Yet the journalism school advantage applies mostly, if not entirely, for beginners. Once you've proved that you can write on deadline, and that it isn't all that difficult, your academic training becomes less and less relevant. In fact, after you've had real world experience, training other than in journalism gives you a broader, more impressive knowledge base.

My international politics major, for example, helped me land the VOA internship and consequently my first radio job. Switching to print was difficult, however, because although I wrote for the college newspaper and had some journalism experience, I had relatively few newspaper clips. I remember one craggy newspaper editor looking at my resume, which included study abroad and foreign languages, staring me in the eye and asking "Would you really be happy covering the school board?" I have now paid those initial dues and find that my international background is a benefit, not a hindrance. It certainly helps in my current job.

If you want to go abroad as a foreign correspondent or freelance writer, a few possibilities exist. The traditional route is to work your way up the career ladder, starting as a reporter for a local newspaper and then moving on to a bigger daily. Once you've proven yourself at a major metropolitan paper, and that typically means years of covering school boards and local politics, you may be tapped for a post abroad—if the paper has one.

The shorter but dicier and less perk-filled route is to head out as a freelancer. But wait until you have at least some professional experience, because you're more likely to know what editors want and how to succeed. Pick a region you know well, especially if you can speak the language, or a region that's not well covered but is of interest to American readers. I have a friend who speaks Russian fluently. After two years as a daily newspaper reporter, he headed to Moscow, landing part-time jobs as a stringer for both the Associated Press and *Newsweek*. He did an outstanding job and eventually was offered a full-time correspondent's job. He was only 29 at the time.

Be aware, though, that neither the freelance route nor the traditional one is easy. With the newspaper world in a downsizing mode, foreign coverage is shrinking. Foreign bureaus, particularly in Japan, can be very expensive and only the largest newspaper companies choose to pay the tab. Knowing a difficult foreign language like Chinese, Japanese, Russian, or Arabic may help set you apart from your competitors. But you'll still need to demonstrate solid journalism skills. A good foreign correspondent will sometimes receive language training, paid by their company, prior to a posting.

One last piece of advice: Be flexible and willing to try other media. Currently, new opportunities are emerging as companies like Microsoft try to establish on-line newsrooms. While many of these attempts may falter, they are growing, and they are worth considering. News companies will increasingly merge their print ventures with on-line and/or broadcast operations to provide the most up-to-the-minute reports. The journalist who can master this more complicated multimedia world, switching from one medium to another, should thrive. He or she need not fear the fate of the dinosaur.

8

Nonprofit and Education Organizations

CASIMIR YOST *

New York Times columnist Thomas Friedman makes the distinction between "making a point and making a difference." His is the distinction between opinion and action. More than ever before, those who want to make a difference are turning to careers in the nonprofit or nongovernmental organization (NGO) sector.

Cutbacks in U.S. government hiring and the significant expansion in recent years of the numbers and programs of nonprofit organizations have helped make this sector more professionally attractive. The collapse or erosion of communist and other authoritarian regimes over the last decade has contributed to the exponential growth of civil societies in countries all over the world. These authoritarian regimes have been replaced not just by more democratic government structures but by private organizations and associations intent on acting or affecting action on issues ranging from poverty to the environment to political rights. At the same time, internal political strife from Africa to Central Asia has expanded the need for not only traditional private relief efforts but also for organizations capable of assisting in building postcrisis democratic institutions and processes.

U.S. organizations, together with those of other countries, have grown to meet these new challenges. NGOs are frequently capable of responding quickly to emerging challenges, are not overly bureaucratic, and are not seen as direct instruments of American foreign pol-

---

* Casimir Yost, a 1973 graduate of Georgetown University's Master of Science in Foreign Service program, is the Director of the Institute for the Study of Diplomacy at Georgetown University. Before assuming his present position, he directed the World Affairs Council of Northern California, a nonpartisan public education organization, for four years and worked for the Asia Foundation. A graduate of Hamilton College, Mr. Yost has also served as a Congressional Fellow on Capitol Hill and worked for Citibank in a variety of posts worldwide.

icy—a plus in some countries. Funding for their efforts has come from individuals, corporations, and private foundations together with the U.S. government. The government has increasingly seen benefit in privatizing its efforts, working through nongovernmental organizations to address priority concerns. The U.S. Agency for International Development (USAID) has channeled significant resources through nongovernmental organizations.

In the United States and around the world, people are discovering that they can pursue professional careers in the nonprofit, nongovernmental sector. They can be careers filled with the satisfaction of working close to problems, with the opportunity to see concrete improvements in the lives of people. At the same time, financial rewards are typically modest and career paths can be unpredictable. It is not unusual for an individual working in the NGO sector to work in a number of organizations over the course of a professional career.

A nonprofit organization's success, by definition, cannot be measured in revenue terms. Despite the absence of the profit motive, nongovernmental organizations must be run professionally. Precisely because budgets are generally tight, efficiencies must be high. Accountability to outside boards of directors and funders must also be high.

These organizations have eclectic staff requirements. Many seek generalists with strong internationalist credentials including academic training, foreign language competence, and prior international experience. Oral and written communication skills are essential. NGOs are looking for people capable of managing budgets and staffs. A premium is placed on individuals able to work as part of a team. Ken Wollack, president of the National Democratic Institute, says "we want people who can move from thinking in the first person singular to thinking in the third person plural." They must be culturally sensitive and flexible. They should be able to build and utilize networks of individuals. They must, above all, be committed to the particular mission of the organization.

Beyond these generalist requirements, every organization has staff needs specific to its particular mission—for some, election specialists; for others, health experts. Many NGOs utilize fixed-term contracts to staff their needs for specialists. All require trained staff to run the financial, personnel, and other needs of a modern organization, including in-house fund-raising capabilities. When an organization's staff is small, the requirements for everyone to fill more than one role can be high.

The growing field of nonprofit/nongovernmental organizations can be grouped under several categories, with some organizations filling more than one role:

- *Humanitarian assistance groups* provide or facilitate the provision of emergency and/or long-term refugee relief, economic development, health care, and other aid to people in need around the world.

- *Exchange organizations* foster the movement of peoples and ideas through cultural and educational exchange programs.

- *Education organizations* disseminate information to members and/or the broader public.

- *Foundations* provide funding for international programs and activities.

- *Political change* organizations assist nations and peoples to broaden citizen participation in political processes.

- *Think tanks* and *research organizations* expand knowledge and disseminate information through research, discussion, and publications.

The nonprofit, nongovernmental sector will offer exciting employment opportunities in the future for people who wish to work directly on problems. As the government and corporations downsize, this sector will remain vibrant, albeit dependent on fund-raising from a variety of sources. Careers in the nongovernmental sector can be exciting, though tinged with the uncertainties inherent in unstable funding and uncertain career paths.

Academy for Educational Development

Founded in 1961, the Academy for Educational Development (AED) is an independent, nonprofit service organization committed to addressing human development needs in the United States and throughout the world. AED is currently active in many areas, including improving the functioning of educational institutions and systems, increasing access to education through applications of modern communication technology; and expanding the sphere of education to health, nutrition, family planning, environment, and development information. AED's activities are supported through grants and contracts from international organizations, U.S. and foreign government agencies, foundations, and private contributions. Under these contracts and grants, the academy operates programs in collaboration with policy leaders, nongovernmental and community-based organizations, businesses, governmental agencies, international multilateral and bilateral funders, and schools, colleges, and universities. In partnership with its clients, AED seeks to meet today's social, economic, and environmental challenges through education and human resource development; to apply state-of-the-art education, training, research and technology, management, behavioral analysis, and social marketing techniques to solve problems; and to improve knowledge and skills as the most effective means for stimulating growth, reducing poverty, and promoting democratic and humanitarian ideals.

When AED hires they look for excellent organizational and analytical skills, several years international or domestic experience related to AED's programs, good language ability, solid research and writing skills, and a master's degree in international relations, education, journalism, communications, or similar fields.

> The Academy for Educational   tel. 202/884-8700
>   Development
> 1255 23rd Street, N.W.
> Washington, D.C. 20037

African-American Institute

The African-American Institute (AAI) seeks to foster development in Africa and to promote mutual understanding between Africans and Americans. AAI sponsors development programs that promote policy dialogue and broaden and sustain a constituency for Africa in the United States through conferences, seminars, and numerous information exchange forums. The organization encourages democratization, trade and investment, and women's political participation. AAI has provided over 3,000 African students with scholarships to pursue graduate education in the United States as well as development training for career professionals in the United States, Africa, Canada, and the Caribbean.

AAI is headquartered in New York City and maintains offices in Washington, D.C., Nigeria, and South Africa. It has field offices in 22 countries, each of which is staffed by African nationals. Its U.S.-based staff numbers 90. Professional positions require master's degrees and some entry-level professionals are hired immediately following school. Travel in or knowledge of Africa is helpful if not required for certain positions. Internships are helpful.

> African-American Institute   tel. 212/949-5666
> 833 United Nations Plaza
> New York, NY 10017

> African-American Institute   tel. 202/667-5636
> 1625 Massachusetts Avenue, N.W.
> Washington, D.C. 20036

Africare

Africare, a private, nonprofit organization, has worked since 1971 to improve the quality of life in rural areas of African countries. The organization promotes development of environmental and water resources, agricultural training, and health care. Dual purposes have been served: education of Americans on conditions in Africa and generation of American commitment to the development process. The organization provides financial and technical assistance to development projects and trains African villagers in everyday maintenance and management.

Africare has about 90 employees, half in its Washington, D.C., headquarters and half in the field. About 40 positions are filled each year. A wide variety of applicants are sought depending on the positions open. Many applicants have graduate degrees and prior overseas work experience. About half of the applicants speak a foreign language.

Africare   tel. 202/462-3614
440 R Street, N.W.
Washington, D.C. 20001

AIESEC

The International Association of Students in Economics and Business Management, better known as AIESEC-U.S. and an affiliate of AIESEC International, operates an international management training program for students and recent graduates educated in a variety of business-related fields. It is the largest nonprofit, student-run organization in the world. More than 500 universities in over 75 countries around the world operate local chapters. Since 1948, more than 110,000 students, 11,000 of them Americans, have taken part in this exchange program. In addition, AIESEC organizes conferences, seminars, and tours for students and members of the business and academic communities. AIESEC works to create opportunities for exposure and interaction between young people of different cultures and nations and complement students' theoretical education with practical business experience. It also seeks to make business more socially aware and responsive to the needs of society in the international arena and to recruit, screen, and provide business with topflight international student talent.

Applications to AIESEC-U.S. are limited to students who belong to one of the U.S. local chapters at institutions of higher learning. Overseas traineeships typically last from 2 to 18 months.

AIESEC-United States, Inc.   tel. 212/979-7400
841 Broadway, Suite 600   http://www.aiesec.org/us/
New York, NY 10003   index.html

American Chemical Society

The American Chemical Society (ACS) is a nonprofit scientific and educational association with a membership of more than 150,000 professional chemists and chemical engineers in industry, government, and academia. ACS has more than 10,000 foreign members representing every nation. It publishes 29 periodicals.

The society fills about 39 positions annually to maintain its professional staff of 1,900. The Office of International Activities employs three professionals and is primarily involved in administering exchange projects between chemists in the United States and abroad. It also acts as a liaison between ACS and similar organizations outside the United States in sponsoring joint international meetings, investigations of alleged violations of scientific freedom, and the promotion of scientific exchanges.

American Chemical Society   tel. 202/872-4600
1155 Sixteenth Street, N.W.   http://www.acs.org
Washington, D.C. 20036

American Friends Service Committee

The American Friends Service Committee (AFSC) was founded in 1917 by the Society of Friends (Quakers) as a public service alternative for conscientious objectors. Its major purpose today is the alleviation of human suffering and injustice in various parts of the world. AFSC maintains nine regional offices in the United States and is involved in programs in more than 20 countries worldwide. Programs are designed to promote self-help and improve basic living standards and social well-being emphasizing integrated community development, construction, agricultural production, cooperative organization, public health services, and refugee assistance. The committee sponsors international conferences on world affairs and publishes a variety of reports on its projects at home and abroad.

The majority of positions at AFSC, either in the United States or abroad, requires persons with a substantial amount of experience in such areas as community development, community organization, self-help projects, communications, and administration. There are very few entry-level positions.

American Friends Service Committee
1501 Cherry Street
Philadelphia, PA 19102–1479

American Society of Association Executives

With more than 23,000 members, the American Society of Association Executives (ASAE) is the leading organization in the field of association management. The membership includes people who manage trade associations, individual membership societies, voluntary organizations, and other not-for-profit associations. ASAE's international section is designed to keep the society's domestic members current on international activities that affect associations and to promote the exchange of ideas and information among colleagues around the world. The section publishes *International News*, a bimonthly newsletter designed to keep members up-to-date on the latest international issues, with articles on overcoming cultural differences to marketing membership and services globally.

The international staff is very small. Interested people should have a knowledge of international activities in associations as well as experience working with overseas counterparts and designing education programs.

American Society of Association   tel. 202/626-2723
   Executives
1575 I Street, N.W.
Washington, D.C. 20005

American Society of International Law

The American Society of International Law (ASIL) is a 4,000-member association committed to the study and use of law in international affairs. As a nonpartisan institution, it provides a forum for an exchange of views among its members from over 100 countries. It publishes books, periodicals and occasional papers, and sponsors research on a broad range of topics in current international law. Outreach to the public on general issues of international law is a major goal of the society. ASIL co-sponsors the Philip C. Jessup International Law Moot Court Competition.

ASIL has a staff of about 20 people, 5 or 6 of whom are in professional-level positions filled by highly qualified individuals with experience in international law. The ASIL internship program enables young professionals to acquire practical experience in international law research and outreach activities.

The American Society of   tel. 202/939-6000
   International Law   e-mail: hdean@asil1.mhs.
2223 Massachusetts Avenue, N.W.   compuserve.com
Washington, D.C. 20008–2864

ARTICLE 19—The International Centre Against Censorship

ARTICLE 19, the International Centre Against Censorship, is a human rights organization concerned with protecting the basic right to free expression and combating censorship. Established in 1986, the organization's name derives from the 19th article of the Universal Declaration of Human Rights, which specifically protects freedom of expression. ARTICLE 19 lobbies to change laws that infringe on international human rights law, to prevent restrictive legislation from becoming law, and on behalf of individuals imprisoned for having expressed their views peacefully. ARTICLE 19 also publishes a series of texts on freedom of speech issues.

ARTICLE 19 employs a professional staff of 15, most of whom have a regional or country-specific and/or human rights law background. In addition, the organization takes on up to four interns a year and any number of volunteers. The campaigning role of ARTICLE 19 is due to be expanded in the coming years, and individuals with a background in political strategy and media relations will be required. ARTICLE 19 makes use of consultancy services for specialist projects, which currently include satellite television, press laws in South and Southeast Asia, and monitoring the independent media in Central and Eastern Europe. The organization's legal office is located in Washington, D.C.

ARTICLE 19   e-mail: article19@gn.apc.org
Lancaster House
33 Islington High Street
London N1 9LH
UNITED KINGDOM

American Baptist Churches in the USA

An evangelical denomination founded in 1814, American Baptist Churches in the USA, through its Board of International Ministries, provides a variety of services designated to help meet basic human needs in developing countries. Assistance is extended in community development, food production, public health and medicine, family planning, social welfare, and disaster relief. The overseas mission programs of the Board of International Ministries utilize approximately $13.5 million and employ about 100 persons in development-related positions. New hires are expected to have at least a master's level academic background plus some professional experience.

American Baptist Churches   tel. 610/768-2200
   in the USA   fax 610/768-2088
Board of International Ministries
P.O. Box 851
Valley Forge, PA 19482–0851

American Political Science Association

The American Political Science Association (APSA), with more than 13,000 members, is the major professional organization in the United States for those engaged in the study of politics. Its members, 10 percent of whom resides abroad, are primarily political scientists doing research and teaching at American colleges and universities. One-fourth of its members pursue careers outside academia in government, research organizations, consulting firms, and private enterprise.

APSA sponsors research, reviews current materials, and provides other services to facilitate teaching and professional development. The association publishes two quarterly journals, *The American Political Science Review* and *PS*. It also operates a personnel service that provides information on available political science positions. APSA administers the Congressional Fellowship Program, a professional-level internship program that places political scientists on congressional staffs.

APSA has a staff of 22, primarily editors and administrators with experience in the discipline.

American Political Science Association   tel. 202/483-2512
1527 New Hampshire Avenue, N.W.   e-mail: apsa@apsa.com
Washington, D.C. 20036–1290

AMIDEAST

The American-Mideast Educational and Training Service, better known as AMIDEAST, was founded in 1951 as a private, nonprofit organization dedicated to improving understanding between Americans and the peoples of the Arab world through education, information, and development programs. Services include educational advising and testing for Arab students and institutions interested in U.S. educational opportunities (mainly through field offices overseas); education and training program administration (mainly in Washington, D.C.); more than 60 programs for a variety of government, corporate, and institutional sponsors of Arab students; English-language programs for the general public and corporate and government agency clients in Bahrain, Egypt, Kuwait, Lebanon, Tunisia, and Yemen; public outreach services in the form of publications and videotapes to support educational exchanges and materials to improve teaching about the Arab world in American secondary schools and colleges; technical assistance to support institution-building in the Arab world, with an emphasis on educational institutions, public administration, judiciary bodies, legislatures, and nongovernmental organizations.

Headquartered in Washington, D.C., AMIDEAST has a network of field offices in Bahrain, Egypt, Jordan, Kuwait, Lebanon, Morocco, Syria, Tunisia, the West Bank/Gaza, and the Yemen Arab Republic. There are 202 staff positions worldwide. Of these, 96 are professional positions in Washington, D.C.; the other 106 professional positions are filled overseas. There are about 10 professional openings a year at AMIDEAST's headquarters. Candidates for employment at headquarters should be U.S. citizens or legal residents of the United States and have at least a bachelor's degree, including some U.S. academic experience. Previous cross-cultural management experience, counseling, or related subjects and foreign language skills are preferred. Positions overseas are mostly filled by local professionals.

America-Mideast Educational   tel. 202/776-9600
   Training Services
AMIDEAST
1730 M Street, N.W., Suite 1100
Washington, D.C. 20036–4505

Amnesty International

Amnesty International is a Nobel Peace Prize winning organization dedicated to the defense of human rights throughout the world. It maintains a global network of affiliated volunteer organizations and counts more than 700,000 members and supporters in more than 150 countries. It mounts letter-writing and publicity campaigns, attempts to secure the release of political prisoners, tries to ensure humane treatment of all prisoners, and works to abolish torture and executions.

The organization's headquarters are in London, where researchers write reports based on visits to countries and interviews with government authorities, current and former prisoners, and local people. Offices are maintained in over 50 countries.

Amnesty International USA has its headquarters in New York where it employs about 50 people. An additional 60 people work in six regional offices and the legislative office in Washington, D.C. A handful of positions are filled annually in the United States. In new employees, the organization usually seeks people with degrees, but for most jobs there are no specialization requirements. Experience in other nonprofit organizations is useful but not required, as is experience in human rights volunteer work.

Amnesty International   tel. 212/807-8400
322 Eighth Avenue
New York, NY 10001

Office of Government Affairs   tel. 202/544-0200
Amnesty International
304 Pennsylvania Avenue, N.E.
Washington, D.C. 20003

Ashoka: Innovators for the Public

Ashoka: Innovators for the Public is an international organization that identifies experts in their fields who have innovative, entrepreneurial ideas in the areas of health, education, women's issues, human rights, or the environment. Based on submitted proposals or business plans, Ashoka grants these individuals fellowships to pay for the implementation of their plans in foreign countries. Ashoka accepts no government funding; a portion of its funding is generated through the membership fees of businesses that are linked with the organization's fellows. Ashoka has representatives in over 30 countries in Asia, Africa, Eastern Europe, and Latin America.

Requirements for candidates for the project manager position include a master's degree, fluency in a foreign language, and experience in marketing and development. Ashoka often looks to graduates of international affairs programs to fill these positions. Project managers are stationed abroad and are charged with overseeing the development of initiatives in foreign countries. They monitor a country's political climate and serve as a point of contact for local fellows.

Ashoka: Innovators for the Public   tel. 703/527-8300
1700 North Moore Street
Arlington, VA 22209

Asia Foundation

The Asia Foundation is a private, nonprofit organization founded in 1954. It provides small grants to indigenous institutions and organizations in Asia working toward the development of more open and just societies through projects that contribute to constructive social change, stable national development, and equitable economic growth in the region. The foundation's primary fields of interest are law and public administration, communications and libraries, rural and community development, Asian regional cooperation, and Asian-American exchange. Through its Books for Asia Program, the foundation has sent more than 35 million American books and journals to libraries, schools, and institutions in Asia and the Pacific islands.

The foundation maintains 12 field offices in Asia. Total professional staff numbers about 50 in the San Francisco headquarters and 20 Americans overseas. An advanced degree in Asian studies, international relations, or a similar field and work experience in foreign affairs, public service, or an educational organization is required for most professional positions. Five to eight professional positions are filled annually.

The Asia Foundation   tel. 415/982-4640
P.O. Box 193223
465 California Street
San Francisco, CA 94119–3223

Asia Society

The Asia Society seeks to strengthen communication between the countries of Asia and the United States and contribute to a greater understanding of Asia and its inhabitants. It promotes Asian arts and humanities and encourages the examination of current economic, political, and cultural issues in Asian society. The Asia Society administers the Asia House Gallery and assists Asian performing musicians touring the United States. Other activities of the society include meetings and study groups of American and Asian scholars to consider contemporary policy issues. The society publishes the bimonthly journal *Asia*, newsletters, occasional papers, and various Asian art reviews.

A staff of more than 90 people keeps the society functioning. Professionals generally have at least a master's degree in international affairs or Asian studies and a foreign language (preferably Asian) is sometimes required. If work experience is required, it usually involves travel or living experience in a specific area related to the position.

The Asia Society   tel. 212/288-6400
725 Park Avenue
New York, NY 10021

CARE

CARE, the Cooperative for American Relief Everywhere, is a federation of agencies interested in assisting the poor of the world to become self-supporting through organizing and utilizing the resources at their command. Programs focus on providing for basic human needs in primary health care, population and family planning, small economic activity development, nutrition, agriculture and natural resources, education, and effective community organization. CARE maintains programs in more than 41 countries that provide supplementary food and nutrition education; furnish materials and know-how to help villagers build clinics, water systems, and farm-to-market roads; help villagers improve agricultural methods; train public health officials; and provide swift emergency relief to disaster victims, among many other types of interventions.

International personnel overseas number 250 and fall into two categories: contract personnel and regular (career) personnel. New employees are hired on a one- or two-year standard contract that may be renewed or changed to career status upon successful completion. Positions may be of an administrative or technical nature. Requirements include a master's degree, at least three years' previous overseas experience, experience in a related field (e.g., nutrition, public health, construction, water resources, administration) and speaking ability in a foreign language—usually Spanish or French. Emphasis on cultural sensitivity is stressed. There are about 50 openings per year.

CARE
Attn: International Employment
151 Ellis Street
Atlanta, GA 30303–2439

The Carter Center

The Carter Center is a nonprofit, nongovernment organization devoted to advancing peace and human rights worldwide. Founded by former U.S. President Jimmy Carter in 1982, it is an independently governed part of Emory University in Atlanta, Georgia. More than 250 staff members implement projects in democracy and development, global health, and urban revitalization in about 130 countries. Areas of specialty include human rights, conflict resolution, disease eradication, African governance, global development, Latin American and Caribbean affairs, democratization and election monitoring, food production in developing nations, tobacco control, and the environment.

Staff are primarily located in the center's Atlanta offices; however, field offices are occasionally established, such as those in Guyana and Liberia. Programs are directed by resident experts, many of whom hold academic appointments at Emory University. Program directors have intense, specialized preparation in their specialties. Strong academic background, experience addressing real-world problems, foreign language, and strong communication skills are desired. In the global health programs, many staff have medical or public health training. In addition, staff work in fund-raising, administration, public information, and conferencing.

The Carter Center   http://www.emory.edu/
One Copenhill   CARTER_CENTER
Atlanta, GA 30084

Catholic Relief Services

Catholic Relief Services (CRS) is the relief and development agency of the U.S. Catholic Church. It was established in 1943 to assist people displaced because of war. CRS now funds programs of assistance, both relief and development, in 76 countries. In 42 of those there is resident staff and, in 34 assistance is directed to local project holders. With an annual budget of more than $300 million, CRS is one of the largest private voluntary organizations in the world.

CRS is continuously seeking to help the poorest, most disadvantaged people in the world with assistance that fosters their self-reliance. Its programs emphasize disaster and emergency relief, mother-child health-care, small enterprise development, aid to farmers, and assistance to refugees. All CRS programs seek to build local capacity and enable communities to formulate solutions to their problems.

Each year, CRS usually has about 20 position openings for overseas or headquarters (Baltimore). These can range from short-term to long-term contract positions. Candidates for positions at CRS should generally have a master's degree along with speaking ability in French or Spanish, and previous relief or development experience in a developing country. In addition, CRS has about 14 intern positions for one-year assignments overseas. This intern program focuses on postgraduate applicants with facility in another language (usually French or Spanish). Experience in the developing world is a plus.

Department of Human Resources   tel. 410/625-2220
Catholic Relief Services
209 West Fayette Street
Baltimore, MD 21201–3402

CDS International

CDS International (CDS) is committed to the advancement of international understanding on an individual and organizational basis. It offers opportunities to gain professional or technical experience abroad, enabling individuals to strengthen their marketability while developing an appreciation of different ways of life and work. Participating individuals benefit from practical training and foreign language instruction. In the long-term these acquired skills translate into a more adaptable and competitive work force for businesses, organizations, and communities.

CDS offers long- and short-term work/study and educational programs, as well as study tours for particular interest groups. CDS administers the following programs: the Congress-Bundestag Youth Exchange for Young Professionals, career training, 6-month internship, German Ministry of Labor (BMA) Internship, Robert Bosch Foundation Fellowship, Corporate Fellowship, United Nations Industrial Development Organization (UNIDO) Fellowship, as well as managing the project "Workforce Solutions for America's Future."

CDS International   tel. 212/760-1400
330 Seventh Avenue, 19th Floor   fax 212/268-1288
New York, NY 10001–5010

The Citizens Network for Foreign Affairs

The Citizens Network for Foreign Affairs (CNFA) is a nonprofit organization dedicated to stimulating international growth and development in the emerging economies of the world—particularly in the Newly Independent States (NIS) of the Former Soviet Union. CNFA works with companies, entrepreneurs, farm groups, business alliances, and other groups to create lasting and effective opportunities in international markets. CNFA's approach to international development encompasses food systems restructuring, the expansion of nongovernmental groups in emerging economies, and the involvement of the U.S. private sector in international development.

CNFA's headquarters are in Washington, D.C., with field offices in Moscow and Krasnodar, Russia; Kiev, Ukraine; and Bishkek, Kyrgyzstan. CNFA has operated since 1986. Among its flagship programs are the Food Systems Restructuring Program, through which CNFA coordinates joint ventures between U.S. agribusinesses and Russian and Ukrainian private businesses with funding from the U.S. Agency for International Development; the agribusiness volunteer program, which arranges for volunteer exchange visits between U.S. agribusiness professionals and their counterparts in the NIS; and the Central Asian Partnership Program, which sets up information and volunteer exchanges between agriculture organizations in Central Asia and similar groups in the U.S.

Last year CNFA hired for 15 positions in the U.S. and overseas. Applicants should have at least a bachelor's degree in international relations or a related field as well as some language expertise (especially Russian or Ukrainian) and/or an agriculture background.

The Citizens Network for   tel. 202/296-3920
   Foreign Affairs   e-mail: demass@cnfa.mhs.
Suite 900   compuserve.com
1111 19th Street, N.W.
Washington, D.C. 20036

Civic Education Project

Founded by American graduate students from Harvard and Yale, the Civic Education Project (CEP) is a not-for-profit organization dedicated to assisting in the revitalization of the social sciences and strengthening the foundations upon which democracy can survive throughout Eastern Europe and the states of the former Soviet Union. CEP accomplishes this goal by developing partnerships with universities and institutions of higher education throughout the region.

Through its Visiting Lecturer Program, CEP places more than 125 highly trained Western scholars in teaching and development positions each year. These lecturers not only teach in the classroom, but engage in a wide variety of outreach and project development activities designed to assist universities in their efforts to revise their curriculum; build strong departmental and university libraries; develop teaching materials in local languages; organize faculty retraining seminars; sponsor academic conferences on topical issues; and create networks through which scholars and government officials can interact and exchange ideas. Program requirements are a master's degree, or preferably a Ph.D., in art history, economics, history, international relations, law, political science, public administration, or sociology; previous teaching experience; and fluency in English.

The Civic Education Project
P.O. Box 205445
New Haven, CT 06520–5445

tel. 203/781-0263
fax 203/781-0265
e-mail: CEP@minerva.cis.yale.edu
http://www.cis.yale.edu/~cep/
cep.html

Council for International Exchange of Scholars

The Council for International Exchange of Scholars (CIES) facilitates international exchange in higher education. Under contract with the United States Information Agency, it cooperates in the administration of the Fulbright scholar program. The council announces the availability of Fulbright awards for university lecturing and advanced research and is responsible for the preliminary review and nomination of candidates for these awards. For foreign scholars coming to the United States, CIES assists in arranging academic affiliations at U.S. universities and provides support services while the scholars are in the United States. Since 1947, CIES has aided in the exchange of more than 25,000 U.S. scholars and 28,000 scholars from abroad.

The council, which has a staff of 80 people including 30 professionals, is affiliated with the American Council on Education.

Council for International Exchange
   of Scholars
Suite M–500
3007 Tilden Street, N.W.
Washington, D.C. 20008

tel. 202/686-4000

Council on International Educational Exchange

The Council on International Educational Exchange, known as Council and often referred to as CIEE, is a nonprofit, nongovernmental organization dedicated to helping people gain understanding, acquire knowledge, and develop skills for living in a globally interdependent and culturally diverse world. Founded in 1947, Council has developed a wide variety of programs and services for students and teachers at secondary through university levels and related constituencies. With 700 professionals in 30 countries working to deliver diverse programs and services, Council has become one of the world's leading operators of international exchange programs and related services. Today, Council operates in six broad business areas: college and university programs, secondary school programs, English language development, work exchanges, voluntary service, and travel services. Regional administrative services are located in North America (New York), Europe (Paris), and Asia (Tokyo).

Council frequently has openings for administrative clerical support staff. Entry-level applicants with excellent organizational and communication skills, foreign language ability, and study or work experience abroad are preferred. Travel opportunities are sometimes available. Council often employs college students for seasonal or short-term jobs. Students able to begin in February or March and continue through August or September are preferred. Most positions are in the student services, work exchanges, and travel divisions; duties range from selling charter flights and student travel products, to processing program applications and handling information requests. Second languages, overseas experience, and office skills are viewed positively.

Council on International Educational   tel. 212/661-1414
   Exchange
Personnel Department
205 East 42nd Street
New York, NY 10017

Cuban American National Foundation

The Cuban American National Foundation is an independent, nonprofit institution devoted to the gathering and dissemination of data about economic, political, and social issues of the Cuban people, both on the island and in exile. The organization supports the concept of a free and democratic Cuba. The foundation maintains a data bank and a research group. Specialized reports are published occasionally and distributed to government officials; members of Congress; journalists; labor, religious, and academic leaders; and the international community. Offices are maintained in

Washington, D.C.; Miami, Florida; San Juan, Puerto Rico; and Los Angeles, California.

The Washington office employs approximately five people, with entry-level openings once or twice per year. Qualities sought in applicants are knowledge of U.S. foreign policy and Latin American issues and good research and writing skills. Proficiency in Spanish also is desired.

Applicants should send a resume, cover letter, and a short writing sample to:

Executive Director   tel. 202/265-2822
The Cuban American National
   Foundation
Suite 505
1000 Thomas Jefferson Street, N.W.
Washington, D.C. 20007

Ford Foundation

The Ford Foundation is the largest foundation in the United States. It aims to advance public welfare by identifying and contributing to the solution of problems of national and international importance. It makes grants primarily to institutions for experimental, demonstration, and development efforts that are likely to produce significant advances within the field of interest. The major portion of the foundation's international budget is devoted to programs in developing countries. These programs include urban poverty, rural poverty and resources, human rights and social justice, governance and public policy, education and culture, international affairs, and reproductive health and population.

The Ford Foundation has assets of $7 billion and expends more than $285 million annually in program activities. The foundation's staff in the international affairs program office numbers 21 and there are 91 people employed in the foundation's programs on Africa, the Middle East, Asia, and Latin America.

The Ford Foundation   tel. 212/573-5000
320 East 43rd Street
New York, NY 10017

German Marshall Fund of the United States

The German Marshall Fund of the United States (GMF) was established as an independent American foundation by a gift from the Federal Republic of Germany. The gift was made in 1972, and renewed in 1985, as a memorial to the

Marshall Plan, the American aid program that helped Europe rebuild after World War II.

Underlying the gift was the belief that by making full use of their interdependence, the United States and the nations of Europe could continue to contribute to world peace and economic growth. The gift was extraordinarily generous in three ways. First, it involved a great deal of money—almost 250 million Deutsche marks (DM), or about $160 million. Second, it mandated a focus on relations between the United States and all of Europe, not just Germany. Third, it was unconditional. Fund decisions are made by a U.S. board of trustees.

Since its inception, the fund's mission has been to increase understanding, promote collaboration, and stimulate exchanges of practical information between the United States and Europe. Since 1989, the GMF has developed programs to assist the emerging democracies of Central and Eastern Europe to work toward political, economic, and environmental reform. Because of the importance of U.S.-German relations, many GMF grants focus on Germany. The fund's office in Berlin assists work with leaders and activists in the new German states. A German advisory board supports grant making in Germany.

Total professional staff number about 30—24 in the Washington, D.C. office, 5 in the Berlin office, and 1 in Paris. A bachelor's degree in international relations or a related field and work experience in foreign affairs, public policy, or nonprofit is required or preferred for most positions. Three to five positions are filled annually.

The German Marshall Fund   tel. 202/745-3950
   of the United States
11 Dupont Circle, N.W., Suite 750
Washington, D.C. 20036

Helen Keller International

Helen Keller International, founded in 1915, is the major U.S. private voluntary agency devoted to fighting blindness overseas. Its present work takes place entirely in developing countries. The agency offers technical assistance to foreign governments that wish to integrate eye care into community-level health care and into a medical referral system. The emphasis is on prevention of nutritional blindness and trachoma and on restoration of sight through cataract surgery. Programs in rehabilitation of the rural blind and education for blind children are offered to serve those whose vision is irretrievably lost.

Helen Keller International works with a small permanent staff at its New York headquarters and hires country representatives on a contractual basis. Members of the program staff include public health professionals, persons with backgrounds in special education, physicians, and administrators with overseas experience. There are 17 professional positions covering the New York and in-country offices. Two individuals were hired last year in the international and program offices. Resumes are reviewed and kept on file. Backgrounds sought are M.P.H., Ph.D., or overseas experience in third world project or program management.

Helen Keller International   tel. 212/943-0890
90 Washington Street
New York, NY 10006

Human Rights Watch

Since its founding in 1978, Human Rights Watch has grown to become the largest and most influential U.S.-based organization seeking to promote human rights worldwide. Human Rights Watch is known for its impartial and reliable human rights reporting, its innovative and high-profile advocacy campaigns, and its success in affecting the policy of the United States and other influential governments toward abusive regimes. Human Rights Watch conducts regular, systematic investigations of human rights abuses in approximately 70 countries around the world. It addresses the human rights practices of governments of all political stripes, geopolitical alignments, and ethnic and religious affiliations. In internal wars it documents violations by both governments and rebel groups. It is an independent, nongovernmental organization supported by contributions from private individuals and foundations worldwide; it accepts no government funds, directly or indirectly.

Headquartered in New York, Human Rights Watch maintains offices in Washington, D.C., Los Angeles, London, Brussels, Moscow, Dushanbe, Hong Kong, and Rio de Janiero. There are five regional divisions covering Africa, the Americas, Asia, the Middle East, and the signatories of the Helsinki accords. In addition, there are five collaborative projects on arms transfers, children's rights, free expression, prison conditions, and women's rights. With a staff of over 100 worldwide, there are approximately 20 opening each year. Candidates for associate positions must have a bachelor's degree, preferably in international relations; researchers should have a master's, law, or other advanced degree. Applicants should have a working knowledge of human rights issues; foreign language skills are desirable.

Human Rights Watch   tel. 212/972-8400
485 Fifth Avenue   e-mail: hrwnyc@hrw.org
New York, NY 10017

Institute of International Education

The Institute of International Education (IIE) develops and administers programs of international educational and cultural exchange and technical assistance under renegotiable contracts with governments, international organizations, corporations, foundations, colleges, and universities in the United States and abroad. Services to students, technicians, and specialists from more than 100 countries are provided at the New York headquarters; the regional offices located in Chicago, Denver, Houston, and San Francisco; a regional and program office in Washington, D.C.; and overseas locations in Hong Kong, Jakarta, Mexico City, and Bangkok. IIE also administers international management services to agricultural research institutes and provides procurement services on behalf of certain sponsors.

In addition, through general support, the institute conducts counseling and information services, issues publications, assists international programs in the performing and visual arts, and conducts conferences, seminars, and other special projects that provide assistance to individuals, colleges, universities, and other organizations on matters of international education and cultural exchange.

Human Resources   tel. 212/984-5324
Institute of International Education
809 United Nations Plaza
New York, NY 10017

InterAction
(American Council for Voluntary International Action)

The American Council for Voluntary International Action, better known as InterAction, is a broadly based coalition of more than 150 private and voluntary organizations (PVOs) dedicated to international relief and development. Members work on a broad range of concerns including sustainable development, refugee assistance and protection, disaster relief and preparedness, public policy, and education of Americans about the developing world. InterAction exists to enhance the effectiveness and professional capabilities of its members and to foster partnership, collaboration, leadership, and the power of the community to strive together to achieve a world of self-reliance, justice, and peace. InterAction serves as an information clearinghouse, works with Congress on international issues, promotes the work of its members, and organizes seminars and conferences. Its biweekly newsletter, *Monday Developments*, contains an extensive listing of job opportunities with international and environmental agencies.

InterAction employs 35–40 professional staff in the United States, all dealing with international issues. On the average 5 to 10 positions are filled each year. A master's degree is preferred but not required; overseas experience and experience with PVOs or other development agencies is desirable. Strong analytical and writing skills are essential.

InterAction
Suite 801
1717 Massachusetts Avenue, N.W.
Washington, D.C. 20036

tel. 202/667-8227
fax 202/667-8236
e-mail: ia@interaction.org
http://www.vita.org/iaction/
iaction.html

International Executive Service Corps

The International Executive Service Corps (IESC) was founded by a group of American businesspeople in 1964 to assist enterprises in developing countries, and now the emerging democracies, by providing technical and managerial expertise and experience developed in the United States. IESC and its volunteers have completed more than 16,000 projects in more than 120 countries. While IESC projects encompass virtually every known type of enterprise, a major number of projects are devoted to basic human needs—food, shelter, clothing, and health care. IESC has 67 offices in 55 countries; since 1990, 34 offices in Central and Eastern Europe, the Baltic States, and the Newly Independent States of the former Soviet Union have opened. IESC's Skills Bank contains the names and qualifications of about 13,000 U.S. men and women who have volunteered their talents and experience for overseas assignments. Although the vast majority are retired, many volunteer executives use their vacation or company leave time to complete projects of two to four weeks or longer. The average length of a project is about two months.

International Executive Service
   Corps
P.O. Box 10005
Stamford, CT 06904–2005

tel. 203/967-6000
fax 203/324-2531

International Peace Academy

The International Peace Academy (IPA) is an independent, nonpartisan, international institution devoted to the promotion of peaceful and multilateral approaches to the resolution of international as well as internal conflicts. IPA activities include: playing a facilitating role in efforts to settle conflicts by providing a middle ground where options for political settlements are explored in an informal, off-the-record setting; a program of research and symposia focusing on preventive action, peacemaking, peacekeeping, internal conflicts, and nonmilitary aspects of security; training seminars on peacekeeping and conflict resolution; and public forum activities. In fulfilling this mission, IPA works closely with the United Nations, regional and other international organizations, governments, and parties to conflicts. The work of IPA is enhanced by its ability to draw on a worldwide network of eminent statesmen, business leaders, diplomats, military officers, and scholars.

Headquartered opposite the United Nations in Manhattan, IPA is staffed by a versatile and culturally diverse group of program associates and administrative personnel. IPA programs typically require foreign language skills and specialization in the affairs of particular regions of the world; this is reflected in the various ethnic backgrounds and national origins of staff members and consultants, currently including individuals from 11 countries. IPA has a staff of 20 which includes 4 executives. Employment opportunities are limited, with most staff members having advanced degrees in international relations and/or substantial military or diplomatic experience at mid-career to senior level.

Personnel   tel. 212/949-8480
International Peace Academy
777 United Nations Plaza
New York, NY 10017

International Rescue Committee

The International Rescue Committee (IRC) helps refugees and other victims of war by providing emergency food, clothing, shelter, and medical assistance. These activities, a major part of which involves helping to resettle displaced persons, include programs in public health, vocational and job training, educational aid, language training, child care, family counseling, and assistance with problems of political asylum. IRC's goal is to enable refugees to become accustomed to life in their new countries with as few problems as possible. The services are provided for refugees from Africa, East Asia and the Pacific, Latin America, the former Soviet republics, and Eastern Europe.

IRC has an annual budget for its international activities of more than $87 million and a total international staff, including volunteers, of more than 280 people. IRC has an ongoing need for health professionals such as physicians and nurses, as well as environmental engineers, educators, and administrators. Last year, IRC had openings for more than 150 professional positions in the international field. Overseas experience in developing countries is preferred.

International Rescue Committee   tel. 212/551-3000
122 East 42nd Street   fax 212/551-3180
New York, NY 10168–1289   e-mail: denise@irc.com

International Research and Exchanges Board

The International Research and Exchanges Board, more commonly known as IREX, administers the principal academic exchange programs between the United States and the countries of Eastern Europe and the Newly Independent States (NIS). Individuals in various research and study programs are placed for periods of 2 to 12 months in participating countries. U.S. citizens must normally be postdoctoral graduate students or faculty members, associated with a recognized North American university. Transportation, room, board, tuition, fees, and research expenses are paid by the United States and the host country. IREX also awards financial assistance for area studies at U.S. universities when necessary as pretravel preparation.

IREX has a permanent staff of 59 based in the United States and 18 field offices. Its annual operating budget is approximately $26 million.

International Research and   tel. 202/628-8188
    Exchanges Board
1616 H Street, N.W.
Washington, D.C. 20006

International Schools Services

International Schools Services (ISS) is a private, nonprofit organization founded in 1955 to support and advance the education of U.S. and other expatriate children attending school overseas. It serves about 200 elementary and secondary schools in U.S. and international civilian communities throughout the world. Schools request staffing assistance, and ISS provides the professional papers of qualified candidates to the schools. Candidates are notified of job openings for which they qualify and arrange contracts with the individual schools. Last year ISS placed almost 500 candidates.

Applicants must have a bachelor' degree and at least two years of current, full-time, elementary or secondary school experience. The two-year experience requirement is sometimes waived in the fields of computers, science, and mathematics. Specialist, guidance counselor, and department head applicants must have advanced degrees. ISS charges a registration fee.

International Schools Services   tel. 609/452-0990
15 Roszel Road   e-mail: ISS@mcimail.com
P.O. Box 5910
Princeton, NJ 08543

International Studies Association

The International Studies Association (ISA) is the premier professional organization for international scholars and policymakers. It fosters scholarly exchange and communication among international studies specialists and has about 3,000 members from 61 countries. The association sponsors an annual conference, several regional conferences, and research and study groups and publishes two journals, *The International Studies Quarterly* and *The Mershon International Review,* and a number of newsletters.

Four or five professionals administer the various ISA programs.

International Studies Association   tel. 520/621-7715
324 Social Sciences
University of Arizona
Tucson, AZ 85721

International Voluntary Services

International Voluntary Services (IVS) works to strengthen the capacities of local organizations and institutions in developing nations through projects that actively help the rural poor through their own efforts and resources. IVS also provides skilled international technicians to fill particular positions at the request of local organizations and governments. The organization's programs focus on community development, small business management and development, food production and agriculture, and medicine and public health. IVS is active in South America, South Asia, and sub-Saharan Africa.

IVS recruits internationally and has approximately 50 full-time staff working in the field. Candidates for program and project manager positions should have degrees in specialized areas of development work, including but not limited to such areas as agronomy, agricultural marketing, irrigation and hydrology, and previous experience working in developing countries.

International Voluntary Services   tel. 202/387-5533
1424 16th Street, N.W.
Suite 204
Washington, D.C. 20036

The Japan Exchange and Teaching Program

The Japan Exchange and Teaching Program (JET) seeks to help enhance internationalization in Japan by promoting mutual understanding between Japan, Australia, Canada, China, France, Germany, Ireland, New Zealand, the Republic of Korea, the Russian Federation, the United Kingdom, and the United States. The program is based upon intensifying foreign language education in Japan and upon promoting international exchange at the local level through fostering ties between Japanese youth and JET Program participants.

JET offers two areas of placement. Coordinators for international relations (CIRs) are engaged in international activities. CIRs are placed in offices of prefectural governments or offices of designated cities. A number of CIRs are placed in municipal governments of nondesignated cities, towns, villages, or other entities through the offices of the prefectures. Assistant language teachers (ALTs) are engaged in language instruction. The participants are placed mainly in publicly run schools or local boards of education.

JET Office   tel. 202/939-6772
Embassy of Japan   tel. 202/939-6773
2520 Massachusetts Avenue, N.W.
Washington, D.C. 20008

MAP International

MAP International is a nonprofit Christian global health organization that provides enabling services that promote total health care for needy people in the developing world. Originally known as Medical Assistance Programs, today MAP provides medicines and supplies, community health development, and emergency relief to bring health to the poor throughout the developing world. MAP's work in community health development includes coordinating projects to improve water supplies, food production, and health education. MAP has provided more than $600 million in donated medicines and supplies through 650 hospitals and clinics in 118 countries since 1954.

The staff of MAP International has included about 10 to 15 professional in recent years. Of the approximately 133 positions at MAP's Georgia headquarters, 6 are considered professional staff. In addition to their U.S. headquarters, MAP also has offices in Latin America and East Africa. About seven U.S. nationals are employed as professionals overseas. In recent years, however, there have been no expatriate openings, nor have there been any professional job openings in the U.S. office. Applicants for professional positions should possess a university degree in public health, nonformal education, or a related field.

MAP International   tel. 912/265-6010
2200 Glynco Parkway   fax 912/265-6170
P.O. Box 215000
Brunswick, GA 31521–5000

Maryknoll Mission Association of the Faithful

The Maryknoll Mission Association of the Faithful, a Catholic community of men and women called to global mission, is a branch of the Maryknoll movement and share in missions with the Maryknoll Fathers and Brothers and the Maryknoll Sisters. Commitments are currently being made in Asia, Africa, and Latin America. A four-month orientation program prior to overseas assignment includes courses in theology, scripture, social justice, missiology, Maryknoll history, and a retreat. A minimum three-and-one-half-year renewable commitment is required. A stipend, transportation to and from the mission site, and room and board are provided.

Applicants generally must be between the ages of 23 and 40 and must be Catholics. In addition to a faith motivation and church commitment, the applicant must have a needed skill or college degree plus a minimum of one year of experience after formal training. Skills in the following areas are currently being sought: agriculture; campus, family, and hospital ministries; communications; community development; counseling; economics; journalism; pastoral work; medicine and nursing; refugee work; social science research; social science; teaching; and various skill professions.

> Maryknoll Mission Association   tel. 914/762-6364
>   of the Faithful
> P.O. Box 307
> Maryknoll, NY 10545–0307

Meridian International Center

Meridian International Center is a not-for-profit educational and cultural institution that promotes international understanding through the exchange of people, ideas, and the arts. For visitors from other countries, Meridian serves as a doorway to the United States through its programming and training services, including conferences and seminars. For Americans interested in global issues, Meridian provides a window on the world through lectures, briefings, educational outreach programs, concerts, and exhibitions. In addition, Meridian coordinates activities for its affiliate, the Hospitality and Information Service, whose volunteers assist Washington's diplomatic community.

Meridian has a staff of 100 employees. The annual budget is about $16 million.

> Meridian International Center   tel. 667-6800
> 1630 Crescent Place, N.W.   e-mail: meridian@dgs.dgsys.com
> Washington, D.C. 20009

NAFSA: Association of International Educators

NAFSA: Association of International Educators is the largest professional membership association in the world concerned with the advancement of effective international educational exchange. NAFSA's 7,700 members—from every state in the U.S. and more than 60 countries—promote the exchange of students and scholars to and from the United States. NAFSA conducts professional training and services for international educators through workshops, seminars, regional and national conferences, and publications.

NAFSA's national headquarters in Washington, D.C. has a staff of 52 that provides membership services, coordinates program activities, and works with U.S. government agencies, embassies, and higher education associations. NAFSA generally has 7 to 10 job openings per year. Applicants must have at least a bachelor's degree in liberal arts and some experience in living or studying in different cultures or working with the foreign student population in the United States. NAFSA also has a job registry service for professionals in the field of international education and exchange.

NAFSA: Association of
  International Educators
Suite 1000
1875 Connecticut Avenue, N.W.
Washington, D.C. 20009–5728

tel. 202/462-4811
fax 202/667-3419
e-mail: inbox@nafsa.org

Near East Foundation

The Near East Foundation, founded in 1915, is America's oldest voluntary agency devoted exclusively to programs of technical assistance in developing countries. It concentrates on community participation, utilizing appropriate technology, building local skill capacity, and providing cofinancing.

The provision of qualified specialists to assist with the transfer of technical skills and human resource development is the foundation's principal mode of operation. It assists only projects that have strong local support and it actively seeks opportunities to extend its work through cooperation with other donor agencies. The annual budgets typically allocate more than $4 million for projects in Middle Eastern and African countries.

A small headquarters staff in New York provides support for field operations. An overseas staff cadre of approximately 100 people includes resident specialists and local professionals. Preferred qualifications for specialist positions are a master's degree (or equivalent) with a development-related specialization and five years' relevant experience.

Near East Foundation
342 Madison Avenue
New York, NY 10173–1030

tel. 212/867-0064

Pact

Pact, a private nonprofit international development organization, targets its efforts on strengthening the community-focused nonprofit sector worldwide and by working with strategic partners to identify and implement participatory development approaches that promote social, economic, political, and environmental justice. Pact concentrates its work in institution-building on organizations dedicated to certain key sectors that have local impact and global relevance, including small- and micro-enterprise development, health care (especially AIDS prevention and treatment), child welfare, environmental protection, participatory governance, nonformal education, women's issues, and human rights. Pact has a portfolio of 17 projects in 10 countries; an annual budget of approximately $18 million; field offices in Asia, Africa, and Latin America; and a staff numbering more than 150 local and expatriate personnel. Pact also has a publications department located in New York, which is the only full service U.S. publishing house offering production and distribution services to individuals and organizations working in international development.

Pact hires at many different levels: program assistant, program officer, associate director for programs, deputy director for programs, and country representative. For new hires, the entry-level position is the program assistant or program officer position. Preferred qualifications for a program assistant position include a bachelor's degree in a related field, foreign language skills, and work experience in a development-related organization. Preferred qualifications for a program officer position include three years' work experience in a development-related organization, experience in administrative procedures, grants management and program backstopping, experience with USAID policies and regulations, foreign language skills, and a master's degree.

Pact
Suite 501
1901 Pennsylvania Avenue, N.W.
Washington, D.C. 20006

Partners for International Education and Training

Partners for International Education and Training (PIET) is a consortium formed by the Asia Foundation, the African-American Institute, AMIDEAST, and World Learning, Inc., to administer a portion of the U.S. Agency for International Development's Worldwide Participant Training Program. People involved in country or regional development projects crucial to the economic, technical, and social progress of their nation are selected and funded to study in the United States. Nondegree, technical training accounts for about 90 percent of PIET's activity, with the remaining individuals enrolled in academic degree programs. All participants are committed to returning home to contribute new skills and knowledge toward their nation's development. To date, PIET has programmed more than 34,000 participants from 143 countries.

There are 100 staff members in the central office in Washington, D.C., and 35 staff members in 10 offices in Central and Eastern Europe, where PIET supports USAID regional activities. Positions come open at various times during the year. For most a college degree and a professional interest in developing and transitional countries are required.

Partners for International   tel. 202/429-0810
   Education and Training
Suite 650
2000 M Street, N.W.
Washington, D.C. 20036

Physicians for Social Responsibility

Physicians for Social Responsibility (PSR) is a national, nonprofit membership organization of more than 20,000 health professionals and supporters working to promote nuclear arms reduction, international cooperation, protection of the environment, and the reduction of violence. PSR was founded in 1961 and is the U.S. affiliate of International Physicians for the Prevention of Nuclear War, which was awarded the Nobel Peace Prize in 1985. PSR supports the downsizing of the nuclear weapons complex and cleanup of radioactive contamination at Department of Energy sites. In addition, PSR promotes an end to nuclear testing, the forging of new arms reduction treaties, a shift in federal budget priorities away from military spending and toward meeting human needs, preservation of the environment, and the reduction of violence and its causes.

PSR's activities include public education about the health impacts of nuclear weapons production and testing, the social costs of the arms race and the links between pollution and public health. PSR's programs range from citizen advocacy with Congress, speaker tours, media work, and educational publications. A background or interest in nuclear weapons and security issues and related legislative policy, as well as an interest in PSR's goals, is sought in prospective hires and interns.

Physicians for Social Responsibility   tel. 202/898-0150
Suite 700   fax 202/898-0172
1101 14th Street, N.W.
Washington, D.C. 20005

Populations Services International

Populations Services International (PSI) is a nonprofit organization established in 1970 and a registered private voluntary organization. PSI designs, develops, and operates maternal and child health, family planning, and AIDS prevention programs in developing countries. These activities include social marketing and promotion of health products in the private sector at prices affordable to the poor, and generic communications and education to motivate target groups to adopt prudent health practices. PSI is an unusual nonprofit in that it operates in the private sector and fashions its management style along the lines of the private sector.

Now the largest private social marketing entity in the world in terms of products delivered and number of projects, and the most cost-efficient, PSI is the only one that focuses on serving lower income people and that distributes products in various health areas for a variety of health interventions. PSI is a flexible, progressive organization that provides challenges and virtually unlimited opportunity for responsibility. The organization encourages innovation and initiative and places a premium on results. They are looking for people with developing country experience and marketing/business experience. Employees need to have strong entrepreneurial skills as well as a desire to help others. PSI is in a growth phase of about 20 percent per year. Approximately one-half of PSI's staff is in Washington, D.C., and the other half are in country. PSI is not a prime contractor with USAID.

Recruitment Director   tel. 202/785-0120
Population Services International
1120 19th Street, N.W.
Suite 600
Washington, D.C. 20036

Project Concern International

Project Concern International (PCI) works with communities worldwide to provide basic, low-cost health care for mothers and children, including child immunizations, diarrheal disease control, nutrition, reproductive health and family planning, HIV/AIDS prevention, and water and sanitation programs.

PCI has an annual budget of $10 million and currently employs about 30 staff members at its San Diego headquarters and domestic locations and 15 to 20 expatriates abroad. For program-oriented positions, PCI seeks candidates with a master's degree in an appropriate field, preferably public health; second or third language skills; prior experience in international nonprofit development; USAID health program experience in areas such as child survival, HIV/AIDS, or family planning; strong written and verbal communication skills; strong communication skills; and the ability to work as part of a team.

Project Concern International   tel. 619/279-9690
3550 Afton Road
San Diego, CA 92123

Project HOPE

Project HOPE (Health Opportunity for People Everywhere) is a private, voluntary, international organization offering multidisciplinary assistance in health-care education in the United States and abroad. It is the principal activity of the People-to-People Health Foundation, an independent nonprofit corporation. Project HOPE's principle objective is to teach modern techniques of medical science to medical, dental, nursing, and allied health personnel in developing areas of the world. Although immediate humanitarian assistance is often an element of its activities, Project HOPE stresses long-term, systemic solutions to health-care problems.

The basic requirement for employment in Project HOPE's international programs is licensure, or in some cases certification, within a health-care profession. Because of the educational nature of HOPE's program, most of their international staff have at least a master's degree and academic and/or clinical teaching experience. Occasionally, internships are available to complement an existing HOPE program, provided the intern has outside funding.

> International Recruitment Section tel. 800/544-4673
> Project HOPE   fax 703/837-1813
> Millwood, VA 22646   e-mail: hope1@netcom.com

Rockefeller Foundation

The Rockefeller Foundation, founded in 1913 to promote the well-being of peoples throughout the world, seeks to identify and relieve the underlying causes of human suffering and need. The foundation works in three broad areas: science-based development; arts and humanities; and equal opportunity. Its programs are carried out through grants and fellowships to institutions and individuals.

The Rockefeller Foundation's development program is of most interest to students of international affairs. This science-based development program has three divisions: agricultural sciences, health sciences, and population sciences. The program is designed to help developing nations, particularly in Africa, use modern science and technology in bringing food, health, education, housing, and work to their people by building partnerships between industrial and developing countries. Although the program is science based, it also emphasizes factors such as local culture and values, equitable policy-making, competent management, and production capability that can determine whether science and technology effectively contribute to the well-being of people in the developing world.

The foundation has a full-time staff of more than 130 people in New York. There are program officers and mid-level program associates in each division. Almost all professional positions are filled by people with extensive experience in the field and often who have published in the area of concentration of the position being filled. Employment opportunities with the foundation are limited.

The Rockefeller Foundation   tel. 212/869-8500
1133 Avenue of the Americas
New York, NY 10036

Salvation Army

Founded in 1865 as a religious and charitable organization, the Salvation Army provides financial and personnel assistance in about 100 countries. Its programs embrace education (primary, secondary, vocational, technical, and teacher training), community centers, disaster relief, health and medical services, agriculture, and a range of community-development projects. A major emphasis of the army's work is to administer spiritual guidance and aid wherever there is human need. It is an integral part of the International Salvation Army of London.

The overseas staff numbers about 80 to 90, most of whom are administrators and have education and experience appropriate to their positions. U.S. staff numbers six to eight.

The Salvation Army   tel. 703/684-5500
National Headquarters
P.O. Box 269
615 Slater's Lane
Alexandria, VA 22313

Save the Children

Save the Children is a private, nonprofit, nonsectarian international organization committed to helping children through the process of community development. Program expenditures are directed primarily to community projects that attack interrelated problems of poverty: poor health, inadequate nutrition, low agricultural productivity, substandard housing and lack of education, skills training and jobs, among others. The organization offers training, technical assistance, tools, and guidance for solving the problems of poor children around the world.

The organization employs over 200 people in its Westport, Connecticut, headquarters with an equal number working in field positions in the United States and abroad. About 5 to 10 professional positions are filled annually.

Increasingly, successful candidates have master's degrees and some professional experience in community development.

> Save the Children   tel. 203/226-7271
> 54 Wilton Road
> Westport, CT 06880

Soros Network of Foundations

The various independent foundations, programs, and institutions established and supported by philanthropist George Soros share a common goal: to foster the development of open societies around the world, particularly in the previously communist countries of Central and Eastern Europe and the former Soviet Union. These organizations help build the infrastructure and institutions necessary for open societies by supporting a broad array of programs in education, media and communications, human rights and humanitarian aid, science and medicine, arts and culture, economic restructuring, and legal reform.

At the heart of this network of organizations are the 24 national foundations in Central and Eastern Europe as well as the foundations in South Africa and Haiti. Each foundation works to promote open society in a country struggling with the legacy of a repressive, totalitarian regime. The national foundations are committed to certain common goals, such as the rule of law; a democratically elected government; a vigorous, diverse society; respect for minorities; and a free market economy. The manner in which they pursue these goals is up to each national foundation, which, with its own board and staff, sets program priorities in response to the particular situation and problems in that country.

Promoting connections and cooperation among the national foundations is the **Open Society Institute (OSI)** in New York and the separate Open Society Institute in Budapest. Both OSIs facilitate the work of the national foundations by creating and funding regional programs on common issues, providing technical assistance, and initiating special projects that address emergencies beyond the capacity and mandate of individual national foundations. As an operating foundation, OSI (New York) also initiates, supports, and promotes a range of programs for the development of open societies around the world, including the United States. In addition, OSI (New York) encourages public policy debate on policy alternatives in controversial fields. The **Open Media Research Institute (OMRI)** has assumed and expanded many of the functions of the Research Institute of Radio Free Europe/Radio Liberty, which was severed from the broadcast operations as part of U.S. government budget cuts. The **Central European University (CEU)** is an accredited, degree-granting educational institution independent of the foundations;

it is dedicated to educating the regions leaders and to researching the transition under way in Central and Eastern Europe.

Other foundations and programs created by George Soros include the **International Science Foundation** and the **International Soros Science Education Program**, which encourage and support the scientists and science teachers in the former Soviet Union so that they are about to continue their work in their home countries. The **Soros Roma Foundation**, located in Switzerland, works with Roma (gypsy) people in Central and Eastern Europe, and a foundation office in Paris aids in coordinating various programs.

OSI (New York) has 130 employees. In addition, there are 1,100 employees in the national foundations' offices, who are hired in the countries where they work. Most OSI (New York) employees speak at least one foreign language (Central and East European) and have some experience living or studying abroad. Their educational background is in international development, international affairs, education, and other related fields.

Communications Department   tel. 212/757-2323
Open Society Institute   fax 212/974-0367
888 Seventh Avenue   e-mail: osnews@sorosny.org
New York, NY 10106   http://www.soros.org

The Tinker Foundation

Established in 1959 by Dr. Edward Larocque Tinker, the Tinker Foundation has since awarded more than $31 million to some 300 institutions in the United States and Latin America. Each year, approximately $2 million is awarded to about 60 organizations. Priority is given to work in economic policy and governance, environmental policy, and the research, training, and public outreach activities associated with these areas. Emphasis is placed on those activities that have strong public policy implications, offer innovative solutions, and incorporate new mechanisms for addressing environmental, economic, political, and social issues.

Tinker Foundation grants are awarded to organizations that promote the interchange and exchange of information within the community of those concerned with the affairs of Spain, Portugal, the Spanish- and Portuguese-speaking countries of the Western hemisphere, and Antarctica. Such activities include research projects, conferences and workshops, and the training of specialists at the postgraduate level. The foundation also promotes collaboration between organizations in the United States and Iberia or Latin America and among institutions in these regions.

The Tinker Foundation has a permanent professional staff of four individuals. Employment prospects are extremely limited.

The Tinker Foundation   tel. 212/421-6858
55 East 59th Street
New York, NY 10022

United Nations Association of the USA

The United Nations Association of the USA (UNA-USA) is the nation's largest foreign policy organization, building public support for constructive U.S. leadership in a more effective United Nations. UNA-USA is a leading center of policy research on the United Nations and global issues like the environment, security, narcotics, development, and human rights. Through the work of its 175 community-based chapters, its 135-member Council of Organizations, and its Washington/New York-based staff, UNA-USA functions as a constructive critic of the U.N. and of U.S. policy at the U.N., and serves as an incubator for new ideas on such issues as conflict resolution, nuclear nonproliferation, and sustainable development. The organization publishes a wide variety of books on the U.N. and international affairs, as well as its quarterly newspaper *The InterDependent.*

Through its offices in New York and Washington and its network of chapters and divisions across the country, UNA-USA offers a larger number of substantive internships; UNA staff are frequently taken from the pool of current and former interns.

United Nations Association   tel. 212/697-3232
 of the USA
485 Fifth Avenue
New York, NY 10017

U.S.-Asia Institute

The U.S.-Asia Institute, founded in 1979, is a national nonprofit, nonpartisan organization devoted to fostering understanding and strengthening ties between the people and governments of the United States and Asia. Through conferences, research, symposiums, international exchanges, and publications, the U.S.-Asia Institute promotes the examination of the economic, political, and cultural issues vital to U.S.-Asia relations.

The board of trustees of the institute encourages the participation of all Americans interested in Asia in this process. The institute currently has three professional staff positions. Openings are rare. The institute also sponsors professional internships for U.S. undergraduate and graduate students as well as international young professionals.

Though academic training in the area of East Asia is certainly preferred, the U.S.-Asia Institute has hired individuals with economic, political science, public policy, and international relations backgrounds who have an interest in Asia. Successful applicants have had a minimum of a B.A. or B.S. and usually one to two years of work experience. They must be well organized and able to communicate effectively in both written and oral form. It is vital that they recognize the importance of teamwork and be willing to do a variety of tasks.

U.S.-Asia Institute   tel. 202/544-3181
232 East Capitol Street, N.E.
Washington, D.C. 20003

World Learning

World Learning is a private, nonprofit organization that has maintained its mission of furthering world understanding since its founding in 1932. World Learning educates people in an international arena, providing skills needed to cultivate the attitudes and knowledge necessary to function as leaders in an interdependent world. World Learning offers citizen exchange program, language training, career-oriented higher education, and programs in international development and training. The organization brings together experimental learning traditions of the educational exchange community, academic traditions of the university, and refugee and development services of the voluntary agency.

World Learning activities overseas are supported by a worldwide federation of more than 30 autonomous international offices. It also undertakes contracts with a number of government agencies and private organizations to provide professional and technical training and international development services both in the United States and abroad.

World Learning has 495 employees plus 600 local hires in Africa, Southeast Asia, and Latin America. It fills about 20 professional positions annually. These positions usually require international/intercultural experience (often country or region specific) and a combination of management and/or technical expertise as determined by the nature of the project. Specific job descriptions are available from the human resource department.

World Learning   tel. 802/257-7751
Kipling Road
P.O. Box 676
Brattleboro, VT 05302–0676

WorldTeach

WorldTeach is an independently incorporated nonprofit organization based at the Harvard Institute for International Development which places volunteers as teachers in countries that request assistance. WorldTeach was founded in 1986 with the goal of contributing to education overseas and creating opportunities for college graduates and students to gain experience in the fields of international development and education. Last year, WorldTeach placed 275 volunteers as teachers in seven developing countries around the world. WorldTeach offers full-year placements in Costa Rica, Ecuador, Namibia, Poland, South Africa, and Thailand. In addition, there is a summer teaching program in Shanghai, China, and a six-month guide-training program in Baja, Mexico. Volunteers receive housing and living stipends for most programs and primarily teach English as a foreign language. Volunteers for the full-year and Mexico programs must have a bachelor's degree, but no prior teaching experience or language skills are required. Before leaving, volunteers raise a fee to cover the cost of airfare, health insurance, training, and support. Applications are accepted from all ages and nationalities.

WorldTeach   tel. 617/495-5527
Harvard Institute for
   International Development
One Eliot Street
Cambridge, MA 02138–5705

Youth For Understanding International Exchange

Youth For Understanding (YFU) International Exchange, one of the world's oldest and largest international exchange organizations, operates a variety of overseas home-stay programs for teenagers in more than 25 countries. Since 1951, YFU has arranged for more than 175,000 high school students to live with families worldwide. Every year, more than 3,000 volunteers assist the YFU staff in providing the students and host families with extensive support services such as cross-cultural orientation, counseling, and language tutoring. The organization has its international center in Washington, D.C., as well as 10 regional offices throughout the United States and national offices abroad. YFU has a staff of about 90 at headquarters and an additional 55 people work in regional offices throughout the United States. To locate the closest regional office, call 800/872-0200.

U.S. National Office   tel. 202/966-6808
Youth For Understanding   fax 202/895-1104
   International Exchange   e-mail: USA@mail.yfu.org
3501 Newark Street, N.W.   http://www.yfu.org
Washington, D.C. 20016

YMCA International Division

The activities of YMCA International center on the provision of technical and financial aid for social and economic development projects and are directed at developing self-sufficiency in indigenous YMCA movements in more than 130 countries. Aid typically includes leadership and vocational training, job creation, health and nutrition services, family management, and agricultural and community development. It also provides disaster relief assistance. The International Division maintains a total salaried staff of approximately 19 personnel, 15 percent of whom serve overseas. All national YMCAs are staffed by host country personnel. YMCA International has an annual budget of about $3.7 million. It maintains educational and work exchange programs and provides overseas employment opportunities in the following areas: Overseas Service Corps (voluntary service), and short-term specialists (up to six months consulting on contract in a specialized subject field). The YMCA of the USA publishes a biweekly roster of all YMCA positions available in the U.S. called *The National Vacancy List*. The list may be obtained by contacting the Human Resources Department at the address below.

YMCA of the USA   tel. 800/872–9622
Human Resources
101 North Wacker Drive
Chicago, IL 60606

9

Research Organizations

CHRISTINE E. CONTEE*

Among western democracies, the proliferation of think tanks is unique to the United States for the several reasons. First of all, as government grew and became more complex in the post–war era, experts were sought to help make decisions. Congressional responsibilities expanded, and several think tanks emerged in response to a perceived need by legislators for policy-oriented analyses. In addition, the U.S. system allows for much more mobility between government, academia, and the private sector than other countries. The so-called revolving door gives individuals outside of government the opportunity to remain active in policy issues through affiliation with think tanks. Last, the strong philanthropic tradition of the United States has generated unmatched levels of support for independent policy research.

Thinks tanks vary considerably in structure and outlook. Some are almost university-like with research driven by individual scholars. Others perform relatively little original in-house research, drawing instead upon the ongoing work of academics and subsequently translating it into policy-relevant analyses and recommendations. Some research organizations work almost entirely under contract for the government. Some think tanks focus far more on creating fora for dialogue and consensus-building among policymakers than on traditional written research.

Think tanks are perhaps traditionally perceived as generating research and analysis that is nonpartisan and independent. Increasingly,

---

* Christine E. Contee, a 1984 graduate of Georgetown University's Master of Science in Foreign Service program, is Director of Public Affairs and Fellow at the Overseas Development Council, an international policy research institute that focuses on development and related global problems.

however, some research organizations tend to edge closer to advocacy by designing and using their information and research agenda to promote certain political goals. Research organizations that operate in this mode may appear more like interest groups than think tanks or research organizations.

There are many variations in the perspectives and agendas of think tanks. Some focus largely on the big picture, long-term basic questions underlying public policy. Others focus on more specific, short-term questions relating directly to policy implementation. Some focus the whole of their attention on a fairly narrow sectoral or regional concern. Others have extremely broad mandates that include many domestic and foreign issues.

Approximately two-thirds of think tanks in Washington, D.C., today have been launched since the 1970s. Some 100 think tanks are located in Washington and over 1,000 are spread across the country, many with at least some aspect of the foreign policy agenda in their portfolio. Financial support for foreign policy research organizations is tight in the 1990s, due to a decline both in government and foundation funding for international research institutions live close to the financial edge, these funding restrictions can certainly be expected to limit employment opportunities in many cases.

Think tanks not only engage in research but also in a variety of communications activities to disseminate the research output, including producing publications, providing policy advice, convening fora to facilitate the exchange of information and/or consensus-building, and working with the media to disseminate their messages. There are employment opportunities in all of these areas.

Employment on the research side of a think tank is possible, but difficult, to obtain with only a bachelor's degree. With this type of degree, the jobs offered will be almost entirely administrative. Entry-level research positions will usually require a master's degree as well as demonstrated administrative skills, communication skills, and research experience of some sort in the field. These positions will usually be administrative, with some opportunity—which will vary substantially—for data collection and writing. For many research positions, an academic background in economics, international relations, public policy, area studies, political science, or history is preferred.

Smaller research organizations often lack the funding to hire permanent research assistants for their senior research staff. These organizations, and larger think tanks as well, rely heavily on interns to meet their staffing needs. For the student and job applicant, internships are a useful way to test future interest in a research career, to gain familiarity with a field, and to make contacts within an organization.

Most senior research positions require a Ph.D. and experience in the chosen field. Because the additional academic credentials and work experience are essential to move from research assistant to senior researcher, upward mobility is extremely rare on the research side of a think tank. It is generally accepted that junior-level research positions will be held by those with master's degrees for a period of not more than a year or two before they move on, usually to pursue doctoral studies.

Entry-level positions on the communications side of a research organization will also require a master's degree, administrative skills, interpersonal skills, and strong written and oral communication skills. Some employers may look for a master's degree in a communications-related field. More frequently, these jobs require a master's degree in an area related to the think tank's substantive portfolio with some job experience in the relevant area, such as editing, media relations, congressional liaison, or conference planning.

Quantitative skills are also important, particularly for certain entry-level and mid-level jobs in research. For both research and related communications positions, training in international economics is increasingly valuable. Knowledge of foreign languages can be helpful for some jobs.

The remainder of this century is likely to be a time of considerable change for most foreign policy research organizations. First, as the number of research organizations grows, as more research organizations tend toward producing material for instrumental purposes, and as budgets tighten, research organizations find themselves in competition for policymakers' attention and funding. It is likely that these trends will have a permanent effect on the way that some think tanks define their research agenda and activities in order to make sure that their ideas get exposure and support.

Second, and more significant, the dramatic changes in the international system have also meant important changes within and among foreign policy research organizations. Just as the United States is groping to define foreign policy interest in the post–Cold War era, international affairs research institutes are rethinking their agendas, methods of operation, and perspectives. Perhaps now more than ever, those interested in a career in foreign policy research should strive to be forward thinking in selecting their area of expertise. Certainly, research on international economic policy and the relationship between economics and politics is likely to be a strong field in the future. Another likely growth area are the cross-border concerns that have been emerging as priorities on the policy agenda—environment, health, refugees, and narcotics, among others.

Predicting problems and proposing solutions in a time of change is critical. As the demand for forecasting and analysis increases, the role of think tanks will continue to expand, change, and grow. A career in this field is not only a challenging one, but it offers individuals a chance to contribute to the creation of the future.

American Enterprise Institute

The American Enterprise Institute (AEI), founded in 1943, is a nonpartisan, nonprofit, research, and educational organization that sponsors original research on government policy, the U.S. economy, and U.S. politics. AEI research aims to preserve and strengthen the foundations of a free society— limited government, competitive private enterprise, vital cultural and political institutions, and a vigilant defense—through rigorous inquiry, debate, and writing. The institute is home to some of America's most renowned economists, legal scholars, political scientists, and foreign policy specialists.

AEI employs 45 resident scholars, recruited mainly from colleges and universities. There are approximately 24 full-time research assistant positions in the disciplines listed above, with four or five new vacancies filled, on average, throughout the year. Holders of bachelor's and master's degrees are eligible to apply.

American Enterprise Institute   tel. 202/862-5800
1150 17th Street, N.W.   fax 202/862-7177
Washington, D.C. 20036

Arms Control Association

The Arms Control Association (ACA) is a small, nonprofit research organization that works to educate the public, government officials, and the press on the importance of arms control to international security. The association has 10 paid staff members, who are primarily engaged in research or work on ACA's publications, notably *Arms Control Today*.

Openings for full-time analysts are relatively rare. Most of those hired have a master's degree. Demonstrated knowledge in the field of arms control is a prerequisite.

Arms Control Association   tel. 202/463-8270
Suite 201   fax 202/463-8273
1726 M Street, N.W.
Washington, D.C. 20036

The Aspen Institute

The Aspen Institute brings timeless ideas and values to bear on issues of practical leadership in today's world. It accomplishes this through nonpartisan seminars and policy programs designed for leaders in business, government, the media, education, and the independent sector from democratic societies worldwide. Headquartered in Washington, D.C., the institute presents programs at its facilities in Aspen, Colorado, and Queenstown, Maryland, as well as in France, Germany, Italy, and Japan. An independent, nonprofit organization, they fund The Aspen Institute through government grants, tuition, and individual and corporate contributions.

Total permanent staff in the U.S. numbers about 100, with some temporary staff for summer activities and special projects. Overseas affiliates operate and hire staff independently from U.S. operations. The annual U.S. operating budget is approximately $16 million.

Office of Personnel   tel. 410/827-7168
The Aspen Institute
P.O. Box 222
Queenstown, MD 21658

The Atlantic Council of the United States

The Atlantic Council of the United States is a nonprofit public policy center that addresses the advancement of U.S. global interests within the Atlantic and Pacific communities. A national, nonpartisan organization, the Council actively engages the U.S. executive and legislative branches in its activities, the national and international business community, media and academia, and diplomats and other foreign leaders.

Building on more than 30 years of leadership in the U.S. international affairs community, council programs identify challenges and opportunities, highlight choices, and foster informed public debate about American foreign security and international economic interests and policies. Cultural programs examine new relationships in Europe and relations between Europe and North America; the transformation of the newly independent Slavic and Eurasian states; new interrelationships between the Asian and Pacific nations, and with North America and Europe; new opportunities for enhancing global and regional security; and increasing global interdependence among energy, environmental, trade, economic growth, and development challenges. Cultural programs also fulfill the educational goals of the Atlantic Council by working to ensure an understanding of the U.S.'s international role by the generations that will succeed to leadership in the next century.

The council has a permanent staff of 25. There are about three openings per year at the staff support level; senior staff openings are far less frequent. Qualifications range from bachelor's to doctoral degrees in foreign affairs.

The Atlantic Council   tel. 202/463-7226
Suite 1000
910 17th Street, N.W.
Washington, D.C. 20006

Brookings Institution

The Brookings Institution is a private, nonprofit, nonpartisan organization devoted to research, education, and publication in economics, government, foreign policy, and the social sciences. Its principal purpose is to bring new knowledge to bear on current and emerging public policy issues facing the United States and to provide an expanded body of knowledge to better inform scholars, decisionmakers, and the U.S. public. Its activities are carried out through three research programs (economic studies, governmental studies, and foreign policy studies), the Center for Public Policy Education, the Social Science Computation Center, and a publications program.

The institution's staff includes about 240 people. Most professional positions are senior fellows and research associates numbering about 55, 17 of whom work on foreign policy issues. Senior fellows primarily hold doctorate degrees in a discipline relevant to a particular topic under research. Research associates usually have a master's degree in international studies with fluency in a foreign language, primarily Arabic, Chinese, or Russian. One or two research associates are hired per year.

The Brookings Institution   tel. 202/797-6000
1775 Massachusetts Avenue, N.W.
Washington, D.C. 20036

Carnegie Endowment for International Peace

An operating as opposed to grant-making foundation, the Carnegie Endowment conducts programs of research, discussion, publication, and education in international relations and American foreign policy. Although its program activities change periodically, emphasis has been on regional and country studies including the Middle East, Central and Latin America, U.S.-Soviet relations, and South Asia. The endowment also has recently pursued a variety of projects concerning Eastern Europe. The organization also engages in joint programs with other tax-exempt organizations to invigorate and enlarge the scope of dialog on international issues. *Foreign Policy* is the quarterly journal published as a public forum for its activities.

The endowment employs about 60 people including about 20 senior associates as well as other professionals associated with research, administration, publications, and support activities. Almost all professional positions are held by well-known experts in particular fields of interest to the endowment. The endowment offers a one-year internship for graduating college seniors.

Carnegie Endowment for   tel. 202/826-7900
   International Peace
2400 N Street, N.W.
Washington, D.C. 20037

Cato Institute

Founded in 1977, the Cato Institute is a public policy research foundation dedicated to broadening the parameters of policy debate and strives to achieve greater involvement of the intelligent, concerned lay public in questions of policy and the proper role of government. To counter what it sees as increasing government encroachment in individual rights, the Cato Institute undertakes an extensive publications program that addresses the complete spectrum of policy issues. Major policy conferences are held throughout the year, from which papers are published three times a year in the *Cato Journal*. The institute also publishes the quarterly magazine *Regulation*.

The Cato Institute employs a total staff of 40, including 4 dealing with foreign affairs. There are approximately five openings per year for support staff; last year none was in foreign affairs. Qualifications for positions range from bachelor's to doctorate degrees in various fields.

Cato Institute   tel. 202/842-0200
1000 Massachusetts Avenue, N.W.   fax 202/842-3490
Washington, D.C. 20001   http://www.cato.org

Center for Defense Information

The Center for Defense Information (CDI) is an independent research organization founded and directed by retired officers of the U.S. military to analyze military spending, policies, and weapon systems. It is dedicated to providing up-to-the-minute, accurate information and appraisals of the U.S.

military, free of the special interests of any government or military, political, or industrial organization. The center believes that sound social, economic, political, and military policies contribute equally to national security and are essential to the strength of the United States. Upon request, the center provides military analyses to government agencies such as the Department of Defense, the Department of State, and Congressional committees. *The Defense Monitor*, the center's best-known publication, is published 10 times per year. CDI produces a weekly television program, *America's Defense Monitor*, carried on public television stations.

The center's staff includes retired admirals, generals, and other former military officers as well as civilians with extensive training and experience in military analysis. An internship program employs undergraduate students, graduate students, and recent graduates with strong interests in U.S. military issues and related public policy questions. Interns generally serve in research or television production positions.

Center for Defense Information   tel. 202/862-0700
1500 Massachusetts Avenue, N.W.   fax 202/862-0708
Washington, D.C. 20005   e-mail: info@cdi.org

The Chicago Council on Foreign Relations

The Chicago Council on Foreign Relations is a diverse and growing foreign policy institute that sponsors both public education and more specialized professional activities. The council's membership consists of more than 7,000 individuals in the greater Chicago area plus 125 corporate sponsors. Public lectures, corporate meetings, seminars, and study groups for the academic community and special research and publication projects are organized on a regular basis. The council has a continuing interest in public opinion and foreign policy, security and defense issues, and international economics. U.S. foreign policy, Europe, and Asia are areas of particular concern. Every four years, the organization publishes *American Public Opinion and U.S. Foreign Policy*, based on a nationwide opinion survey conducted by Gallup. The council also publishes policy-oriented books on a range of international relations topics as well as occasional paper series. It administers the Atlantic Conference, attracting leaders from Western Europe and the Americas and has close ties with the quarterly journal *Foreign Policy*.

The council has a staff of about 20 people. Employment opportunities are limited.

The Chicago Council on   tel. 312/726-3860
   Foreign Relations
116 South Michigan Avenue
Chicago, IL 60603

Council on Foreign Relations

The Council on Foreign Relations, established in 1921, is a nonprofit and nonpartisan membership organization dedicated to improved understanding of U.S. foreign policy and international affairs. As a leader in the community of institutions concerned with U.S. foreign policy, the council conducts a comprehensive meetings program. The meetings sponsored by the council reflect the issues of current concern in international affairs and are led by top foreign policy officials and experts who are critical to the discussion of policy. The council's studies program examines key issues in U.S. foreign policy today through a combination of individual scholarly research, group discussions, and conferences. The council also publishes books and papers on international issues and since 1922 has published *Foreign Affairs*, the leading journal in the field. The council's research, editorial, and administrative staff is located at its headquarters in New York and in Washington, D.C., offices.

The council provides excellent opportunities for recent graduates who are considering careers in international relations or political science through its entry-level professional position of staff assistant. Staff assistants can identify different career options in the field of international relations, as well as increase their knowledge of world events by taking advantage of the council's many resources. Those applying for staff assistant positions should possess a strong interest in international affairs and a willingness to assist with administrative work. Graduate degrees are not required. About 10 positions open annually, generally from late spring to early fall.

Council on Foreign Relations   tel. 212/734-0400
58 East 68th Street
New York, NY 10021

East-West Center

The East-West Center was established in 1960 by the U.S. Congress "to promote relations and understanding between the United States and nations of Asia and the Pacific through cooperative study, training and research." It is operated by a quasi-public, educational, nonprofit corporation with an independent and international board of governors. The center's research activities focus on critical issues of importance to the Asia-Pacific region. It is organized into programs: culture and communication; environment and policy; population; resource systems; Pacific island development; and international relations. Activities concern Asian and Pacific issues in U.S. public schools and universities and journalism.

There are about 60 research fellows. The center also offers visiting fellowships and shorter-term grants. Each year the center provides scholarships for about 50 graduate students from the United States and the Asia-Pacific region who are studying at the University of Hawaii. The center hires research associates, usually on three-year contracts, for which it seeks Ph.D.s or the equivalent in practical experience. There are other employment opportunities for research and program support positions and for technical and clerical work.

Personnel Office   tel. 808/944-7973
East-West Center
1777 East-West Road
Honolulu, Hawaii 96848

Foreign Policy Association

The Foreign Policy Association (FPA) is devoted to developing informed, thoughtful, and articulate public opinion on international affairs. Through the *Great Decisions* program, its *Headline Series*, television and other media exposure, and meetings of experts on international affairs, FPA reaches more people than any other foreign policy education effort.

FPA has a total staff of 30 in its New York headquarters and two in Washington, D.C. Most of its professional staff are editorial researchers, program coordinators, or experts on educational programs concerned with foreign policy issues.

Foreign Policy Association   tel. 212/481-8100
Second Floor
470 Park Avenue South
New York, NY 10016–6819

Foreign Policy Research Institute

The Foreign Policy Research Institute (FPRI) is a private, nonprofit, nonpartisan organization dedicated to scholarly research and public education in international affairs. Since its founding in 1955, the institute has served as a catalyst for ideas about the more effective pursuit of U.S. interests abroad. The institute publishes *Orbis*, a quarterly journal of world affairs, and research bulletins such as the *FPRI* and *Middle East Council Wires*.

FPRI has 21 full-time staff assisted by 20 part-time employees. The full-time staff includes one scholar selected by FPRI on an annual basis as the Thornton D. Hooper Fellow in International Affairs. Virtually all professional positions are filled with doctoral degree candidates or recipients or by writers with extensive publishing experience.

Foreign Policy Research Institute   tel. 215/382-0685
3615 Chestnut Street
Philadelphia, PA 19104

Heritage Foundation

The Heritage Foundation is a public policy research institute devoted to the advancement of conservative policy ideas in government and the economy. Heritage addresses critical issues of the day in a variety of forums including newsletters, monographs, and policy papers ranging from several to several hundred pages in length. About 200 policy papers are published per year. Diverse issues are addressed such as defense and foreign policy (including State Department and United Nations assessment projects); international economic development; housing; energy; the environment; and other domestic and international issues. An Asian Studies Center was founded in 1982 focused on issues particular to that region.

The Heritage Foundation also acts as a liaison between the academic and research communities linking them to decisionmakers in government. It frequently organizes lectures and seminars featuring speakers from all branches of the government as well as scholars.

The foundation's professional staff numbers about 135 people, 60 of whom are research personnel. Most of the latter are candidates for or recent recipients of doctoral degrees. Several professional positions are filled annually. The foundation also maintains a Washington Executive Bank (WEB) that places qualified conservative applicants in policy-making positions throughout the administration and Congress.

The Heritage Foundation   tel. 202/546-4400
214 Massachusetts Avenue, N.E.
Washington, D.C. 20002

Hoover Institution

Founded by Herbert Hoover in 1919, the Hoover Institution on War, Revolution and Peace is one of the world's leading centers devoted to interdisciplinary scholarship and advanced research in domestic and international affairs. Located on the campus of Stanford University, it houses one of the world's largest private archives and major libraries on political, economic, and social change in the 20th century. The focus of the institution's international research is to identify and analyze major issues and potential crises that may face U.S. government policymakers in the future.

The Hoover Institution has about 120 researchers consisting of both resident and visiting scholars from throughout the world with an extensive support staff. Another 120 staff members are associated with the library and archives. Research results are made public through a wide variety of books, journal articles, lectures, interviews, programs in the news media, seminars, conferences, expert congressional testimony, and consultative services.

The Hoover Institution   tel. 415/723-0603
Stanford University
Stanford, CA 94305-6010

Hudson Institute

Hudson Institute is a private, not-for-profit research organization headquartered in Indianapolis, Indiana, with offices in Washington, D.C.; Montreal, Canada; Brussels, Belgium; and Madison, Wisconsin. The institute analyzes and makes recommendations about public policy for business and government executives, as well as for the public at large. Hudson Institute operates a Center for European and Eurasian Studies. Hudson's work on Eastern Europe, Russia, and the other states of the former Soviet Union focuses on identifying and analyzing the emerging economic, political, and security trends in this rapidly changing, often volatile region, and providing those governments and the U.S. government with specific, realistic policy recommendations for promoting the difficult transition to democracy and free-market economies.

Hudson is also examining the future of U.S.-Japanese relations; evolving relations between Taiwan and the People's Republic of China; the European political economy; and new transatlantic security arrangements.

Hudson Institutes staff of 76 includes 34 research professionals. Qualifications for entry-level research positions generally include advanced academic training and/or some professional experience in an area related to the institute's research interests. Excellent written and oral communication skills are also required.

Hudson Institute   tel. (317) 545-1000
Herman Kahn Center   http://www.indy.net:80/~web/
P.O. Box 26–919   hudson
Indianapolis, IN 46226

Institute for Defense and Disarmament Studies

Founded in 1979, the Institute for Defense and Disarmament Studies (IDDS) is a nonprofit center for research and education on ways to minimize the risk of war, reduce the burden of military spending, and promote the growth of democratic institutions. Institute staff members study worldwide military forces and military and arms control policies. The institute's monthly journal, the *Arms Control Reporter*, is the leading international reference source on arms control negotiations. In 1992, the IDDS organized the International Fighter Study, a collaborative effort with scholars from the main arms-producing and arms-importing nations to study ways of restricting the production and export of weapons with long-range attack capability. IDDS also produces a new reference work, *IDDS Almanac: World Combat Aircraft Holdings, Production, and Trade.*

IDDS currently has six full-time staff positions, including four full-time research positions. The institute also has volunteers and interns working on substantive research. For research positions, IDDS prefers college graduates with a degree in an appropriate discipline with statistical and research experience.

Institute for Defense &
   Disarmament Studies
Eighth Floor
675 Massachusetts Avenue
Cambridge, MA 02139

tel. 617/354-4337
fax 617/354-1450
e-mail: idds@world.std.com

Institute for Policy Studies

The Institute for Policy Studies (IPS), founded in 1963, has been described as the first "respectable" offspring of the new left. A center of scholarship and education, the institute's staff conducts not only scholarly research but is involved in teaching, conferences, seminars, lecture projects, and social investigations as well. The institute conducts research programs in the following areas: national security and foreign policy; domestic public policy; international economic order; and human rights.

The formal educational aspect of the institute includes the Social Action Leadership School for Activists, which provides continuing education for many community activists and an intern program providing research experience for undergraduate and graduate students under the supervision of IPS fellows. In addition, IPS maintains a European office, the Transnational Institute, in Amsterdam. An array of pamphlets, articles, and books is published.

The institute's staff numbers 25, about half being professional research positions. Researchers generally have advanced degrees in the humanities, social sciences, or law and a breadth of travel, publication, and public policy analysis experience.

Institute for Policy Studies
1601 Connecticut Avenue, N.W.
Washington, D.C. 20009

tel. 202/234-9382

Institute of Peace, United States

The United States Institute of Peace is an independent, nonpartisan federal institution created and funded by Congress to strengthen the nation's capacity to promote international peace. The institute works to expand basic and applied knowledge about the origins, nature, and processes of war; sponsors research by scholars and others who represent the widest spectrum of approaches to these questions; and elicits the personal reflections of practitioners of statecraft and international negotiations. The institute then disseminates this knowledge, and practical lessons from it, to officials, policymakers, diplomats, and other practitioners, in the United States and abroad. In addition, the institute conducts and supports educational programs for the U.S. public on aspects of international peace.

Candidates for positions with the United States Institute of Peace should have a background in international affairs and strong research and writing skills.

United States Institute of Peace   tel. 202/457-1700
Suite 700
1550 M Street, N.W.
Washington, D.C. 20005–1708

Institute of War and Peace Studies

The Institute of War and Peace Studies was organized in 1951 under the sponsorship of Dwight D. Eisenhower. It is affiliated with the School of International Affairs at Columbia University. In addition to its ongoing program of research and publications, the institute sponsors speakers, faculty seminars, and joint student-faculty workshops on a variety of topics. The institute is currently undertaking research and training programs on regional security in an era of strategic parity (funded by the Ford Foundation) and the political economy of national security (funded by the Pew Charitable Trusts' Program for Integrating Economics and National Security).

The research program of the institute has two main parts. One deals with peace and security, including relevant problems of U.S. foreign policy, strategic studies, and arms control. The other involves theoretical and empirical investigations in international and comparative politics, international political economy, and international institutions. In addition to a wide variety of articles in scholarly journals, numerous books and symposia, more than 62 volumes have been produced under institute auspices.

The institute has a small professional research staff conducting about 20 individual studies. Research assistants are appointed from within the university.

Institute of War and Peace Studies   tel. 212/854-4616
Columbia University   fax 212/864-1686
420 West 118th Street
New York, NY 10027

International Institute for Environment and Development

Established in 1971, the International Institute for Environment and Development (IIED) is an independent, nonprofit policy research institute linking environmental concerns and with the development needs of the South and with other global environment and development priorities. IIED's work is undertaken with, or on behalf of, governments and international agencies, the academic community, foundations and nongovernment organizations, community organizations and groups, and the people they represent. The institute advises decisionmakers and raises public awareness on such crucial issues as sustainable agriculture, tropical forestry, human settlements, drylands management, environmental economics, and business and the environment.

IIED works worldwide, though its principal focus is the developing world. Some of the areas IIED is most active in are: Argentina, Burkina Faso, Cape Verde, Ethiopia, Gambia, Ghana, India, Indonesia, Kenya, Laos, Lesotho, Nigeria, Papua New Guinea, Philippines, Senegal, Thailand, Uganda, Vietnam, Zaire, Zambia, and Zimbabwe. IIED's permanent staff of 45 consists of many disciplines organized into eight programs. In addition, IIED maintains a register and deploys consultants worldwide.

IIED London   tel. (+44) (71) 388-2117
3 Endsleigh Street
London WC1H ODD
UNITED KINGDOM

IIED America Latina   tel. (+54) (1) 961-3050
Piso 6, Cuerpo A
Corrientes 2835
1193 Buenos Aires
ARGENTINA

Associated organization:

WRI/CIDE   tel. 202/638-6300
Seventh Floor
1709 New York Avenue, N.W.
Washington, D.C. 20006

International Republican Institute

The International Republican Institute is a nonprofit organization funded by the U.S. Congress through the National Endowment for Democracy, founded in December 1983. Its objective is to encourage democratic development abroad through assistance to political parties and various affiliated institutions. The institute's activities center on party organization, policy development, aid to democratic multilateral political organizations, and electoral assistance.

The present staff includes a 23-member board of directors, 60 staff members, and interns. Employment qualifications require a background in international political and economic affairs and democratic processes and development. Also important is a strong understanding of political party organization and structure.

> International Republican Institute   tel. 202/408-9450
> Suite 900   fax 202/408-9462
> 1212 New York Avenue, N.W.
> Washington, D.C. 20005

The Middle East Institute

The Middle East Institute (MEI) is a membership organization founded in 1946 to promote U.S. understanding of the Middle East, North Africa, the Caucasus, and Central Asia. MEI is a nonprofit, nonadvocating resource center that sponsors classes in Arabic, Hebrew, Persian, and Turkish; coordinates cultural presentations and an annual garden series; convenes political and economic programs and an annual conference; publishes the *Middle East Journal*; and maintains a 25,000-volume library. MEI also has a scholar-in-residence program and a college internship program.

The MEI has a staff of 15, half of whom are professionals with extensive experience in Middle Eastern affairs.

> The Middle East Institute   tel. 202/785-1141
> 1761 N Street, N.W.   fax 202/331-8861
> Washington, D.C. 20036–2882

National Democratic Institute

The National Democratic Institute (NDI) was started with the National Endowment for Democracy. Its purpose is to teach democracy and the democratic process. It has a budget of $20 million and a staff of 160 full-time employees, 25 consultants, and 25 interns. The organization has field offices abroad in Africa, Latin America, and Europe. Currently 12 NDI officers are stationed in Johannesburg and 30 in Moscow. NDI's major initiative since 1990 has been voter registration in South Africa. A recent focus has been on ways to broaden recruitment efforts of the organization.

Ideal candidates for positions at all levels of NDI should be knowledgeable in accounting, governance, development, political party structure, and the parliamentary process and be able to speak at least one foreign language. Resumes received at NDI are generally organized by region of familiarity, functional expertise, and political party experience. The position of program assistant is primarily administrative, providing full project support to program officers. About half of all program assistants possess master's degrees. Program officers survey missions abroad to monitor developments with local governments and help determine which projects are funded. A master's degree is required for this position. Regional directors, or senior program officers, are stationed abroad and oversee projects in the field offices in foreign countries.

National Democratic Institute   tel. 202/328-3136
1717 Massachusetts Avenue, N.W.
Washington, D.C. 20036

Overseas Development Council

The Overseas Development Council (ODC) is an independent nonprofit organization established in 1969 to increase U.S. understanding of the economic and social problems confronting developing countries and to highlight the importance of these countries to the United States in an interdependent world. The council functions as a center for policy research and analysis, a forum for the exchange of ideas, and a source of publications in the development field. ODC seeks to promote the consideration of development issues by the U.S. public, policymakers, educators, and the media through its research, conferences, publications, and liaison with U.S. mass membership organizations interested in U.S. foreign relations. Current research efforts include: analysis of economic interrelatedness between the United States and developing countries; alternative development strategies for developing countries; U.S.-Mexican relations; U.S. trade policy and the developing countries; problems of economic adjustment; the role of commercial banks in developing countries; development in sub-Saharan Africa; and the interrelationship between the environment and sustainable development. ODC has a staff of 20 professionals.

Overseas Development Council   tel. 202/234-8701
Suite 1012
1875 Connecticut Avenue, N.W.
Washington, D.C. 20009

The Population Council

The Population Council, a nonprofit, nongovernmental research organization established in 1952, seeks to improve the well-being and reproductive
health of current and future generations around the world and to help
achieve a humane, equitable, and sustainable balance between people and
resources.

The council analyzes population issues and trends; conducts research in
the reproductive sciences; develops new contraceptives; works with public
and private agencies to improve the quality and outreach of family planning
and reproductive health services; helps governments design and implement
effective population policies; communicates the results of research in the population field to diverse audiences; and helps strengthen professional resources
in developing countries through collaborative research and programs, technical exchange, awards, and fellowships.

Research and programs are carried out by three divisions—the Center
for Biomedical Research, the Research Division, and the Programs Division—
and two Distinguished Colleagues. Council headquarters and the Center for
Biomedical Research are located in New York City; the council has 4 regional
and 14 country offices overseas. About 365 women and men from 62 countries work for the council, more than a third of whom hold advanced degrees.
Roughly 40 percent are based in developing countries. Council staff collaborate with developing country colleagues to conduct research and programs in
some 50 countries in South and East Asia, West Asia and North Africa, sub-
Saharan Africa, and Latin America and the Caribbean. A listing of current job
openings at the Council is available from their internet World Wide Web site.

The Population Council   tel. 212/339-0500
One Dag Hammerskjold Plaza   http://www.popcouncil.org
New York, NY 10017

RAND

From its inception in the days following World War II, RAND has focused
on the nation's most pressing policy problems. The institution's first hall-
mark was high quality, objective research on national security, and it began
addressing problems of domestic policy in the 1960's. Today, RAND's broad
research agenda helps policymakers strengthen the nation's economy, maintain its security and improve its quality of life by helping them make the
choices in, among other areas, education, health care, national defense, and
criminal and civil justice.

RAND staff is housed in five departments: Defense and Technology Planning; Human and Material Resource Policy; International Policy; Social Policy; and Washington Research. Research divisions include Project AIR

FORCE, the only federally funded research and development center charged with policy analysis for the U.S. Air Force, Army Research, and National Security. The European-American Center for Policy Analysis is a special program that brings together joint, multidisciplinary teams of U.S. and European researchers to collaborate on projects and to exchange data and research methods. Smaller research centers dealing with international affairs include the Center for Asia-Pacific Policy, the Center for Russian and Eurasian Studies, and the Greater Middle East Studies Center. RAND also operates a graduate school that awards more doctoral degrees in policy analysis than any other institution in the country.

RAND employs more than 600 research professionals; more than 500 professional consultants provide the equivalent of approximately 90 more full-time researchers. Most researchers work in RAND's Santa Monica headquarters, though a few others are based in Washington, D.C., and a few operate from RAND's European-American Center for Policy Analysis in Delft, the Netherlands. Nearly 80 percent hold advanced degrees in a wide variety of disciplines; among RAND researchers the most common degree is the doctorate.

RAND   tel. 310/451-6913
1700 Main Street   http://www.rand.org
Santa Monica, CA 90407–2138

Resources for the Future

Resources for the Future (RFF) is a nonprofit, multidisciplinary research and educational organization that promotes the development, conservation, and wise use of natural resources and the environment. Most of its studies are in the field of the social sciences and are concerned with the relationship between people and their natural environment. Although the major part of its activities is domestic, RFF undertakes a range of international activities, including cooperative research with organizations in other countries, awarding research grants to foreign organizations and participating actively in international conferences, workshops, seminars, and study teams.

RFF employs 60 professionals as administrators, senior fellows, fellows, and research assistants. The organization typically hires five research assistants per year. Successful candidates usually have graduate degrees in economics and work experience relative to a particular project.

Resources for the Future   tel. 202/328-5000
1616 P Street, N.W.   e-mail: info@rff.org
Washington, D.C. 20036   http://www.rff.org

Royal Institute of International Affairs

The Royal Institute of International Affairs is an independent, London-based organization founded in 1920 to encourage, facilitate, and inform the debate on international affairs. The institute organizes research by individual scholars and expert study groups; publishes books, periodicals, and pamphlets; arranges lectures and discussions; and maintains a specialized library of books and documents. The institute is responsible for the publication of the journal, *International Affairs*; the magazine, *The World Today*; and the *Chatham House Papers*. The institute has a Scottish branch.

The Royal Institute has more than 3,000 members and associates and maintains a staff of about 86 people. Opportunities for careers are open to a very small number of individuals.

Royal Institute of International Affairs tel. 071/930-2233
Chatham House
10 St. James Square
London, SW 1Y4LE
UNITED KINGDOM

Woodrow Wilson International Center for Scholars

The Woodrow Wilson International Center for Scholars was established as a living memorial to the 28th President of the United States to commemorate President Wilson's lifelong commitment to uniting scholarship with public affairs. Through an annual fellowship competition, the center awards approximately 35 residential fellowships to individuals with outstanding proposals representing the entire range of scholarship, with a strong emphasis on the humanities and the social sciences. In addition, the center sponsors public meetings and generates publications exploring contemporary issues and trends. The center's programs, including the Division of Historical, Cultural, and Literary Studies; the Division of International Studies; the Division of United States Studies; and the Division of Regional Comparative Studies, which includes the Kennan Institute for Advanced Russian Studies and programs on Asia, East and West Europe, and Latin America, provide the structure through which the center carries out its activities. In addition to its fellowship competition for senior scholars, the center offers internships to outstanding undergraduate and graduate students.

The Wilson Center is administered by a small staff of scholar/administrators, program specialists, and support staff.

The Woodrow Wilson
   International Center for Scholars
SI MRC 022
1000 Jefferson Drive, S.W.
Washington, D.C. 20560

tel. 202/357-2429
tel. 202/357-2841
   (Fellowship Office)
tel. 202/357-3362 (Internships)
tel. 202/357-3000, x313
   (Personnel)
fax 202/357-4439

Worldwatch Institute

Worldwatch Institute is a nonprofit, public-interest research institute concentrating on global environmental and environmentally related issues. Founded in 1974, it is the most frequently cited research institute in the world today. Worldwatch Institute is dedicated to fostering a sustainable society—one in which human needs are met in ways that do not threaten the health of the natural environment or future generations. To this end, the institute conducts interdisciplinary research on emerging global issues, the results of which are disseminated to decisionmakers, the media, and the public. In many countries in the world today, Worldwatch has become the principal source of environmental information, including countries as different as Norway and China. The institute has several publications, including the *Worldwatch Papers*, the annual *State of the World* report (which is translated into 26 languages), *World Watch* magazine, the *Environmental Alert* book series, and *Vital Signs*, a series on trends shaping the future.

The Worldwatch Institute has a staff of 30 professionals, half engaged in research, the other half in support positions. No set criteria exist for employment, although employment experience plays a large role. All have employees have at least a B.A. and many have M.A.s.

Worldwatch Institute
1776 Massachusetts Avenue, N.W.
Washington, D.C. 20036

tel. 202/452-1999
gopher://gopher.igc.apc.org:70/
   11/orgs/worldwatch
http://www.econet.apc.org/
   econet/

10

The Internet Job Search

MICHAEL TRUCANO*

The internet—until recently the domain of academics and scientists— has exploded onto computer screens and into the public conscious- ness. Although attention has largely focused on the its commercial and entertainment potential, it is increasingly apparent that the inter- net is a job-search asset. Why use the internet in your international career search? The short answer is: because it's there. Using the inter- net can yield some big rewards. The internet connects you to a truly staggering amount of information and knows no geographic con- straints. If the information is on the internet, it doesn't matter where you are. Scanning job openings for a United Nations post in Ethiopia, doing background research on Japanese banks, exploring environmen- tal projects outside Vancouver—it's all possible on the internet. The internet also provides an means of communication—e-mail—for quickly contacting hard-to-reach individuals and organizations. And finally, it's relatively cheap! If you're a student, you have internet access through your school. If not, private service providers offer access that, compared with the cost of being on hold during long dis- tance phone calls, is a real bargain. Internet job searches are still a nov- elty for most outside of the high-tech industry. For now, it will help differentiate you from the pack. Soon, however, it will be a necessity.

What Should I Do?

The basics of what the internet is and how to use it are best left to other resources, some of which are listed in the bibliography at the

---

* Michael Trucano, a 1996 graduate of Georgetown University's Master of Science in Foreign Service program, works in consulting. Before coming to Georgetown, he worked for International Education Systems on a series of guides to international busi- ness culture and management, and at consulting firms in Washington and Prague. A graduate of Bowdoin College, Mr. Trucano also studied at universities in Munich and Prague.

end of this book. This chapter focuses on how the internet can support your job search.

E-mail

E-mail is electronic mail, faster than a fax, swifter than the U.S. Postal Service. E-mail can often provide the best and most immediate connection to contacts at a given organization. While most people can screen calls and cover letters, many people will respond quickly when approached via e-mail. Focused and appropriate use of e-mail can be very fruitful when conducting a job search.

Some notes on e-mail culture and etiquette (or "netiquette") are in order, for e-mail's informal, immediate, and often quirky nature can create problems if it's used inappropriately.

- Treat all correspondence via e-mail with the same professionalism and respect that you would letters sent through the post office. You have time to rethink what you said in your cover letter as you stuff it in an envelope and take it to a mailbox. E-mail, however, is gone seconds after you finish typing your name, so allow yourself at least 15 minutes after finishing your e-mail before sending it off.

- Always proofread whatever you write! Spelling errors and typos are difficult to spot on the computer screen, so be extra careful about reviewing what you have written before you hit that send key!

- DON'T USE ALL CAPITAL LETTERS! This is the e-mail equivalent of shouting and is considered bad form.

- Note that you can usually tell to what country you're sending an e-mail from the last two digits of the e-mail address (French e-mail addresses end in .fr, for example).

- Don't expect e-mail to be confidential. Until the courts rule otherwise, employers believe they have the right to monitor employees' e-mail. Assume that all e-mail is stored somewhere (perhaps forever) and act accordingly.

You should design and keep an electronic version of your resume ready to e-mail whenever necessary. Keep a copy on disk and in the saved messages folder of your e-mail program. Your best bet is to save your resume as a plain text or ASCII file, which you can do in all widely used word-processing programs. Then you can cut-and-paste it into an e-mail file that you can send out over the internet. While this may not be the most pleasing format to the eye, it will ensure that whoever you e-mail it to will be able to read it. Sending snazzy, formatted word-processing files would be best, of course, but more often than not their recipient will either be unable to read them or the format will be scrambled. ASCII may not be attractive, but it is reliable.

If you send an electronic version of your resume to a company, it is often entered into a human resource database. Therefore, when constructing your electronic resume, you should take time to consider incorporating certain key words to ensure that your resume pops up as often as possible when the company searches its database. For example, a company may search for certain skills, experiences, academic institutions and degrees, geographic areas, languages, or previous employers. Thus, anticipating which words a particular employer will think important can help your resume rise to the top of a database search.

There are ways to keep your e-mail anonymous. Many third-party servers (which usually charge a fee) can forward your resume to job banks or employers while withholding certain information until you are comfortable with the party with whom you are dealing. If you send in an electronic resume to an employer or data bank, it is best to omit the name of your current employer unless you are comfortable with the fact that your boss might see it.

"Internetworking"

To keep abreast of the latest trends in a your field, join relevant internet mailing lists and monitor discussion groups (called "usenet"). Information about mailing lists can often be found in a web site of related interest. As a general rule of thumb, the more specific the topic, the higher the quality of the information. Therefore, put some time and thought into any questions you have before posting them to a usenet group. Avoid basic questions that are probably answered in the FAQ (frequently asked questions) guide that accompanies any usenet group. A word of warning: never post your resume to a usenet group—you will most likely receive a barrage of e-mail in reply, all negative! Whether responding to individual postings in a usenet group or when sending e-mail to a mailing list, remember that what you write could be seen by hundreds (if not thousands) of people—make sure the tone of your letter is appropriate for the most discriminating and demanding reader and you won't go wrong.

World Wide Web sites

A great deal of career-related research can be done by visiting organizations' home pages (and their competitors) on the World Wide Web (the Web), the multimedia component of the internet. How do you find these? With creative search techniques and diligence and by keeping your eyes and ears open, it can be done without much trouble. Use a search engine (or "spider"), a means of scanning the internet in search of specific words or phrases, to target certain types of jobs or subject areas that could be of value in your career exploration. Popular search engines can be found at www.lycos.com, www.altavista.com, and www.excite.com.

Navigating the internet can be difficult. Finding the right key words to search for is real art—and sometimes an entertaining exercise in lateral thinking! If you are interested in finance, searching for bank, for example, would yield an unwieldy number of matches ("hits"), while a search for high-yield bond trading is probably too specific and would result in no hits. Including city names or the postal abbreviations for states can often be a useful way to streamline a search that yields an unmanageable number of hits. Different search engines yield different results when searching for the same word or words, so don't restrict yourself to just one. Browse a hierarchical internet Web library like yahoo! in its business or employment sections. There are also a number of on-line career-related resources that contain links to a wide variety of employer home pages.

The content of company home pages, like all Web sites, varies widely. Some provide a wealth of information useful to the job seeker, including basic company information and background, press releases, job postings, contact names for recruiting, profiles of current employees, and samples of current work and reports related to the firm. Others serve primarily as advertisements for the company's products and services. Still others serve no really useful purpose (yet) except to establish that the firm intends to maintain a presence on the web in the future.

One characteristic of information on the internet is that it is constantly changing. Many organizations update their Web sites regularly, so check back periodically. Remember to always check the "last updated" line usually found at the bottom of a Web site; a lot of information on the Web is out of date.

Career-related sites on the internet

The number of sites on the internet exclusively dedicated to providing career resources and employment listings has mushroomed. These sites fall into two general categories—private employment or job banks and university-sponsored career sites. Both types of sites can provide a variety of useful information, including advice, job listings, interview schedules, and links to a myriad of related sites. Well-known private sites include the want ad listings at CareerPath (www.career-path.com) and the comprehensive Riley Guide (www.jobtrak.com/job-guide). Check the employment sections at sites like yahoo! (www.yahoo.com) to find links to areas of interest. Don't forget to visit the Web site of your university career center, which should have a good variety of links to other sites as well. Most university career centers are linked to the school's home page, which can be found by using a search engine or even by guessing at the school's Uniform Resource Locater. Most school addresses follow the following format: www.georgetown.edu, with the school name appearing after the code for the World Wide Web (www) but before the code assigned to educational institutions (edu). Full access to a university's career resources on the web is sometimes restricted to its students and alumni/ae, but more and more schools are making their resources available to the internet community as a whole. Some private career sites have begun charging user fees. Be wary, however, of any site that asks for your credit card information before you are allowed a trial peek at their services. Private on-line networks like America Online have extensive employment sections.

Your own home page

Creating your own home page on the World Wide Web can be useful when conducting your internet job search. Increasingly, schools are providing space on their servers for student Web pages—if yours does not, talk to your computer center. Most internet service providers also offer the opportunity to create personal web pages for a small fee. Following some basic guidelines should help maximize your potential benefit from your home page:

• Keep it simple. Stay away from incorporating innovative new internet technologies unless you know they will work as planned and enhance what you're advertising—you. Keep extras to a minimum unless they add definite value, such as papers or presentations that could be of interest to potential employers.

- Be selective in your choice of links to other Web pages, if you decide to use them at all. Consider the purpose of posting your resume on the Web: Do you really want to entice a potential employer to click on a link and leave your resume site for somewhere more interesting?

- Be professional. Be careful about what you put on the page—it may be the only chance you get to impress a potential employer, so it's best to leave out links to information about your favorite rock bands or television shows.

- If you don't want people to know something about you—your telephone number, address, photograph, current or previous employer, and so on—don't post it on the World Wide Web! Unfortunately, abuses of information can and do occur, so exercise good judgment.

If you don't feel comfortable designing your own Web page, there are lots of people out who can do it for you. Ask around, check the want ads in computer publications or call a university computer center to find someone who can help you.

Some Words of Caution

While the internet can be very valuable in your job search, you should be aware of some potential problems that could arise. It may be difficult sometimes to judge the reputation of the organization with which you are dealing—the quality of a Web site of a one-man firm operating from someone's basement can be the same as that of a *Fortune 500* company, so be careful when making any assumptions about the size or prestige of an organization only on the basis of its Web site.

When you're on the internet it can be easy to forget that you are communicating with people all over the world. Personal questions, such as those relating to marital status, while against the law in the United States, may be standard practice elsewhere. If you are uncomfortable revealing personal information about yourself, just don't do it.

Final Words of Advice

Used wisely, the internet can alert you to a vast body of information and contacts that you can tap for subsequent leads in the job search process. However, it is only one part of a broader career-search strategy. Use of the internet is no substitute for the telephone and face-to-face networking that in the end usually result in a job offer.

And finally: Don't forget to reference your home page and e-mail address on all hard copies of your job correspondence! Now that you're using the internet to aid in your job search, this serves two functions—it points the way to additional information about you and shows potential employers that you are at least a little familiar with this emerging medium. Good luck!

Bibliography

Advertising Career Directory. 1995. Ronald W. Fry. Hawthorne, N.J.: The Career Press Inc.

Almanac of International Jobs and Careers. 1991. Ronald L. Krannich and Caryl Rae Krannich. Woodbridge, Va.: Impact Publications.

American Foreign Service Officer. 1993. New York: Prentice Hall.

American Jobs Abroad. 1994. Detroit, Mich.: Gale Research.

American Register of Exporters and Importers. Annual. New York: American Register of Exporters and Importers Corporation. Covers 30,000 U.S. manufacturers and distributors in the import/export trade and service firms assisting foreign customers, both private and public. Lists company name, address, and products in which firm deals.

Ayers Directory of Publications. Annual. Bala Cynwyd, Pa.: Ayer Press. Lists the newspapers and periodicals in United States, Puerto Rico, Virgin Islands, Canada, Bahamas, Bermuda, Panama, and the Philippines. Entries include circulation figures, address, telephone numbers, and the names of editors and publishers.

Broadcasting Yearbook. Annual. Washington, D.C.: U.S. Government Printing Office. Provides a complete listing of U.S. and Canadian television and radio stations. Along with addresses and telephone numbers, it provides the names of the licensee, owner, general manager, and other principal personnel.

Bureau of International Commerce, Trade Lists. Annual. Washington, D.C.: U.S. Department of Commerce. Lists American firms, subsidiaries, and affiliates in each country with brief descriptions and addresses.

Career Choices for the Political Science and Government Student. 1990. Peggy Schmidt and Ramsey Walker. Hawthorne, N.Y.: Walker Publishing Company, Inc.

Career Choices for Students of Economics. 1990. Peggy J. Schmidt. New York: Walker Publishing Company, Inc.

College Placement Annual. Bethlehem, Pa.: College Placement Council, Inc. Information on U.S. employers that hire college graduates. Includes brief description of the nature of the business or organization, name of the college recruiting officer, number of employees, and occupational openings for which the organization will recruit.

Commerce Business Daily. Washington, D.C.: U.S. Department of Commerce, International Trade Administration. Good source for consulting leads. Includes information on unclassified requests for bids and proposals, procurements reserved for small business, prime contracts awarded, federal contractors seeking subcontract assistance, and upcoming sales of government property. Published daily.

Congressional Directory. Annual. Joint Committee on Printing. Washington, D.C.: U.S. Government Printing Office.

Congressional Staff Directory. Annual. Box 62, Mount Vernon, Va.: Information covering the current Congress with emphasis on the staffs of the members and of the committees and subcommittees.

Consultants and Consulting Organizations Directory. 10th ed. 1990. Detroit, Mich.: Gale Research Company. A listing of consulting firms by location, subject, and firm names.

CPC Annual: A Guide to Career Planning, the Job Search, Graduate School, and Work-Related Education 1994–95. 33rd ed. Vol. 1 Bethlehem, Pa.: College Placement Council, Inc.

CPC Annual: A Directory of Employment Opportunities for College Graduates in Administration, Business, and Other Non-technical Options 1989/90. 33rd ed. Vol. 2 Bethlehem, Pa.: College Placement Council, Inc.

Current Technical Service Contracts and Grants (AID Contracts). 1995. Washington, D.C.: Office of Procurement, Agency for International Development.

Directory of American Firms Operating in Foreign Countries. 18th ed. 1994. New York: World Trade Academy Press. A three-volume compilation of information on 3,200 U.S. corporations that operate abroad cataloged by firm names and geographic location.

Directory of Consultant Members. Annual. Washington, D.C.: American Management Association.

Directory of Foreign Firms Operating in the United States. 6th ed., 1989. Juvenal L. Angel. New York: World Trade Academy Press. Names and addresses of enterprises owned wholly or in part by more than 2,700 foreign firms that have invested in American manufacturing, banking, petroleum, merchandising, finance, insurance, and other industrial and service fields.

Dun and Bradstreet Exporter's Encyclopedia, World Marketing Guide. Annual. New York: Dun and Bradstreet International. A guide to exporting, organized by country.

Editor and Publisher International Yearbook. Annual. New York: Editor and Publisher Company.

Electronic Job Search Revolution. 2nd ed. 1995. Joyce Lain Kennedy. New York: John Wiley & Sons.

Employment Abroad: Fact and Fallacies. 1990. Washington, D.C.: U.S. Chamber of Commerce.

Encyclopedia of Associations. 24th ed. 1990. Burck, Koek, and Norallo, eds. Detroit, Mich.: Gale Research, Inc. Five-volume guide to national and international organizations. Volume 4 specifically deals with international organizations by an alphabetical and subject index. Gives names of chief officer, brief statement of activities, number of members, and publications.

European Markets. 3rd ed. 1990. Washington, D.C.: Washington Researchers Publishing.

Europe's 10,000 Largest Companies. Annual. New York: Dun and Bradstreet International. Source of financial and statistical information for the largest companies in the 16 countries of Western Europe and Scandinavia. Companies are ranked by profit figures and sales.

Federal Jobs Overseas. Annual. Washington, D.C.: U.S. Civil Service Commission.

Fortune World Business Directory. Annual. Chicago: *Fortune*, August. Ranks by sales the "500 largest industrial corporations outside the U.S."; presents tables of data including country, industry groups, sales in dollars, assets, net income, stockholders' equity, and number of employees.

The Foundation Directory. 13th ed. 1990. Marianna O. Lewis, ed. New York: The Foundation Center. Listing of various foundations and areas of interest.

Great Careers: A Guide to Internships and Volunteer Opportunities in the Non-Profit Sector. 1990. Devon Smith, ed. Garrett Park, MD: Garrett Press.

Guide to Careers in World Affairs. 1994. New York: Foreign Policy Association.

Guide to Foreign Information Sources. Washington, D.C.: International Division, Chamber of Commerce of the United States. Lists foreign embassies and legations in the U.S. and other organizations and services relating to major areas of the world and selected references.

A Guide to Hispanic Organizations. 1989–91. New York: Phillip Morris, Inc.

The Guide to Internet Job Searching. 1996. Margaret F. Riley. New York: Public Library Association.

Harvard Guide to Careers. 1995. Cambridge, Mass.: Harvard University Office of Career Services.

Harvard Guide to Careers in Consulting. 1992. Cambridge, Mass.: Harvard University Office of Career Services.

Harvard Guide to Careers in Government & Politics. 1992. Cambridge, Mass.: Harvard University Office of Career Services.

Hook Up, Get Hired, 1995. Joyce Lain Kennedy. New York: John Wiley & Sons.

How to Find an Overseas Job with the U.S. Government. 1992. New York: World Wise Books.

How to Get a Job in the Pacific Rim. 1992. Robert Sanborn and Anderson Brandao. Chicago: Surrey Books.

How to Get a Job in Europe. 1993. Robert Sanborn. Chicago: Surrey Books.

International Agriculture: Challenging Opportunities. 1990. Warnken, Ragsdale, and Flain, eds. Columbia, Mo: University of Missouri Extension Publications.

International Bankers Directory. Semiannual. New York: Rand-McNally.

International Division, International Policy Development and Business Diplomacy. Annual. Washington, D.C.: International Division, Chamber of Commerce of the United States. Briefly describes each of the division's policy units with the names of chairmen and executive secretaries given. Also lists selected research reports on international investment.

International Internship and Volunteer Programs. 1992. New York: World Wise Books.

International Jobs. 1993. Eric Kocher. Reading, Mass.: Addison-Wesley.

Internships in Foreign and Defense Policy: A Complete Guide for Women (and Men). 1990. Women in International Security. Cabin John, MD.: Seven Locks Press.

Jane's Major Companies of Europe. Annual. London, England: Jane's Yearbooks. Detailed information about finances and operations for more than 1,000 companies based in Europe.

Journalism Career and Scholarship Guide. 1990. Princeton, N.J.: The Dow Jones Newspaper Fund.

Lists of Foreign Firms Operating in the United States. 1995. New York: World Trade Academy Press, Inc. A series of books on individual countries containing the names and address of the American branch or affiliate, with name of its foreign parent company.

Major Companies of Europe. J. Love, ed. New York: McGraw-Hill. Description of Fortune 500 companies of Western Europe.

Making It Abroad. 1990. Howard Schumann. New York: Wiley Press.

Marketing Your Skills Overseas. 1992. New York: World Trade Academy Press Inc. National profiles stating the advantages and disadvantages of working and living in the country described and employment possibilities. Includes a list of U.S. firms with subsidiaries or affiliates in that country.

Moody's International Manual. Annual. New York: Moody's Investors' Services.

Occupational Outlook Handbook. Annual. U.S. Department of Labor, Bureau of Labor Statistics. Washington, D.C.: U.S. Government Printing Office.

The 100 Best Companies to Work for in America. 1992. Robert Levering, Milton Moskowitz, and Michael Katz. New York: Signet Book/NAL Penguin, Inc.

Opportunities for Teaching Abroad. Annual. Washington, D.C.: U.S. Information Agency.

Overseas Development Network Opportunities Catalogue. 1990. San Francisco, Calif.: Overseas Development Network.

Overseas Employment Opportunities for Educators. 1990. Washington, D.C.: Department of Defense. Lists general and specific requirements for working in schools for children of military personnel.

Passport to Overseas Employment. 1990. Dale Chambers. New York: Prentice Hall Press.

The Perfect Resume. 1990. Tom Jackson. Garden City, N.Y.: Anchor Press/Doubleday. The best, most straightforward book on how to plan and prepare a resume and cover letter.

Peterson's Annual Job Guides: Business and Management Jobs 1995. Christopher Billy and Mark Geoffroy, eds. Princeton, N.J.: Peterson's Guides, Inc.

Principal International Businesses: The World Marketing Directory. Annual. New York: Dun and Bradstreet International. Names, addresses, chief officers, SIC numbers, and so on for approximately 51,000 companies around the world.

Standard and Poor's Register of Corporations, Directors and Executives. Annual. New York: Standard and Poor's Corporation.

Trade Lists. Annual. Washington, D.C.: U.S. Department of Commerce. A series of listings of foreign firms and individuals classified under major commodity groups published by country.

Using the Internet in Your Job Search. 1995. Fred Jandt and Mary Nemnich. Chicago: JIST.

Volunteer! The Comprehensive Guide to Voluntary Services in the U.S. and Abroad. 1989–90. Marjorie Adoff Cohen, ed. New York: Council on International Educational Exchange.

What Color is Your Parachute? 1996. Richard Nelson Bolles. Berkeley, Calif.: Ten Speed Press.

Work, Study, Travel Abroad: The Whole World Handbook. 1990–91. Marjorie Adoff Cohen. New York: Council on International Educational Exchange.

Worldwide Chamber of Commerce Directory. Annual. Loveland, Colo.: Johnson Publishing Company, Inc. A complete list of chambers of commerce in the United States, foreign chambers of commerce in principal cities throughout the world, and foreign embassies and consulates.

Yearbook of International Organizations. Annual. Brussels, Belgium: Union of International Associations.

Index